Social Media and Strategic Communications

Social Media and Strategic Communications

Edited by

Hana S. Noor Al-Deen
University of North Carolina Wilmington, USA

and

John Allen Hendricks
Stephen F. Austin State University, USA

First published 2013 by
PALGRAVE MACMILLAN

Palgrave Macmillan in the UK is an imprint of Macmillan Publishers Limited,
registered in England, company number 785998, of Houndmills, Basingstoke,
Hampshire RG21 6XS.

Palgrave Macmillan in the US is a division of St Martin's Press LLC,
175 Fifth Avenue, New York, NY 10010.

Palgrave Macmillan is the global academic imprint of the above companies
and has companies and representatives throughout the world.

Palgrave® and Macmillan® are registered trademarks in the United States,
the United Kingdom, Europe and other countries

ISBN: 978–1–137–28704–5

This book is printed on paper suitable for recycling and made from fully
managed and sustained forest sources. Logging, pulping and manufacturing
processes are expected to conform to the environmental regulations of the
country of origin.

A catalogue record for this book is available from the British Library.

A catalog record for this book is available from the Library of Congress.

To all abused, homeless, and shelter animals that are in desperate need of human compassion and support

Hana S. Noor Al-Deen

To Stacy, Abby, and Haydyn

John Allen Hendricks

Contents

Part I Social Media and Advertising

Part II Social Media and Public Relations

Part III   Social Media Policies/Practices and Legal/Ethical Considerations

List of Illustrations

Figures

Tables

Appendixes

Foreword

Anyone who has followed the evolution of digital media from its early theoretical formulation to the latest social networking via Twitter and Facebook, among others, could be misled into thinking that social media are a populist phenomenon invented by the young and led by them. While the young have been enthusiastic users of social media from the get-go, these media and their Internet, wireless and mobile platforms do not reside exclusively in the world of the young and never have. It is clearly grown-ups at the keyboard and behind the screen making systematic and strategic use of social media to engage the young, yes, but also to connect and interact with every imaginable demographic and interest. While some traditional media lagged behind in social media applications and thus delayed their participation in this whole new virtual world, many of those involved in strategic communications in the fields of advertising and public relations were among the first to embrace this movement and make immediate applications to their work. Social media and online connection experts quickly established boutique practice areas and departments in ad agencies and PR firms before social networking through social media was as all-pervasive and widespread as it is today among individual users. Its engagement today is widespread and simply taken for granted as essential to any modern communication program and strategy.

Two imaginative scholars, Hana S. Noor Al-Deen and John Allen Hendricks, have produced this edited collection of original work with the help of 29 insightful, faculty contributors from 14 institutions. The result is an orderly anthology set out in three parts: Social Media and Advertising; Social Media and Public Relations; and Social Media's Legal/Ethical Considerations. Here we learn about advertising in social network games, relationship marketing, digital techniques and strategies generally, across both 50 large corporations as well as social networking as a revenue generator. Yes, these networks and communities of "friends," an overused and distorted term, are also all about money and monetizing clusters of individuals into larger saleable audiences. Facebook's 2012 IPO surely signaled that, even if in fits and starts. In the PR realm, we learn about the ways that crisis communication has harnessed social networking to its advantage, how social media have empowered public relations practitioners, giving them identity where anonymity was once the rule. A look at virtual reality tunes in on the uses of Second Life, one of the early virtual reality sites, which has implications for good works and the nonprofit sector while also making money. Next comes a case study of how NGOs use Twitter to push causes. What we get in the advertising and PR sections of the book are close-up examinations of how commercial and not-for-profit enterprises are harnessing social media for purposes greater than online chatter among teenagers. Indeed, social media are now pervasive across these industry segments, just as they are in nearly every other aspect of individual and institutional life. Everyone it seems has a social media strategy and needs in order to avoid missing out on the connectedness of networks, which have replaced old media as society's central nervous system.

Especially useful are the chapters on legal and ethical implications of social media, often remarked upon but usually bypassed by those enthralled by the latest Tweet from a Hollywood celebrity or politician. The notion that social media operate outside the realm of media law is quickly dispelled as one chapter points up the systemic reach of the legal system, in spite of the free-spirited nature of social media. This is followed by a study on best practice for organizations using social media as well as codes of ethics that even YouTube, Facebook and Flickr should, and in some cases have, considered. In this world of apparent "anything goes freedom" for many, three authors remind us that "the FTC [and presumably other surveillance agencies] are watching." The idea that social media do not run free and without constraint is well documented in several chapters while not undervaluing the somewhat runaway-train nature of the medium and its problems with privacy, piracy and other transgressions of the social compact. Indeed many of the myths and partial truths about social media's unconstrained, sometimes anarchistic, nature are confronted head-on in subtle and more overt ways. These insights into how the commercial world uses social media for its own ends and how the interests of nonprofit enterprises from noble causes to hard-fisted ideological efforts, are treated in accessible and intelligent ways.

In short, we have here a thoughtful, sometimes counterintuitive collection with matter of fact examinations of how social media contribute to and extend strategic communication. There is real value added here for all readers, but especially the young, who grew up with social media as it evolved incrementally and seamlessly with few hints of their larger organizational context.

For students who have grown up with social media and who have been its biggest promoters and users, this book is an eye-opener as it reveals how the appearance of creative messaging and unfettered freedom actually masks a much more complex and strategic enterprise. And who knows, this may presage a fragmentation of social media along more predictable demographic, and especially age, lines. As one analyst has said, the day when teenagers discovered with horror and amusement that their parents and grandparents are on Facebook should have been a wake-up call that this was no longer exclusively their space and enclave. Little did they know the deeper meaning of that discovery. *Social Media and Strategic Communications*, while intended as an updated and orderly analysis of the socializing uses of social media, offers much more with a profound and informative message for its readers. It is also an exemplary collaboration between scholars, that one imagines was itself a product of social media use and understanding.

Everette E. Dennis

Preface

The adoption and usage of social media have skyrocketed in less than a decade. This cutting-edge technology has basically delivered channels of communication that connect masses of people. Social media have consequently become very appealing to businesses, both profit and nonprofit organizations, that deal directly with selected consumers or the general public. Such businesses have embraced social media and in the process these media have become an integral part of their operations. Among the leading industries that have exploited social media are advertising, marketing, and public relations. Essentially, the interactive nature of social media has furnished strategists in such businesses with a platform and an opportunity to communicate directly with selected consumers which enables them to develop mutual understanding and ongoing enduring relationships with those consumers and the public. Although social media have been heavily used by various industries, policies, codes of ethics, rules, and regulations pertaining to such media are still in the making.

Because businesses have shown a rapidly increased propensity to use social media and integrate them into their daily operations, a demand for an intellectual analysis of this amalgamation has naturally become indispensable. Therefore, this book provides comprehensive and original scholarly research that exhibits the strategic implementation of social media in both advertising and public relations. It also examines policies, codes of ethics, and recommendations that are set by such businesses for best practices.

The book serves as an indispensable source for academic curriculum, educators, advertisers, marketers, public relations practitioners as well as for libraries, a personal source, and many wide-ranging needs of those who are interested in incorporating social media into their professions. It is designed as a reader for upper-level undergraduate and graduate level courses and it constitutes a truly valuable choice for courses in academic programs that deal with advertising, marketing, and public relations. The chapters are grouped into three major parts, each containing four chapters.

Part I: Social Media and Advertising demonstrates the utilization of social media by advertisers and marketers to build and maintain long-lasting relationships with consumers. Chapter 1 analyzes advertising in Social Network Games (SNGs). Through regression analysis, this chapter examines how the variables persuasion, knowledge, and electronic word-of-mouth (eWOM), along with perceived advertiser sincerity, product knowledge, and game involvement have influenced consumer eWOM behavior in SNGs. Chapter 2 focuses on Twitter as an advertising strategy that aids in relationship building with consumers within the context of professional sports teams. A content analysis of professional sport (NBA) team Twitter accounts is employed to examine the usage of social media by brand managers. Chapter 3 explores the techniques that were implemented to achieve success in the social media marketing of the product Old Spice. Using textual analysis, this chapter scans the social media activity of Old Spice across Twitter, Facebook, and YouTube. Chapter 4 analyzes the strategy of Fortune 500 companies in utilizing Facebook to disclose company information, disseminate company/product information, and interact with consumers. Content analysis is employed to provide insight for companies seeking to increase their brand awareness and improve their relationship with their public.

Part II: Social Media and Public Relations exhibits how public relations practitioners have included social media in their strategies to cultivate and sustain relationships with the public and other stakeholders. Chapter 5 discusses the strategic implications of social media for risk and crisis communications. Exploratory case studies are used to analyze such issues. Chapter 6 explores the social media empowerment of public relations. A case study technique is utilized to inspect health communication practitioner roles and the use of social media to cultivate relationships with the public. Chapter 7 investigates the Twitter engagement which has become an increasingly important part of the public relations strategy of leading U.S. nonprofit organizations in the health sector. Content analysis is employed for this research. Chapter 8 identifies strategic public relations principles and practices that facilitate awareness and fund-raising efforts in a virtual world like Second Life. Through direct observations, a holistic model of the context surrounding that event is examined.

Part III: Social Media Policies/Practices and Legal/Ethical Considerations explains policies, codes of ethics, rules, and regulations pertaining to the usage of social media. Chapter 9 conducts an in-depth examination of existing organizational social media policies and best practices for the construction and implementation of organizational social media policies. Content analysis was carried out for such analysis. Chapter 10 provides an ethical and legal framework for strategic communication professionals to use when employing social media. Codes of ethics as well as social media guidelines and the policies of leading strategic communication companies are scrutinized. Chapter 11 studies the use of Twitter hashtags as recommended by the Federal Trade Commission (FTC) to disclose compensation. A survey technique was employed to inspect student understanding of FTC and Twitter regulations. Chapter 12 examines how traditional media law has been adapted to address the unique characteristics of social media and what legal issues strategic communicators should watch as they expand their offerings in social media. Court cases, statutes, and administrative guidelines are used to illustrate these potential dangers.

Acknowledgements

The editors wish to express their gratitude to the contributors of this book for their enthusiastic and diligent work throughout the process. It was most certainly a mutual interest in social media that made this book possible.

The editors wish to express appreciation to Felicity Plester, Senior Commissioning Editor of Film, Culture & Media Studies at Palgrave Macmillan, who was very supportive of this venture from its outset and who provided professional assistance throughout the project. Appreciation is also extended to Chris Penfold, Assistant Editor, for his diligence and efficiency. Moreover, the editors wish to thank the anonymous reviewers for their endorsement of this project.

John Allen Hendricks wishes to acknowledge the support of Stephen F. Austin State University.

Lastly, but perhaps most importantly, the editors wish to express appreciation to their families for continued support and understanding when time was spent focused on this book. Hana S. Noor Al-Deen wishes to thank her husband, Omar, for his unwavering support and to express special appreciation to her four-legged little boy, Culee, for his devotion in waiting for his two-legged buddy during the wee hours of the night while she was working on this project. John Allen Hendricks wishes to thank his wife, Stacy, and his children, Abby and Haydyn.

About the Editors

Hana S. Noor Al-Deen is a professor of communication at the University of North Carolina Wilmington (UNCW) where she has been teaching since 1985. Noor Al-Deen, who holds a Ph.D. from the State University of New York at Buffalo, has been involved with digital technology for almost 30 years starting with her doctoral dissertation 'Corporate Teleconferencing: Audio, Video, and Computer'. She has been teaching courses in digital multimedia, 3D computer animation, social media, advertising, and intercultural/international communication.

She was the lead editor of *Social Media: Usage and Impact* and the sole editor of the book *Cross-Cultural Communication and Aging in the United States*. Her work has appeared in books and journals. Among her journal articles was 'The Evolution of Rai Music' published by *Journal of Black Studies* in 2005 and republished by Sage Publications in 2011 in the four-volume distillation of the best that has been thought and published in the academic study of Popular Music. Noor Al-Deen was a consulting editor for the *International and Intercultural Communication Annual*, a book proposal reviewer for Sage Publications and Allyn & Bacon Publishing, a reviewer for the *Journal of International & Intercultural Communication* (JIIC), and a convention paper reviewer for the Newspaper Division of the Association for Education in Journalism and Mass Communication (AEJMC) and various Divisions of the Southern States Communication Association (SSCA). She has conducted research and presented academic papers in Canada, China, Egypt, France, and Turkey.

Noor Al-Deen is a past Chair of the SSCA Mass Communication, Popular Communication, and Intercultural Communication divisions. Furthermore, she served on the Executive Council of the SSCA and as the Web Manager for the International Division, Broadcast Education Association (BEA). She was the founder and faculty advisor of UNCW Advertising Chapter, affiliated with American Advertising Federation (AAF). And, she is a member of the Honor Society of Phi Kappa Phi.

Moreover, Noor Al-Deen has devoted more than 25 years of her life toward helping abused, homeless, and shelter animals. She is a proud and active member of various animal rights organizations such as the American Society for the Prevention of Cruelty to Animals (ASPCA), World Wildlife Fund (WWF), and Animal Legal Defense Fund (ALDF).

John Allen Hendricks is Chair of the Department of Mass Communication at Stephen F. Austin State University (SFA) in Nacogdoches, Texas, and he holds the rank of Professor. The department includes the academic units of strategic communication, radio/television, and journalism/photojournalism.

He is the former Director of the Division of Communication & Contemporary Culture at SFA which included the academic units of media studies, communication studies, philosophy, Greek, and Latin. Hendricks is the former Chair of the Department of Communication & Theatre at Southeastern Oklahoma State University which included the academic units of media studies, communication studies, and theatre where he held the rank of Professor.

Hendricks holds a Ph.D. from the University of Southern Mississippi. He has edited/co-edited five books about the topic of social media/new media technologies in society: *Communicator-in-Chief: How Barack Obama Used New Media Technology to Win the White House* (with Robert E. Denton, Jr.), *Techno Politics in Presidential Campaigning: New Voices, New Technologies, and New Voters* (with Lynda Lee Kaid), *The Twenty-First-Century Media Industry: Economic and Managerial Implications in the Age of New Media*; *Social Media: Usage and Impact* (with Hana S. Noor Al-Deen), and *The Palgrave Handbook of Global Radio*.

Hendricks served as a member of the Board of Directors of the Broadcast Education Association representing Texas, Oklahoma, Kansas, Missouri, and Arkansas from 2009 to 2013. He is past President of the Oklahoma Broadcast Education Association and is a former *ex-officio* member of the Board of Directors of the Oklahoma Association of Broadcasters. He is past Chair of the Southern States Communication Association's Political Communication and Mass Communication divisions. He serves on the Editorial Advisory Board of the *Journal of Radio and Audio Media* and is a past member of the Editorial Advisory Board of the *Southwestern Mass Communication Journal*.

Notes on Contributors

Genelle I. Belmas is an associate professor of communications at California State University, Fullerton. She is the co-author of a media law textbook (*Major Principles of Media Law*, 2009) and has published articles on topics including judicial speech, judges and social media, broadcast indecency, and online anonymity. She holds a Ph.D. from the University of Minnesota. Her work has appeared in *Communication Law and Policy*, the *Journal of Mass Media Ethics*, the *Federal Communications Law Journal*, and the *South Carolina Law Review*. She teaches courses in media law, communications technologies, and media ethics.

Linda Thorsen Bond is an assistant professor of mass communication at Stephen F. Austin State University. She holds a Ph.D. from the Texas A&M University, College Station. Her research interests include media convergence, collaborative learning, and advertising. She is the author of the book, *Women Negotiating Collaborative Learning: Making the Grade* (2011).

Heather Carithers is a marketing and public relations professional in the medical field. She holds a master's degree from the University of Southern Mississippi. Her research specialization includes social media and health communication.

Catherine A. Coleman is an assistant professor of strategic communication in the Schieffer School of Journalism at Texas Christian University. Coleman has received her Ph.D. from the University of Illinois, Urbana-Champaign. Her research examines issues of representation, particularly of gender and race, advertising ethics, and consumer culture, and recent work can be found in the journal *Consumption, Markets and Culture* and in the book *Gender, Culture and Consumer Behavior*. She teaches courses in advertising, research methods, and media ethics.

Everette E. Dennis is the dean of Northwestern University in Qatar. Dean Dennis is a highly regarded educator, institution builder, author and media expert who has collaborated with leaders in media industries, foundations and other organizations for four decades. He holds a Ph.D. from the University of Minnesota. Dennis has researched and written widely about technological convergence and its impact on media organizations and careers. Prior to his appointment, Dennis was the Felix E. Larkin Distinguished Professor and Chair of Communication and Media Management at Fordham University Business School in New York City. He is a member of the Council on Foreign Relations and has held advanced fellowships at Harvard Law School, Harvard Business School, Harvard's Institute of Politics, and Stanford University. Dennis was founding director of the Media Studies Center at Columbia University and concurrently a senior vice president at the Gannet and Freedom Forum foundations. He was also founding president of the American Academy in Berlin. Dean Dennis is the author or editor of some 45 books and many monographs and articles on media and communications, higher education, and institution building, including *Understanding Media in the Digital Age*, *Media Debates: Great Issues for the Digital Age*, *Higher Education in the Information Age*, *Demystifying Media Technology*, *Understanding Mass Communication*, *Media Freedom and Accountability*, and *Reshaping the Media: Mass Communication in an Information Age*.

Melissa D. Dodd is an assistant professor of public relations at the State University of New York, Oswego. She holds a Ph.D. from the University of Miami. Her research interests include social capital theory, individual/ interpersonal variables, social media, reputation, ethics, and measurement as they relate to public relations.

Karen Freberg is an assistant professor in strategic communication at the University of Louisville. She holds a Ph.D. from the University of Tennessee. Her research has been published in several book chapters and in academic journals such as *Public Relations Review, Media Psychology Review,* and *Health Communication.* She also serves on the editorial board for *Psychology for Popular Media Culture* and *Case Studies in Strategic Communication.*

Meghan Graham is a media relations practitioner. She has a master's degree from the University of Southern Mississippi. Her area of specialization and research interests include the effects of mass media and social networking on adolescents and young adults.

Sara Green-Hamann is a doctoral student at the University of Maine. She holds a master's degree from the University of Maine. Her research interests include computer-mediated communication, health communication, persuasion, and public relations. She has published research in the *Journal of Computer-Mediated Communication.*

Holly Kathleen Hall is an assistant professor of journalism at Arkansas State University. She holds a J.D. from the University of Arkansas, Little Rock. Her research interests are in the areas of U.S./U.K. comparative media law and social media. She currently teaches classes in media law, social media and public relations and is Accredited in Public Relations (APR) by the Public Relations Society of America.

Sara Steffes Hansen is an assistant professor of strategic communication in the Department of Journalism at the University of Wisconsin Oshkosh. She has obtained her Ph.D. from the University of Wisconsin. Her research focuses on brands in interactive media, including social media and games. She previously worked in public relations and marketing for high-tech companies, and teaches advertising, public relations, and new media.

Casey Hart is an assistant professor of mass communication at Stephen F. Austin State University. He holds a Ph.D. from the University of Southern Mississippi. His research interests include race and gender representations in movies and advertising and he has presented several papers at PCA/ACA conferences. His teaching specialization is convergent broadcast techniques and technology.

Nicole Hendricks is a doctoral student in the School of Mass Communication and Journalism at the University of Southern Mississippi. She holds a master's degree from Ball State University. Her research interests include crisis communications, public relations theories, and sports communications. She has taught undergraduate courses in media studies.

Myleea D. Hill is an associate professor of journalism at Arkansas State University. She holds an Ed.D. from Arkansas State University. Her research interests include journalism pedagogy and strategic application of online communication and social media. She serves as a media relations volunteer and consultant to several educational and youth non-profits, which informs her teaching in advertising and public relations.

Yan Jin is an associate professor in the School of Mass Communications at the Virginia Commonwealth University. She has completed her Ph.D. from the University of Missouri-Columbia. Her research interests are in crisis communication and strategic conflict management, as well as how emotions influence public relations decision-making and public responses.

Jin Kyun Lee is an assistant professor of advertising in the Department of Journalism at the University of Wisconsin Oshkosh. He has a Ph.D. from the University of Texas, Austin. His research explores consumer psychology and behavior in technology-mediated environments, and cross-border strategic brand alliance. He previously worked in brand consulting, and teaches advertising courses including campaigns and design.

Seungae Lee is a doctoral student at the University of Texas at Austin. She has received her master's degree from the University of Southern Mississippi. Her research interests include advertising strategies, new media behavior, and media effects.

Regina Lewis is an associate professor at the University of Alabama. She holds a Ph.D. from the University of North Carolina, Chapel Hill. Her research interests include branding, consumer behavior and new media. She teaches Consumer Insights, Strategic Media Planning and Strategic Campaigns, at both undergraduate and graduate levels.

Shana Meganck is a doctoral candidate in the Media, Art and Text program at Virginia Commonwealth University. She holds a master's degree from the University of Georgia. Her research interests include women in the media, the effects of advertising and public relations on society, public relations and new media technologies, and ethical issues in public relations and advertising.

Vivian Medina-Messner is a full-time journalism instructor in the School of Mass Communications at the Virginia Commonwealth University. She has completed her master's degree from Florida International University. Prior to entering academia, she worked as a content producer for Media General Interactive (TimesDispatch.com) and as an online producer for MiamiHerald.com.

Marcus Messner is an assistant professor in the School of Mass Communications at the Virginia Commonwealth University. He has a Ph.D. from the University of Miami. His research interest is in new and social media and how they are adopted and used in journalism and public relations. He teaches in social media, multimedia journalism and global communication.

Sally K. Norton is a public health research consultant and wellness educator. She holds an MPH from the University of North Carolina at Chapel Hill. Her career history includes public health service and education in academic health care. Previous employers include the Program on Integrative Medicine at UNC and VCU's Department of Social and Behavioral Health.

Michael J. Palenchar is an associate professor and founding co-director of the Risk, Health and Crisis Communication Research Unit at the University of Tennessee, and has more than two decades of professional and academic public relations experience. He has received his Ph.D. from the University of Florida. His research interests include risk and crisis communication and issues management. His research has been published in numerous journals and he is co-author with Robert L. Heath of *Strategic Issues Management* (2nd edn).

Mary Jackson Pitts is a professor of radio-television at Arkansas State University. She holds a Ph.D. from the University of Southern Mississippi. Her research focuses on new media applications with a current interest in iPad technology. She teaches graduate level research and theory classes. Most recently she oversaw the conversion of Arkansas State University's television studios to high-definition.

Scott C. Quarforth is a graduate student in the Master of Social Work program at Virginia Commonwealth University. He holds a master's degree from Springfield College. He has published research on student athlete retention at D-III schools. His current research focus is on marriage and family counseling, as well as the impact of the digital divide on healthcare for low-income families.

John C. Sherblom is a professor of communication and journalism at the University of Maine and past editor of *The Journal of Business Communication* and *Communication Research Reports*. He holds a Ph.D. from the University of Maine. He regularly publishes research and teaches courses on computer-mediated, organizational, small group, and persuasive communication.

Jae-Hwa Shin is an associate professor in the School of Mass Communication and Journalism at the University of Southern Mississippi. She has a Ph.D. from the University of Missouri-Columbia. Her research interests include strategic conflict management, public relations theories, agenda-building process and health communication. She teaches undergraduate and graduate courses in public relations, conflict/issue/crisis/risk management, campaigns, theories, and research methods.

Brian G. Smith is an assistant professor of communication in the Brian Lamb School of Communication at Purdue University. He researches and teaches public engagement, interactive media, and integrated communication (iComm). He holds a Ph.D. from the University of Maryland. His work on social media and iComm has been featured in the *Journal of Communication Management, Public Relations Review,* and the *Journal of Public Relations Research,* among others; and he has also contributed chapters to the *Sage Encyclopedia of Public Relations* and *The Digital Public Relations Guidebook, 2.0.* (3rd edn).

Don W. Stacks is a professor of public relations at the University of Miami. He has written more than 150 scholarly articles and papers, winning numerous accolades. He serves on the editorial boards of most premier communication and public relations journals and directs the annual International Public Relations Research Conference. He holds a Ph.D. from the University of Florida.

Daxton R. "Chip" Stewart is an associate professor at the Schieffer School of Journalism at Texas Christian University, where he teaches courses in media law and ethics. He has received his Ph.D. from the University of Missouri and J.D. from the University of Texas. He is the editor of *Social Media and the Law: A Guidebook for Communication Students and Professionals* (2012), and his recent research has focused on social media intellectual property and defamation issues.

Brandi A. Watkins is a doctoral student at the University of Alabama. She holds a master's degree from the University of Alabama. Her research interests include consumer–brand relationships and social media. Her teaching interests include introduction to mass communications, theory, public relations, and advertising.

Part I
Social Media and Advertising

1

Advertising in Social Network Games: How Consumer Persuasion Knowledge and Advertiser Sincerity Impact eWOM of Marketer-Generated Messages

Jin Kyun Lee and Sara Steffes Hansen

Popular social network games (SNGs), casual online games played via social network sites (SNSs) like Facebook, offer an appealing channel for advertisers to reach hundreds of millions of consumers globally (Baker, 2012). In the U.S., SNGs drew 53 million players in 2010, representing 24 percent of the online population (Verna, 2011). By 2011, half of Americans aged 18 to 44 played social games daily, a habit intensified with a growing use of tablets and smartphones (Web users, 2011). Such trends show good news for SNG advertisers like McDonald's, BestBuy, and DreamWorks (Shields, 2012). Two in five SNG players prefer online games for new product knowledge, outpacing traditional media advertising (Web users, 2011).

SNG play is free. However, players seeking enhanced status or enjoyment may purchase game currency and virtual goods; or consumers may be given currency and goods in exchange for clicking on an SNG advertisement and taking an advertiser's survey, watching a product video, or engaging in another activity. At times, advertisers also make requests enabled by the SNG being nested within social media: asking consumers to pass along advertiser messages to their Facebook friends. As such, consumers are sharing marketer-generated electronic word-of-mouth (eWOM) or "exogenous WOM" (Godes & Mayzlin, 2009, p. 723).

Ample studies have explored the determinants of eWOM. However, there has been limited examination of eWOM behavior related to consumer persuasion knowledge – knowledge consumers use to cope with marketer attempts (Friestad & Wright, 1994). Persuasion knowledge and eWOM have been studied in virtual consumer communities (Hung & Li, 2007) and online video sharing (Hsieh, Hsieh, & Tang, 2012). Within the context of social gaming, this study examines eWOM stemming from the persuasion knowledge model (PKM), and extending into sincerity, consumer product knowledge, and game involvement. Consumers playing SNGs regularly encounter engagement advertisements. Though game motivations may spark advertisement activities and eWOM, consumer behavior may differ depending on levels of persuasion knowledge.

Past studies have found connections between persuasion knowledge and consumer feelings of sincerity toward advertisers (Campbell & Kirmani, 2000). Understanding and coping with advertiser messages in persuasive environments, such as SNGs, is a major effort for consumers (Friestad & Wright, 1994). Consumers assess what advertisers are attempting to achieve, and their persuasion tactics to achieve ulterior goals. In SNGs, consumers might be suspicious of advertisers' underlying motives (Fein, 1996) and may not understand any economic incentives related to advertiser requests. If consumers perceive advertiser insincerity, they may be less likely to forward marketer-generated messages.

Also, consumer product knowledge is an important variable that affects eWOM behavior. According to Feick and Price (1987), opinion leaders tend to have high product class-specific information and act as disseminators of product information, thus playing an essential role in influencing others' purchases. Opinion leaders may be considered more credible than salespeople, print, or broadcast media (Gremler, Gwinner, & Brown, 2001). Further, as consumers are overloaded with information and products, reliable and valid information from others with high product knowledge lessens cognitive elaboration (Walsh, Gwinner, & Swanson, 2004).

In the SNG context for eWOM, game involvement is also key, defined as "a motivational state to exert cognitive effort at playing a game, and that its primary antecedents are a game player's desire to beat the game or improve his/her game score" (Lee & Faber, 2007, p. 77). Consumers may be more likely to engage in eWOM related to game incentives to enhance game performance.

Though many different studies have attempted to understand impacts of these constructs, this work is the first to examine how persuasion knowledge, sincerity, product knowledge, and game involvement affect eWOM behavior. The objectives of this study are (a) to help broaden academic understanding of this consumer behavior and (b) to provide implications for practitioners embracing the highly popular new media channel of SNGs for marketer-generated eWOM.

Literature Review

Persuasion Knowledge

Persuasion has been extensively researched for several decades. Friestad and Wright (1994) first examined how consumers develop and employ their knowledge about persuasion to cope with marketers' persuasion attempts. When consumers experience marketing messages, their awareness of marketer intentions may impact how they interpret these messages and respond. This awareness, or persuasion knowledge, is conceptualized in Friestad and Wright's (1994) persuasion knowledge model. The PKM outlines how people develop personal awareness or knowledge, and in turn, use it to cope with persuasion attempts.

Persuasive attempts, such as an advertisement, a salesperson's greeting or a product message, aim to "influence someone's beliefs, attitudes, decisions, or actions" (Friestad & Wright, 1994, p. 2). Consumers who are aware of persuasion tactics coming from an agent – such as a salesperson or an advertising vehicle – may not be persuaded, or counteract the attempt. As consumers cope with marketing attempts, they activate personal persuasion knowledge, agent knowledge, or topic knowledge about the product or service (Friestad & Wright, 1994).

Individuals structure beliefs about marketers' psychological approaches and tactics, and self-views of how they cope with persuasive attempts. These beliefs are operationalized into effects that individuals think advertisers are trying to achieve via different tactics (Boush, Friestad, & Rose, 1994; Wright, Friestad, & Boush, 2005). For example, middle school students with higher persuasion knowledge were more likely to be skeptical of advertising (Boush et al., 1994). Higher persuasion knowledge among adolescents with more exposure to television also aligned with higher skepticism (Mangleburg & Bristol, 1998).

Past experimental studies show how consumers may develop attitudes and take actions related to marketer interactions in different marketing scenarios. Pertinent to SNGs, several studies have conducted experiments in video games and interactive environments that include billboard advertisements and product placements (Chaney, Lin, & Chaney, 2004; Lee & Faber, 2007; Nelson, 2002; Nelson, Yaros, & Keum,

2006). Chaney et al. (2004) found immersion, even with multiple product placements of brands, limiting brand recall in games. Lee and Faber (2007) saw brand memory influenced by location of placements, involvement with the game, and prior play experience. However, improved recall emerged when brands were key to game play, relevant to players, or showing unique qualities (Nelson, 2002). Further, Nelson et al. (2006) found higher brand recall for product placement among game watchers versus players, who extended more cognitive demand during play.

Related to the few studies of marketer-generated eWOM, persuasion knowledge has been acknowledged as a potential contributor to consumer attitudes and behaviors (Godes & Mayzlin, 2009). Persuasion knowledge, developed via interactions in a virtual consumer community with messages from marketers and consumers, impacted ways consumers share information (Hung & Li, 2007). Also, persuasion knowledge negatively related to online video sharing of marketer messages (Hsieh et al., 2012).

Given previous findings, consumers bring persuasion knowledge to SNG play. Cognitive capacity may be demanded by the game experience. When seeing a marketer-generated eWOM message, consumers use persuasion knowledge and agent knowledge to understand the message as a tactic. Past research found that consumers tend to show greater compliance to advertisers' attempts when they did not perceive tactics to achieve ulterior goals (Friestad & Wright, 1994). Also, it was found that priming consumers' awareness of an advertisement would negatively affect advertisement effectiveness in traditional and non-traditional media (Yoo, 2009). In other words, increased awareness of advertisers' ulterior motives and tactics negatively impacted advertising effectiveness.

Deeper knowledge may be involved as a consumer decides whether to forward the marketer-generated message, and potentially become a persuasion agent carrying the message to others. Consumers would be expected to decrease opinion passing and opinion giving when persuasion knowledge is heightened about marketer-generated messages in SNG play, leading to the following hypotheses:

H1: Higher levels of persuasion knowledge will negatively impact opinion passing.

H2: Higher levels of persuasion knowledge will negatively impact opinion giving.

Sincerity

Perceived sincerity that consumers feel about the ulterior motives behind a marketer's attempt closely relates to their persuasion knowledge (Campbell & Kirmani, 2000). In the PKM literature, consumers access and use agent knowledge in persuasive attempts. The concept of sincerity emerges as a factor in how consumers evaluate the motives of persuasion agents.

Related to SNGs, sincerity may play a part in consumer decisions about clicking on game advertising, engaging in advertising activities, and spreading marketer-generated eWOM. When consumers play SNGs, accessing persuasion knowledge could raise suspicions of the sincerity of advertisers' ulterior motives. When exposed to embedded advertising messages in SNGs, consumers may wonder why advertisers repeatedly ask them to take a survey or watch a video. Consumers may infer that advertisers have ulterior motives and perceive them to be less sincere.

The PKM framework depicts a consumer who processes persuasion attempts based on multiple pieces of information about the message, agent, and topic (Friestad & Wright, 1994). In this processing, with activated persuasion knowledge and ample cognitive capacity, consumers in experimental studies were more likely to rate an agent as less sincere (Campbell & Kirmani, 2000; Tuk, Verlegh, Smidts, & Wigboldus, 2005). These consumers may suspect ulterior motives of a persuasion agent, which lessens perceived sincerity (Campbell & Kirmani, 2000). However, Campbell and Kirmani (2000) emphasized that findings may differ depending on situations in which consumers value particular attributes, and cognitive demands vary. Tuk et al. (2005) studied relationship norms between consumers and agents, finding that when different norms were activated with limited cognitive capacity, sincerity levels changed.

Alternatively, Carl (2008) found consumers expressing higher feelings of credibility toward human agents who disclosed that they were communicating marketer-generated messages. In fact, motives may not be as much of an issue as the honesty of marketers – who make intentions clear to gain credibility and lessen skepticism (Forehand & Grier, 2003). The consumer playing an SNG may experience a marketer-generated eWOM attempt, viewing the persuasive agent as the advertiser. Marketer-generated messages in SNGs from different advertisers tend to follow similar mechanisms that make it easy for consumers to pass them along to their social networks.

SNGs are a new channel for the study of advertiser sincerity. Based on previous findings, consumers who experience an advertiser message in SNGs may decide to forward a marketer-generated message based on judgments of the sincerity of the advertisers. Further, consumers in the SNG eWOM situation may rely more on sincerity judgments because they are, in turn, passing along the marketer-generated message. Also, SNGs are within social media, which represent transparent qualities of communication and may enhance perceptions of advertiser sincerity. When consumers believe that advertisers do not have hidden motives, they are more likely to pass along and give information to their Facebook friends. Hypotheses support a positive direction of consumer perceptions of sincerity on eWOM behavior:

H3: Higher levels of sincerity will positively impact opinion passing.

H4: Higher levels of sincerity will positively impact opinion giving.

Consumer Product Knowledge

Consumer product knowledge is also an important factor that affects eWOM behavior. Knowing a person or an object means increased knowledge structure, affecting consumer information processing activities in several ways (Alba & Hutchinson, 1987, 2000; Rao & Monroe, 1988; Wood & Lynch, 2002). Product knowledge stored in a consumer's memory tends to facilitate easier and more efficient processing of information (Johnson & Russo, 1984). Additionally, knowledgeable consumers are able to make more refined product class or category-related judgments, allowing them to compare products and brands. As such, knowledgeable consumers are more likely to identify and choose products of relatively superior quality than consumers with low product knowledge (Kerin, Kalyanaram, & Howard, 1996; Kotler, 2000).

Söderlund (2002) found that, compared to low product knowledge, high product knowledge was associated with more extreme post-purchase responses for consumer satisfaction, repurchase intentions, and word-of-mouth intentions. More specifically, when service performance was high, consumers with high product knowledge expressed a higher level of satisfaction and behavioral intentions than did those with low product knowledge. On the other hand, when the service performance was low, consumers with high product knowledge expressed lower levels of satisfaction and behavioral intentions than did those with low product knowledge. This is because consumers with high product knowledge may use a different frame or set of reference for evaluations. Knowledgeable consumers have extensive networks of knowledge reflecting substantial prior thoughts and brand evaluations. Therefore, they are likely to make inferences that are more polarized than those with a less elaborate knowledge structure (Söderlund, 2002). Muthukrishnan (1995) also supports the notion that a higher level of elaboration and experience could lead to a stronger preference for the target brand and higher confidence in the decision.

Consumer-created information is likely to be more credible than seller-created information since consumers with high product knowledge are perceived to be a trustworthy information source (Chen & Xie, 2008; Wilson & Sherrell, 1993). Related to eWOM in SNGs, consumers with high product knowledge tend to be regarded as experts among peers, and are more likely to pass along and give information to their Facebook friends. Therefore, the following hypotheses predict:

H5: Higher levels of product knowledge will positively impact opinion passing.

H6: Higher levels of product knowledge will positively impact opinion giving.

Involvement

Feelings of involvement with media channels, such as television or video games, may influence responses to embedded advertising that encourages eWOM. Involvement perspectives for the newer gaming form of SNGs stem from studies related to video games with advertising product placement, and extended with eWOM literature. Consumers who play SNGs may feel varying levels of involvement with this entertainment being personally relevant based on "inherent needs, values and interests" (Zaichkowsky, 1994, p. 61). Zaichkowsky's (1994) definition relates to the personal involvement inventory, which describes consumer feelings that may motivate engagement with products, advertisements, and purchase situations.

Within experimental studies, in which consumers experienced product placements in video games, involvement contributed to advertising outcomes. Higher levels of involvement with the game environment, moderated by experienced presence or immersion, led to higher evaluation of advertising messages (Nicovich, 2005). Game involvement may also relate to how a consumer is motivated to use cognitive skills in play. Higher involvement in play may demand more cognitive skills, which lessens attention paid to advertising product placement, while lower involvement lessens attention to advertisements for different reasons. However, moderately involved consumers are more likely to pay attention to advertisements than consumers with low or high involvement. An inverted U-shape pattern depicts the relationship (Chaney et al., 2004; Lee & Faber, 2007).

Consumers experience SNG play while regularly checking in to social media. Given high levels of SNG play within the popular activity of Facebook use, consumer involvement with games may lead to feelings about SNGs as a form of entertainment and a personal interest area, which may be shared with Facebook friends. Further, consumer involvement in playing different SNGs may support positive feelings toward advertising messages. Higher personal interest in SNGs should positively influence decisions to pass along or share information related to marketer-generated messages in play. Hypotheses to reflect this expected direction include:

H7: Higher levels of game involvement will positively affect opinion passing.

H8: Higher levels of game involvement will positively affect opinion giving.

Method

An observational study of popular SNGs was conducted in 2011. Observations, captured in notes and screenshots, documented types of engagement advertisements primarily in four Facebook games: FarmVille, CityVille, PetVille, and Café World. An online survey of people who play Facebook games, based on the literature and on observational study, was conducted in late 2011 and completed in 2012. Facebook was chosen as a platform because of the popularity of the social network and its games, its avid promotion of many free games, and the high number of Facebook game players (Baker, 2012). Following Institutional Review Board approval, 319 participants were surveyed via a convenience sample. Participants were sought via email requests at a Midwestern university, messages on social media, and as an extra-credit opportunity in media courses. The sample was 33.1 percent male and 66.9 percent female. About 94.7 percent were ages 18–25, 2.5 percent were 26–35, 1.2 percent were 36–45, and 1.6 percent were 46–55. A series of regression analyses was conducted. Independent and dependent variables were analyzed based on the hypotheses. A conceptual model appears in Figure 1.1.

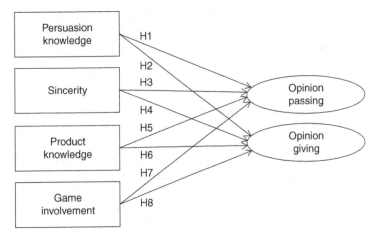

Figure 1.1 Hypothetical conceptual model

Independent Variables

Four independent variables were studied: persuasion knowledge, sincerity, product knowledge, and game involvement.

Persuasion knowledge is conceptually defined as "consumers' theories about persuasion and includes beliefs about marketers' motives, strategies, and tactics" (Campbell & Kirmani, 2000, p. 69). The measure for persuasion knowledge (Boush et al., 1994) was eight items on a seven-point Likert scale (1 = not trying at all; 7 = trying very hard) for the question, "When an ad asks you to pass along a message to your Facebook friends, how hard is an advertiser trying to..." (p. 167). The variables were the following statements:

a) Grab your attention, b) Make you want to buy something, c) Help you learn more about something you may want to buy, d) Make you like the game, e) Make you like the product, f) Get you to remember an advertisement, g) Get you to believe an advertisement, and h) Get you to think that having their product will make you feel good (Cronbach's α = .95). (Boush et al., 1994, p. 167)

The concept of sincerity shows ways a consumer may perceive a persuasion agent as honest, or alternatively, lacking straightforwardness because of ulterior motives (Campbell & Kirmani, 2000). Sincerity was measured with four items from Campbell and Kirmani (2000, p. 73), applied to SNG advertisers, through a rating scale for the question, "Select the number that best represents how you feel about advertisers in online games on Facebook." The seven-point semantic differential scale was:

a) 1 = insincere/7 = sincere, b) 1 = dishonest/7 = honest, c) 1 = manipulative/7 = not manipulative, and d) 1 = pushy/7 = not pushy (Cronbach's α = .83). (Campbell & Kirmani, 2000, p. 73)

In identifying the effects of product knowledge on consumer product evaluation, measuring both objective knowledge and subjective knowledge is common (Alba & Hutchinson, 1987; Park & Lessig, 1981). This study employed the subjective knowledge dimension, based on its relationship to consumer heuristics and decision-making strategy. Brucks (1985) defined subjective knowledge as the individual's perception of how much a consumer knows. The measure was slightly modified from the study of Alba and Hutchinson (1987). Four variables were measured on a seven-point Likert scale (1 = strongly disagree; 7 = strongly agree) to which respondents rated responses to the following statements:

a) I know a great deal about the products I post on my wall, b) I do not feel very knowledgeable about the products I post on my wall, c) Compared to my Facebook friends, I know less about the products I post on my wall, and d) When it comes to the products I post on my wall, I really don't know a lot (Cronbach's α = .75). (Flynn, Goldsmith, & Eastman, 1996, p. 59)

Lastly, Zaichkowsky (1985) defined involvement as perceived relevance for an object based on inherent needs, value, and interests. Zaichkowsky's (1994) personal involvement inventory was used by asking 10 items with a seven-point semantic differential scale such as:

a) 1 = unimportant/7 = important, b) 1 = irrelevant/7 = relevant, c) 1 = means nothing to me/7 = means a lot to me, d) 1 = worthless/7 = valuable to me, e) 1 = boring to me/7 = interesting to me, f) 1 = unexciting/7 = exciting to me, g) 1 = unappealing/7 = appealing to me, h) 1 = not needed/7 = needed by me, i) 1 = mundane/7 = fascinating to me, and j) 1 = uninvolving/7 = involving to me (Cronbach's α = .94). (p. 70)

Dependent Variables

Two dependent variables were studied: eWOM beliefs for opinion passing and opinion giving. Chu and Kim (2011), studying eWOM in SNSs specifically, conceptualized eWOM as opinion seeking, opinion giving, and opinion passing. Adding opinion passing operationalized SNS behaviors given the ease of passing along information and messages to other members of one's network. Based on the study from Chu and Kim (2011), seven-point Likert scales ranging from "strongly disagree" to "strongly agree" were used for eWOM measures. To measure opinion passing, respondents were asked their feelings about the statements:

a) When I receive product-related information from an advertiser while playing a game, I pass it along to my Facebook friends, b) While playing a game, if an advertiser asks me to post a message about a product to my wall, I'm likely to do it, and c) One way that I give my opinion about products is by posting an advertiser's message on Facebook (Cronbach's α = .78). (Chu & Kim, 2011, p. 60)

The important dependent variable is opinion giving. In considering marketer-generated messages in the game context within SNSs, Chu and Kim's (2011) conceptualization shows opinion giving with more persuasion. In contrast to opinion passing, opinion giving relates to opinion leadership as based on Flynn et al. (1996) and Sun, Youn, Wu, and Kutaraporn (2006). The measure asks respondents their feelings about the statements:

a) I often persuade my Facebook friends to buy products that I like, b) My Facebook friends pick their products based on what I have told them, and c) I often influence my Facebook friends' opinions about products (Cronbach's α = .89). (Chu & Kim, 2011, p. 60)

Results

Hypotheses Testing

Opinion passing and opinion giving were predicted from variables of persuasion knowledge, sincerity, product knowledge, and game involvement. Standard multiple regression was performed with all predictor variables entered in one step. To assess whether there were any multivariate outliers, the standardized residuals were plotted against standardized predicted values. No indications of pattern, trend, outliers, and heteroscedasticity were found, indicating that the assumption required for multiple regressions was reasonably met for hypotheses testing.

The overall regression to opinion passing, including all four predictors, was statistically significant, $R = .31$, R square = .10, adjusted R square = .08, $F(4, 314) = 8.25$, $p < .01$. A series of regression analyses showed that out of four predictors sincerity ($\beta = .26$, $t(314) = 4.65$, $p < .01$) and game involvement ($\beta = .11$, $t(314) = 2.02$, $p < .05$) significantly affected opinion passing, as demonstrated in Table 1.1. As such, H3 and H7 were supported.

The overall regression to opinion giving, including all four predictors, was statistically significant, $R = .35$, R square = .12, adjusted R square = .11, $F(4, 314) = 10.95$, $p < .01$. A series of regression analyses showed that out of four predictors, sincerity ($\beta = .27$, $t(314) = 4.98$, $p < .01$), product knowledge ($\beta = .11$, $t(314) = 2.14$, $p < .05$), and game involvement ($\beta = .14$, $t(314) = 2.50$, $p < .05$) significantly affected opinion giving, as displayed in Table 1.2. As a result, H4, H6, and H8 were supported.

Table 1.1 Results of standard multiple regression to predict opinion passing

Model	Unstandardized coefficients		Standardized coefficients		
	B	Std Error	Beta	T	Sig.
(Constant)	1.295	.327		3.963	.000
Persuasion knowledge	−.009	.034	−.014	−.254	.799
Sincerity	.226	.049	.260	4.645	.000**
Product knowledge	−.045	.052	−.046	−.856	.392
Game involvement	.108	.054	.111	2.015	.045*

Note: Dependent variable: opinion passing; * p < .05, ** p < .01.

Table 1.2 Results of standard multiple regression to predict opinion giving

Model	Unstandardized coefficients		Standardized coefficients		
	B	Std Error	Beta	T	Sig.
(Constant)	.423	.443		.954	.341
Persuasion knowledge	.005	.047	.005	.101	.920
Sincerity	.329	.066	.274	4.976	.000**
Product knowledge	.151	.071	.113	2.135	.034*
Game involvement	.182	.073	.136	2.493	.013*

Note: Dependent variable: opinion giving; * p < .05, ** p < .01.

Furthermore, correlation testing was conducted to understand the relationships between variables. Correlation testing found that opinion passing and opinion giving were significantly correlated (r = .58, p < .01). This result shows that the distinct concepts of opinion passing and giving are closely related. Correlation testing also found that sincerity is positively correlated with involvement (*r* = .23, p < .01), opinion passing (*r* = .29, *p* < .01), and opinion giving (*r* = .30, *p* < .01), respectively. High persuasion knowledge is negatively correlated with sincerity (*r* = −.11, *p* = n.s.), although it is not statistically significant. Perhaps the more consumers know about persuasion knowledge, the more sophisticated they are about differentiating the persuasion agent's true motives. Also, game involvement is positively correlated to both opinion passing (*r* = .17, *p* < .01) and opinion giving (*r* = .21, *p* < .01). Lee and Faber (2007) and Campbell and Kirmani (2000) found that the more consumers are involved in cognitive elaboration, the more the consumers' cognitive capacity to infer ulterior motives becomes restricted.

Additional Analysis: Mediation Effects of Attitude toward Advertisement and Brand

Further study was conducted regarding why persuasion knowledge did not directly impact opinion passing and opinion giving during hypotheses testing. A closer evaluation was conducted for sincerity, which Campbell and Kirmani (2000) saw heightened with less-activated persuasion knowledge. Attitude toward advertising (Aad) in SNGs and attitude toward brands (Abrand) in SNGs were evaluated, based on Homer's (1990) measurement, as intermediating variables for potential effects between sincerity and both eWOM behaviors. A series of regression analyses was conducted to check the assumption test (Baron & Kenny, 1986). When considering Aad, the estimated regression model showed that persuasion knowledge significantly affects sincerity ($\beta = -.20$, $p < .05$). With the direction of beta value, consumers with higher persuasion knowledge were less likely to perceive advertisers as being sincere. Also, sincerity significantly affects Aad ($\beta = .39$, $p < .00$). Therefore, the more consumers perceived advertisers as sincere, the more positive Aad increased. However, persuasion knowledge did not significantly affect Aad ($\beta = -.02$, $p = $ n.s.), meaning the assumption for mediation effect was not met.

Regarding Abrand, a full mediation effect of sincerity between persuasion knowledge and Abrand was found. Persuasion knowledge significantly impacts both sincerity and Abrand respectively ($\beta = -.20$, $p < .05$; $\beta = -.18$, $p < .05$). Also, sincerity significantly influences Abrand

($\beta = .50$, $p < .00$). Finally, when persuasion knowledge and sincerity were considered simultaneously, it was expected that the formerly significant effect of persuasion knowledge on Abrand would lose significance, and, indeed, it was found to be insignificant ($\beta = -.09$, $p = $ n.s.). Yet, the effect of sincerity on Abrand remained significant ($\beta = .48$, $p < .00$). This result illustrates that sincerity fully mediates the relationship between persuasion knowledge and Abrand. Of note, the direction of impact shows that persuasion knowledge negatively impacts sincerity, and sincerity positively impacts Abrand. This finding could explain why persuasion knowledge did not directly impact eWOM behaviors in hypotheses testing. Put another way, persuasion knowledge could be an antecedent of sincerity, which aligns with Campbell and Kirmani's (2000) study. Therefore, subsequent analysis was conducted without persuasion knowledge.

To further understand the underlying relationships between three antecedents and opinion passing and opinion giving, a series of

Table 1.3 Mediating effects of Aad and Abrand on sincerity

Independent variable	Dependent variable	Total	
		β	P
Sincerity	Opinion passing	.29	.00**
Sincerity	Aad	.45	.00**
Aad	Opinion passing	.38	.00**
Sincerity	Opinion passing	.15	.05*
Aad		.32	.00**
Sincerity	Opinion giving	.30	.00**
Sincerity	Aad	.45	.00**
Aad	Opinion giving	.28	.00**
Sincerity	Opinion giving	.22	.00**
Aad		.18	.00**
Sincerity	Opinion passing	.29	.00**
Sincerity	Abrand	.48	.00**
Abrand	Opinion passing	.26	.00**
Sincerity	Opinion passing	.21	.00**
Abrand		.16	.05*
Sincerity	Opinion giving	.30	.00**
Sincerity	Abrand	.48	.00**
Abrand	Opinion giving	.29	.00**
Sincerity	Opinion giving	.21	.00**
Abrand		.19	.00**

Note: Aad: attitude toward ad; Abrand: attitude toward brand. Adapted from Homer (1990) with permission. *: p <.05, **: p < .01.

regression analyses was performed to examine the mediating roles of Aad and Abrand. It was found that Aad and Abrand partially mediate the impact of sincerity on opinion passing and opinion giving. These results illustrate that consumers tend to form positive Aad and Abrand when they perceive advertisers are sincere in SNGs, and then engage in opinion passing and giving behaviors as shown in Table 1.3.

Similarly, it was found that Aad and Abrand partially mediate the impact of involvement on opinion passing and opinion giving. In particular, Abrand fully mediates the impact of involvement on opinion passing behavior. As such, consumers tend to form positive Aad and Abrand when they are highly involved with SNGs, which results in opinion passing and opinion giving behavior, as shown in Table 1.4. Regarding product knowledge, no mediation effect was found for opinion passing and opinion giving.

Table 1.4 Mediating effects of Aad and Abrand on game involvement

Independent variable	Dependent variable	Total	
		β	P
Involvement	Opinion passing	.17	.00**
Involvement	Aad	.16	.00**
Aad	Opinion passing	.38	.00**
Involvement	Opinion passing	.11	.05*
Aad		.37	.00**
Involvement	Opinion giving	.21	.00**
Involvement	Aad	.16	.00**
Aad	Opinion giving	.28	.00**
Involvement	Opinion giving	.17	.00**
Aad		.25	.00**
Involvement	Opinion passing	.17	.00**
Involvement	Abrand	.25	.00**
Abrand	Opinion passing	.38	.00**
Involvement	Opinion passing	.11	.06
Abrand		.24	.00**
Involvement	Opinion giving	.21	.00**
Involvement	Abrand	.25	.00**
Abrand	Opinion giving	.29	.00**
Involvement		.15	.05*
Abrand	Opinion giving	.25	.00**

Note: Aad: attitude toward ad; Abrand: attitude toward brand. Adapted from Homer (1990) with permission. *: p <.05, **: p < .01.

Discussion

Research Implications

The goal of this study was to understand the role of persuasion knowledge, sincerity, product knowledge, and game involvement on eWOM in SNGs. In initial regression analysis, all factors, except persuasion knowledge, were positive antecedents of eWOM behavior for consumers playing SNGs. Sincerity and game involvement significantly influenced opinion passing, and along with product knowledge, significantly influenced opinion giving. With additional mediation analysis, persuasion knowledge that did not influence eWOM indeed emerged as impacting the sincerity consumers felt toward advertisers. In turn, higher sincerity led to positive consumer attitudes toward advertisements and brands in SNGs, and enhanced eWOM behaviors.

These findings support Campbell and Kirmani's (2000) study of the interplay between accessibility of persuasion knowledge and cognitive capacity affecting inference of persuasion motives and, eventually, perceptions of the agent. When persuasion knowledge was evaluated in mediation analysis as preceding sincerity feelings – via perceptions of the agent or SNG advertisement – its influence on attitudes and subsequent eWOM behaviors was evident.

Sincerity fully mediates the impact of persuasion knowledge on Abrand. Subsequently, both Aad and Abrand partially mediate the impact of sincerity on opinion passing and giving behavior. Therefore, it can be concluded that persuasion knowledge indirectly impacts opinion giving and passing via sincerity and Abrand. It is interesting to note that the more persuasion knowledge consumers have, the less likely they are to perceive advertisers as being sincere. It could be that consumers with high persuasion knowledge are able to assess persuasion tactics in memory structures (Campbell & Kirmani, 2000). In addition, significant positive impacts of Aad and Abrand on opinion giving and passing behavior illustrate how important it is for companies to form positive consumer attitudes toward advertisements and brands. Underlying mechanisms of how persuasion knowledge negatively impacts sincerity from the psychological perspective could be the subject of future research.

As predicted in the initial analysis, sincerity significantly impacts opinion passing and giving. Past studies found that suspicion of an advertiser's underlying motives could result in a less favorable perception of the advertiser (Fein, Hilton, & Miller, 1990; Vonk, 1998, 1999). When consumers were exposed to engagement advertisements, they were likely to assess the advertisers' ulterior motives. Consumers are

uncertain about the claims in the advertisements and normally companies know more about their product than do consumers (Erdem & Swait,
2004). When advertisers are perceived as credible, consumers regard them
as sincere. As Carl (2008) found, when advertisers' motives are disclosed,
consumers see heightened sincerity and honesty, which may increase
their passing along and giving information about marketer-generated
messages to Facebook friends.

Product knowledge significantly affected opinion giving, although
it did not significantly impact opinion passing. Consumers with high
product knowledge tend to evaluate product quality accurately and have
a strong preference toward a certain brand (Kerin et al., 1996; Kotler,
2000; Muthukrishnan, 1995). Therefore, consumers with high product
knowledge are more likely to give information to Facebook friends to
influence their purchase decisions. Flynn et al. (1996) defined opinion
leaders as people who directly influence others by providing advice and
verbal directions for product searching and purchase. Consumers with
high product knowledge help their networks by transferring useful information. However, it was found that both Aad and Abrand do not mediate
the impact of product knowledge on opinion giving. Put another way,
consumers with high product knowledge do not necessarily form Aad
and Abrand before giving opinions to Facebook friends.

Game involvement significantly affects opinion passing and giving.
It is important for consumers to advance and perform well in the game.
Particularly in SNGs, consumers are repeatedly asked by advertisers to
engage in different types of activity to receive game currency or virtual
goods. Therefore, voluntarily posting marketer-generated messages on
their Facebook walls relates to economic benefits. Other researchers
found that playing the game is the primary task for players, whereas
processing advertisements embedded in the game is a secondary task
(Grigorovici & Constantin, 2004). In SNGs the border between game
and advertisements is blurred. Mediation analysis also supports the
concept that consumers with high involvement tend to form positive
Aad and Abrand and that subsequently they impact opinion passing and
giving. The more consumers engage in SNGs, the more they are likely to
be exposed to advertisements and brands. They will form positive Aad
and Abrand, which aids eWOM related to game performance.

Practical Implications

Advertising fuels the fast growth of free-to-play SNGs. This activity,
popular with the global public, is positioned to grow as game titles,
features, and advertisement interactions expand (Baker, 2012; Shields,

2012), and evolve as social media platforms mature. Practitioners find that SNG advertisements not only engage with consumers to complete activities related to a product or brand but also successfully encourage consumers to become persuasion agents. As such, consumers may forward a marketer-generated message to social media when advertisers are seen as sincere and the games are involving.

When consumers view SNG advertisers as sincere, significantly more opinion passing and giving happens. Attitudes that consumers develop toward advertising and brands in SNGs influence eWOM behaviors. SNG developers and advertisers, at the time of this study, developed a positive relationship with consumers regarding eWOM. Potentially, advertisements in the game take on the transparent and straightforward qualities of Facebook and other social media. The friendly ways in which consumers interact with each other may transfer to inclusion of eWOM messages. Also, observational play revealed that SNG advertisement campaigns focused less on promotional selling and more on brand building as consumers interacted with advertisements – taking surveys, watching videos, or uploading consumer-generated content – to receive economic game incentives. Messages tended to be brand-related interactions versus a 'hard sell.' This message approach may support positive Aad and Abrand that helped enhance sincerity and involvement impacts on eWOM behavior. Further, observations showed that consumers were free to choose whether to forward these messages, which may have limited feelings of advertisers being pushy or manipulative. As SNGs and SNG advertisements evolve in game features and new campaigns, practitioners should ensure they interact with consumers in a way that maintains an honest and optional approach.

Since advertisements play a key role in SNGs, their presence may influence involvement. As SNGs regularly release new titles and ways to interact with other players and advertisements, game features may enhance involvement. Potentially, game features that integrate with advertisements could impair player interactions and entertainment value, and limit involvement. An ideal mix of cognitive demand may be particular to SNGs at the time of this study – involvement happened, yet the advertisement outcomes support consumers forwarding marketer eWOM and giving persuasive opinion. With the heightened use of mobile devices, consumers have increasing opportunities to play SNGs, experience advertisements, and increase personal investment in casual games. Given these trends, advertisers should choose campaigns that build on involvement and game features. SNGs should encourage user-friendly games with a continued focus on entertainment, achievement, and other fun features for ongoing play. With a potential to reach consumers that is growing compared to traditional channels, more advertising may be proposed for SNGs. Game designers and advertisers need to be watchful to ensure that engagement advertisements and new advertisement functions do not detract from the SNG experience. Detractions may decrease involvement, and in turn, lessen eWOM potential.

The impact of product knowledge shows that advertisers should use marketing objectives to determine the type of eWOM campaign. Logically, consumers who like to share product knowledge to persuade others' purchase decisions are more likely to persuasively share marketer-generated eWOM via opinion giving. These opinion leaders are less likely to pass along a message if their product knowledge does not support it. This opinion leader behavior, discerning which messages to forward based on product knowledge, can alert SNG advertisers to realities based on their marketing objectives. As Godes and Mayzlin (2009) found, less loyal customers may indeed spread more information simply by passing along marketer-generated eWOM. In a related way, advertisers seeking broad eWOM pass-along should consider SNG campaigns that are less about product features and facts, and more focused on promotion or fun. However, if SNG campaigns seek to influence consumers with product knowledge, who in turn influence others via eWOM, advertisers should consider product-specific campaigns that detail features, competitor comparisons, and other insights for the more knowledgeable and persuasive consumer.

SNGs and SNSs are dynamic and evolving platforms. Consumer habits and trends, platform popularity, game features, and mobile intersections continue to shift as forms of new media mature. Ongoing change tends to impact the ways consumers experience social media, and how advertisers leverage new media environments for strategic communications.

References

Alba, J. W., & Hutchinson, J. W. (1987). Dimensions of consumer expertise. *Journal of Consumer Research, 13*(4), 411–454.

Alba, J. W., & Hutchinson, J. W. (2000). Knowledge calibration: What consumers know and what they think they know. *Journal of Consumer Research, 27*(2), 123–156.

Baker, L. B. (2012, April 29). Madison Avenue turns to social game advertising. *Reuters*. Retrieved from http://www.reuters.com/article/2012/04/29/us-videoga mes-ads-idUSBRE83S09P20120429

Baron, R. M., & Kenny, D. A. (1986). The moderator-mediator variable distinction in social psychological research: Conceptual, strategic, and statistical considerations. *Journal of Personality and Social Psychology, 51*(6), 1173–1182.

Boush, D. M., Friestad, M., & Rose, G. M. (1994). Adolescent skepticism toward TV advertising and knowledge of advertiser tactics. *Journal of Consumer Research, 21*(1), 165–175.

Brucks, M. (1985). The effects of product class knowledge on information search behavior. *Journal of Consumer Research, 12*(1), 1–16.

Campbell, M. C., & Kirmani, A. (2000). Consumers' use of persuasion knowledge: The effects of accessibility and cognitive capacity on perceptions of an influence agent. *Journal of Consumer Research, 27*(1), 69–83.

Carl, W. J. (2008). The role of disclosure in organized word-of-mouth marketing programs. *Journal of Marketing Communications, 14*(3), 225–241.

Chaney, I. M., Lin, K., & Chaney, J. (2004). The effect of billboards within the gaming environment. *Journal of Interactive Advertising, 5*(1), 37–45. Retrieved from http://jiad.org/article54

Chen, Y., & Xie, J. (2008). Online consumer review: Word-of-mouth as a new element of marketing communication mix. *Management Science, 54*(3), 477–491.

Chu, S., & Kim, Y. (2011). The determinants of consumer engagement in electronic word-of-mouth (eWOM) in social networking sites. *International Journal of Advertising, 30*(1), 47–75.

Erdem, T., & Swait, J. (2004). Brand credibility, brand consideration, and choice. *Journal of Consumer Research, 31*(1), 191–198.

Feick, L. F., & Price, L. L. (1987). The market maven: A diffuser of marketplace information. *Journal of Marketing, 51*(1), 83–97.

Fein, S. (1996). Effects of suspicion on attributional thinking and the correspondence bias. *Journal of Personality and Social Psychology, 70*(6), 1164–1184.

Fein, S., Hilton, J. L., & Miller, D. T. (1990). Suspicion of ulterior motivation and the correspondence bias. *Journal of Personality and Social Psychology, 58*(5), 753–764.

Flynn, L. R., Goldsmith, R. E., & Eastman, J. K. (1996). Opinion leaders and opinion seekers: Two new measurement scales. *Journal of the Academy of Marketing Science, 24*(2), 137–147.

Forehand, M. R., & Grier, S. (2003). When is honesty the best policy? The effects of stated company intent on consumer skepticism. *Journal of Consumer Psychology, 13*(3), 349–356.

Friestad, M., & Wright, P. (1994). The persuasion knowledge model: How people cope with persuasion attempts. *Journal of Consumer Research, 21*(1), 1–31.

Godes, D., & Mayzlin, D. (2009). Firm-created word-of-mouth communication: Evidence from a field test. *Marketing Science, 28*(4), 721–739.

Gremler, D. D., Gwinner, K. P., & Brown, S. W. (2001). Generating word-of-mouth communication through customer-employee relationships. *International Journal of Service Industry Management, 12*(1), 44–59.

Grigorovici, D. M., & Constantin, C. (2004). Experiencing interactive advertising beyond rich media: Impact of ad type and presence on brand effectiveness in 3D gaming immersive virtual environments. *Journal of Interactive Advertising, 5*(1). Retrieved from http://jiad.org/article53/

Homer, P. M. (1990). The mediating role of attitude toward the ad: Some additional evidence. *Journal of Marketing Research, 27*(1), 76–86.

Hsieh, J., Hsieh, Y., & Tang, Y. (2012). Exploring the disseminating behaviors of eWOM marketing: Persuasion in online video. *Electronic Commerce Research, 12*(2), 201–224.

Hung, K. H., & Li, S. Y. (2007). The influence of eWOM on virtual consumer communities: Social capital, consumer learning, and behavioral outcomes. *Journal of Advertising Research, 47*(4), 485–495.

Johnson, E. J., & Russo, J. E. (1984). Product familiarity and learning new information. *Journal of Consumer Research, 11*(1), 542–550.

Kerin, R. A., Kalyanaram, G., & Howard, D. J. (1996). Product hierarchy and brand strategy influences on the order of entry effect for consumer packaged goods. *Journal of Product Innovation Management, 13*(1), 21–34.

Kotler, P. (2000). *Marketing management, the millennium edition.* Upper Saddle River, NJ: Prentice Hall.

Lee, M., & Faber, R. J. (2007). Effects of product placement in on-line games on brand memory. *Journal of Advertising, 36*(4), 75–90.

Mangleburg, T. F., & Bristol, T. (1998). Socialization and adolescents' skepticism toward advertising. *Journal of Advertising, 27*(3), 11–21.

Muthukrishnan, A. V. (1995). Decision ambiguity and incumbent brand advantage. *Journal of Consumer Research, 22*(1), 98–109.

Nelson, M. R. (2002). Recall of brand placements in computer/video games. *Journal of Advertising Research, 42*(2), 80–92.

Nelson, M. R., Yaros, R. A., & Keum, H. (2006). Examining the influence of telepresence on spectator and player processing of real and fictitious brands in a computer game. *Journal of Advertising, 35*(4), 87–99.

Nicovich, S. G. (2005). The effect of involvement on ad judgment in a video game environment: The mediating role of presence. *Journal of Interactive Advertising, 6*(1), 29–39. Retrieved from http://jiad.org/article67

Park, C. W., & Lessig, V. P. (1981). Familiarity and its impact on consumer decision biases and heuristics. *Journal of Consumer Research, 8*(2), 223–230.

Rao, A. R., & Monroe, K. B. (1988). The moderating effect of prior knowledge cue utilization in product evaluations. *Journal of Consumer Research, 15*(2), 253–264.

Shields, M. (2012, March 5). How ads could ruin Zynga and why they (probably) won't: Post IPO does the gaming giant need to see the advertising light? *Adweek.* Retrieved from http://www.adweek.com/news/advertising-branding /how-ads-could-ruin-zynga-and-why-they-probably-wont-138716

Söderlund, J. (2002). Managing complex development projects: Arenas, knowledge processes and time. *R&D Management, 32*(5), 419–430.

Sun, T., Youn, S., Wu, G., & Kutaraporn, M. (2006). Online word-of-mouth (or mouse): An exploration of its antecedents and consequences. *Journal of Computer-Mediated Communication, 11*(4), 1104–1127.

Tuk, M. A., Verlegh, P. W. J., Smidts, A., & Wigboldus, D. H. J. (2005). Activation of salesperson stereotypes affects perceptions of word-of-mouth referral. *Advances in Consumer Research, 32*(1), 1–38.

Verna, P. (2011, January). Social gaming: Marketers make their move. *eMarketer.* Retrieved from http://www.iab.net/insights_research/industry_data_ and_landscape/1675/1552062

Vonk, R. (1998). The slime effect: Suspicion and dislike of likable behavior toward superiors. *Journal of Personality and Social Psychology, 74*(4), 849–864.

Vonk, R. (1999). Impression formation and impression management: Motives, traits, and likability inferred from self-promoting and self-deprecating behavior. *Social Cognition, 17*(4), 390–412.

Walsh, G., Gwinner, K. P., & Swanson, S. (2004). What makes mavens tick? Exploring the motives of market mavens' initiation of information diffusion. *Journal of Consumer Marketing, 21*(2), 109–122.

Web users welcome brands to social games (2011, June 23). *eMarketer*. Retrieved from http://www.emarketer.com/Article.aspx?R=1008456

Wilson, E. J., & Sherrell, D. L. (1993). Source effects in communication and persuasion research: A meta-analysis of effect size. *Journal of the Academic Marketing Science, 21*(2), 101–112.

Wood, S. L., & Lynch, Jr., J. G. (2002). Prior knowledge and complacency in new product learning. *Journal of Consumer Research, 29*(3), 416–426.

Wright, P., Friestad, M., & Boush, D. M. (2005). The development of marketplace persuasion knowledge in children, adolescents, and young adults. *Journal of Public Policy & Marketing, 24*(2), 222–233.

Yoo, C. Y. (2009). The effects of persuasion knowledge on click-through of keyword search ads: Moderating role of search task and perceived fairness. *Journalism and Mass Communication Quarterly, 86*(2), 401–418.

Zaichkowsky, J. L. (1985). Measuring the involvement construct. *Journal of Consumer Research, 12*(3), 341–352.

Zaichkowsky, J. L. (1994). The personal involvement inventory: Reduction, revision, and application to advertising. *Journal of Advertising, 23*(4), 59–70.

2

Twitter as Gateway to Relationship Marketing: A Content Analysis of Relationship Building via Twitter

Brandi A. Watkins and Regina Lewis

Relationship marketing has been cited as an umbrella term for service sector marketing strategies and in marketing literature is considered a move away from finding ways to attract new customers to attaining, maintaining, and enhancing relationships with existing customers (Berry, 1995, 2002). In recent years, researchers have devoted considerable attention to studying the nature of the relationship between brands and consumers; however, much of the research has focused on marketing-related outcomes (Ashworth, Dacin, & Thomson, 2009). Bhattacharya and Sen's (2002) research sought to understand why consumers enter into relationships with brands, and found that consumers seek out relationships with brands that "satisfy one or more key self-definitional needs" (p. 77). Gwinner, Gremier, and Bitner (1998) studied consumer benefits to engaging in consumer–brand relationships. Their findings indicate that consumers experience confidence, and social and special treatment benefits through involvement in consumer–brand relationships.

Social media have changed the way consumers and brands interact and are potentially a valuable tool for advertisers in building consumer–brand relationships (Wallace, Wilson, & Miloch, 2011). Wallace et al. (2011) wrote, "the ability to communicate direct and unfiltered messages via social media provides a significant and strategic means of establishing and maintaining a strong brand identity for encouraging repeat consumption" (p. 423). Kittle and Ciba (2001) suggested that relationship marketing should include high levels of consumer involvement, and that social media, especially Twitter, promotes high levels of interaction among users (Williams & Chinn, 2010; Kaplan & Haenlein, 2010). The interactive structural features of Twitter allow for the possibility of continuous dialogue between brands and consumers (Kwon & Sung, 2011). Java, Song, Finin, and Tseng (2007) found that micro-blogging networks, including Twitter, have "a high degree of correlation and reciprocity, indicating close mutual acquaintances among users" (p. 64). Additional research is necessary to determine how social media sites, such as Twitter, can be used as a tool in creating consumer–brand relationships.

Drawing on traditional relationship building scholarship, previous work conducted by the authors adopted the five levels of a relationship building framework (Kotler, 1992) to use in Twitter (Watkins, 2012). In the research, the authors redefined and used the existing levels in terms of the consumer–brand interaction on Twitter. In an effort to work toward a better understanding of the role of social media in establishing consumer relationships, the authors refined the previous definitions to provide a more comprehensive examination of how all Twitter's features can be used in building consumer–brand relationships. The new definitions were studied and worked on in tweets from professional sports teams to gauge the amount of interaction between the brand and its followers.

Sports are classified as a service sector brand (much like universities, the setting for the original study) that is defined by intangible products and highly involved consumers (Underwood, Bond, & Baer, 2001). Bee and Kahle (2006) argued that, "sports consumers are often highly involved and their commitment to the sports organization is often displayed through repeat purchase of tickets, continued attendance at sporting events and the purchase of sport-related products" (p. 104). Through these high levels of involvement, consumers demonstrate a desire to engage in a relationship with the sports brand (Bee & Kahle, 2006). Additionally, social media allows sports fans unprecedented access to sports teams, coaches, players, and other fans. Hambrick, Simmons, Greenhalgh, and Greenwell (2010) wrote, "this accessibility to teams, and, more important, to players is an important antecedent to the development of team identification" (p. 455); the authors argued that team identification can be equated to brand identification. For these reasons, sports provide an interesting context for studying consumer–brand relationships. The goal of this chapter is to study the consumer–brand relationship by identifying the social media activity that precedes the consumer–brand relationship.

Relationship Marketing

Service-based industries are based on intangible products that cannot be packaged like goods, for instance, shampoo or soap (Berry, 2000). For this reason, the branding and marketing of service brands becomes even more important. Berry (2000) argued, "branding plays a special role in the service companies because strong brands increase customers' trust of the invisible purchase" (p. 128). One strategy for enhancing a consumer's experience of a brand is to engage the consumer in a long-term relationship that is mutually beneficial for both brand and consumer (Berry, 2000; Bhattacharya & Bolton, 2000; Williams & Chinn, 2010). Fournier (1998) explained, "brands can and do serve as viable relationship partners, consumer–brand relationships are valid at the level of lived experience" (p. 344). Through shared experiences with a brand, consumers become relationship partners with the brand.

Relationship marketing is defined as "attracting, maintaining and – in multi-service organizations – enhancing customer relationships" (Berry, 2002, p. 61), and represents a paradigm shift to focusing on retaining current customers rather than attracting new ones (Berry, 2002; Bhattacharya & Bolton, 2000). Parvatiyar and Sheth (2000) assert, "the core theme of all relationship marketing perspectives and definitions is a focus on cooperative and collaborative relationships between the firm and its customers and/or other marketing actors" (pp. 6–7). Relationship marketing operates on the assumption that it is more efficient and effective for brands to retain customers than to attract new ones (Sheth & Parvatiyar, 2000). This framework emphasizes establishing a relationship with existing customers, turning indifferent customers into loyal customers, and treating customers as if they were clients (Berry, 1995). Customer retention leads to repeat purchase behavior (customer loyalty), psychological attachment and the development of a positive attitude toward the brand.

However, as Gronroos (2004) argued, relationship marketing does not exclude attracting new consumers. By establishing a relationship with existing consumers, a company can also attract new ones, and engage existing and potential consumers in a relationship, which is mutually beneficial for all parties. Loyal customers who engage in repeat activity with a brand help the brand meet its economic goals while the consumer meets emotional goals of belonging and acceptance (Gronroos, 1994). Berry (1995) suggested, "services [brands] that are personally important, variable in quality and/or complex" (p. 237) are more likely to attract customers who would want to be "relationship customers" (p. 237).

This implies a willingness on the part of the consumer to engage in a relationship with a brand. Relationship marketing is ineffective if there is not a customer base interested in engaging in such a relationship. Thus, the type of communication (one- or two-way) between the brand and the consumer becomes an important aspect of the relationship building process.

Five levels of relationship building

Service–product consumption is a process rather than an outcome; therefore, maintaining a long-term relationship with consumers is an important goal for service oriented brands (Gronroos, 2004). Gronroos (2004) describes this process as "identifying potential customers to establishing a relationship with them, and then maintaining the relationship that has been established and enhance it so that more business as well as good references and favorable word of mouth are generated" (p. 101). Kotler (1992) developed a model for five levels of building relationships with consumers; these levels are: basic, reactive, accountable, proactive and partnership. Within this model, brands engage in different levels of relationship building ranging from virtually no effort to a two-way conversation. Social media, and Twitter in particular, provide an outlet for brands to engage in two-way conversation with potential consumers.

Building on the proposition that brands operate at different relationship building levels with consumers, the authors operationalized Kotler's (1992) five levels of relationship building in the context of Twitter. Twitter's structure offers a unique opportunity for brands to engage in direct conversation with consumers, making it ideal for studying the use of social media in establishing consumer–brand relationships. Each level represents an increase in activity by both brand and consumers (i.e., other Twitter users).

The basic level, as conceived by Kotler (1992), does not include following-up with the consumer after the point of sale. For Twitter, this level is defined as one-way communication with followers with no intention to respond (Watkins, 2012). This was operationalized as the broadcast of an original message by the brand with no additional links or information in the tweet.

The reactive level builds on the basic level in that the brand invites the customer to initiate a post-sale communication. The reactive level is defined as one-way communication with followers and is characterized by the broadcast of an original message with links to external sources for additional information. The onus is on the consumer to seek out the additional information. A tweet containing a link to an external website, or the presence of an @ mention, was operationalized as the main characteristic of this level.

The third level of relationship building is the accountable level. Kotler's (1992) definition suggests the seller initiates one post-transaction contact. Applying this level to Twitter includes having the brand "follow" the user. Following a user on Twitter is viewed as a one-time courtesy that acknowledges the presence of a user but does not necessarily imply that future interaction will take place. The number of Twitter users the brand follows should indicate how responsive they are at the accountable level.

At the proactive level, there is periodic contact with the brand and the consumer. Watkins (2012) operationalized this level as engaging in one-way, multi-time communication with followers represented through the act of "retweeting" a message from followers. Retweeting is defined as "the act of forwarding another user's tweet to all of your followers" (Twitter, 2012, para. 61). The act of retweeting a message is still a form of one-way communication but can occur multiple times.

Finally, the fifth level of relationship building is the partnership level in which there is continual contact with the customer. Brands can use Twitter to engage in two-way, dialogic communication with followers. This can be accomplished through replying directly to tweets posted by users.

An initial study completed by the authors utilized these definitions in a content analysis of university Twitter activity (Watkins, 2012). The top twenty-five universities on the *U.S. News and World Report* National University Rankings were used in the analysis. Tweets were collected from each school for a one-week period over three months (October 2011, November 2011, December 2011) to determine the level of relationship building universities were employing. Results revealed that most of the universities engaged in reactive level relationship marketing; based on the operational definition of the reactive level, the study found that most universities were engaging in one-way communication with little to no response to followers. These findings suggest that the two-way dialogic capabilities of using Twitter are currently not being fully utilized by universities.

To continue working toward identifying antecedents that precede consumer–brand relationships using social media, the previously discussed relationship level definitions need to be refined and applied across multiple industries to ensure generalizability. For these reasons, the current study builds upon previous research by adjusting the accountable and proactive levels of relationship building to include user response, and examines tweets collected from professional sports teams.

After further examination of the structure and composition of tweets, the authors decided that these operational definitions should be refined to better represent actual Twitter activity. The basic level retained its current definition, as a one-way communication with followers defined by the broadcast of an original message with no outlet for response from followers. The reactive level also retains its initial definition as one-way communication with followers but the presence of additional information invites consumers to initiate follow up communication. In this case, the coding definition has been changed to include not only the presence of links to external websites but also the presence of a hashtag (#), which is used in Twitter as a way to organize broad topics of tweets (Twitter, 2012). By including a hashtag with the tweet, the brand not only broadcasts a message but also provides a method for the user to respond to the tweet (by identifying their response with the same hashtag). Applied to Twitter, the accountable level is defined as one-way, one-time communication with followers; while initially this was defined as the number of Twitter users a brand followed, the authors now posit that the act of retweeting other messages from Twitter users by a brand is more representative of one-way, one-time communication. The rationale for this change is that while a brand can retweet a particular user more than once, the actual message (or tweet) is still a one-way, one-time broadcast message. As Kotler's (1992) definition suggests, the proactive level is characterized by *periodic contact* with the consumer; following this, the Twitter definition was adjusted to include two-way, multi-time communication. The brand sends messages via Twitter at either the basic or reactive level and the consumer responds to these levels by retweeting the initial tweet from the brand or by marking it as a favorite. By accounting for user interaction with the brand's original tweets, this new definition is more representative of two-way, multi-time communication between the consumer and the brand. The coding definition for the proactive level is a summation of the number of user retweets and the times a tweet (from the brand) was marked as a favorite by users who followed the brand. Finally, the definition of partnership level changes slightly to be a two-way, multi-time dialogue with followers. This change better represents Kotler's (1992) initial definition of *continual contact* with consumer (emphasis added). The coding definition remains the same as a direct reply to a tweet from a follower. Table 2.1 summarizes the revised definitions employed in the current study.

This research works toward developing a more comprehensive model of relationship marketing in the service sector by attempting to identify antecedents to building consumer–brand relationships. To ensure generalizability of the refined relationship building levels across service sector brands, professional sports was used as a context for the study. Sports, like universities, are considered a service sector industry. Research has suggested that through the shared experience and high involvement of sports fans, sports products should be considered a service rather than a typical consumer product. Underwood et al. (2001) suggest that service brands lie on a continuum of involvement, with sports consumers at the highly involved end. High consumer commitment and involvement with a service brand underscores the importance of establishing a relationship with consumers. The intangible nature of the

Table 2.1　Updated operationalization of five levels of relationship building

Level	Kotler (1992)	Application to Twitter	Coding definitions
Basic	No follow-up after sale	One-way communication with followers; no response	Broadcast of an original message with no additional information
Reactive	Customer is encouraged to initiate contact after the sale	One-way communication with followers; no response	Broadcast of an original message with additional information or the presence of a hashtag
Accountable	One post-transaction contact initiated by the seller	One-way, one-time communication with followers	Act of retweeting a message from followers
Proactive	Periodic contact with the Customer	Two-way, one-time communication with followers	The number of users who have retweeted or marked the tweet as a favorite
Partnership	Continual contact with the customer	Two-way, multi-time dialogue with followers	Reply directly to tweets from followers

Note: Adapted from Kotler (1992, p. 50). Copyright 1992 by Emerald Publishing Group Limited.

sport product and the highly involved nature of sports consumers (i.e., fans) (Ross, 2006; Underwood et al., 2001) make sports an ideal environment to study consumer–brand interactions through social media. As Apostolopoulou and Biggers (2010) suggested, "sport should thus design and promote opportunities for interaction among fans and the team/athletes and invest in fan appreciation and relationship building initiatives in an effort to strengthen fan's emotional connection to their team" (p. 234).

Method

Sample

Content analysis methodology was used to examine tweets produced by professional sports teams, specifically a sample of teams from the National Basketball Association (NBA). The NBA was selected because the ending of the NBA season coincided with the data collection for the study, allowing the authors easy access to a sample of tweets spanning the entire regular season. This season provides an especially interesting context for study. The 2011 to 2012 NBA season was shortened due to a player lockout; because of the lockout, one could speculate that teams were more likely to engage consumers in higher levels of communication to recover some goodwill that may have been lost during the lockout. Eight teams were selected for the analysis, with careful attention to even distribution from conferences and an effort to include a representative sample (i.e., teams that did or did not make the playoffs, large and small market teams, teams with higher or lower winning percentages). The teams included in the sample were: Boston Celtics, Chicago Bulls, Cleveland Cavaliers, Dallas Mavericks, New Orleans Hornets, Oklahoma City Thunder, and San Antonio Spurs.

To generate a sample that was representative of an entire NBA regular season (excluding playoffs), the teams were divided into two groups to represent each half of the season. Group one (Boston, Dallas, Oklahoma City, and New Orleans) represented the first half of the season (December 25, 2011–February 25, 2012). Tweets from each team were pulled during alternating weeks starting January 1, 2012, and ending February 18, 2012. Group two (Chicago, Cleveland, Miami, and San Antonio) represented the second half of the season (February 26–April 26, 2012). Tweets from each of these teams were pulled during alternating weeks starting March 4, 2012, and ending April 21, 2012. To maintain consistency in the number of tweets used in the analysis, a random number generator was used to select 150 tweets from each team. The resulting sample used in the analysis was 1,200 tweets (150 from each team). Table 2.2 summarizes the sample.

Table 2.2 NBA team sample

NBA Team	Conference	Playoffs	Twitter ID	Tweets	N
Boston Celtics	Eastern	Yes	celtics	219	150
Dallas Mavericks	Western	Yes	dallasmavs	416	150
Oklahoma City Thunder	Western	Yes	okcthunder	430	150
New Orleans Hornets	Western	No	Hornets	417	150
Chicago Bulls	Eastern	Yes	chicagobulls	851	150
Cleveland Cavaliers	Eastern	No	cavs	153	150
Miami Heat	Eastern	Yes	MiamiHEAT	489	150
San Antonio Spurs	Western	Yes	spurs	233	150

Procedure

Tweets were copied to an Excel document along with standard information about the tweet including whether the tweet was an original post, retweet, or a direct reply as well as the presence of an @ mention, link to an external website, video, or picture. Tweets were then coded according to two variables: relationship level and message orientation. Relationship level was defined according to the previously discussed definitions (basic, reactive, accountable, proactive, or partnership). Message orientation was adopted from previous research (Lin & Pena, 2011), which utilized Bales' Interaction Process Analysis to determine the instrumental or task orientations of the tweets. The message orientation variable provided additional insights into specific messages transmitted by brands on Twitter. Message orientations include: give opinion (e.g., the team fought hard in the third quarter), give suggestion (e.g., you should take exit 108 to avoid road construction near the arena), give information (e.g., you can watch the game on ESPN), ask opinion (e.g., what did you think about the team's effort tonight?), ask suggestion (e.g., what restaurants would you suggest that fans visit near the arena?) and ask information (e.g., what are the strengths/weaknesses of the opposing team?). Finally, tweets were coded for the presence of information on team promotions. This category was included to determine how often teams in the sample used Twitter to communicate team promotional events to fans. All categories, except the components of the tweets, are mutually exclusive. When indications of multiple levels were present, the highest relationship level was used.

Results

Of the 1,200 tweets analyzed in the study, 1,037 (86%) were original tweets, 183 (15%) were retweets of posts from other users, and 84 (7%) were direct replies to other users. The presence of @ mentions, $n = 523$ (44%), and hashtags, $n = 524$ (44%), occurred most frequently in the analysis followed by links to external websites, $n = 350$ (29%). Regarding multimedia information in tweets, $n = 9$ (1%) included video and $n = 100$ (8%) included pictures. Table 2.3 shows a breakdown of these components by team. The characteristics of tweets were relatively consistent among teams in the sample. Some notable exceptions include that Miami Heat used hashtags considerably more than other teams, $n = 125$ (83%), and the Cleveland Cavaliers had no direct replies to followers.

Relationship Levels

For the overall sample, the reactive level was the most frequently used relationship level, $n = 680$ (57%). The reactive level was operationalized as an original post with the presence of an external link or hashtag. At this level, consumers are encouraged to initiate the post-sale (post-communication) interaction by clicking on the link or replying using the hashtag. The basic level, defined as a one-time communication between brand and consumer and operationalized as an original tweet with no additional information or follow-up, was the second most used level, $n = 270$ (23%). Inherently, all original tweets are basic level tweets. The presence of additional information such as hashtags or @ mentions indicate higher levels of interactivity and relationship building. The third level of relationship building was the accountable level, which is defined as the team retweeting tweets from other users. For the sample, the accountable level was the third most frequent level, $n = 166$ (14%). The partnership level represents the highest level of interaction with consumers. For the current study, the partnership level was operationalized as direct replies to other Twitter users such as @ replies or replies including a retweet. Of the sample, $n = 84$ (7%) of the tweets represented the partnership level.

When individual teams were examined, the reactive level was the most frequently used for Chicago ($n = 116$, 77%), Cleveland ($n = 113$, 75%), Miami ($n = 110$, 73%), San Antonio ($n = 106$, 71%), and Oklahoma City

Table 2.3 Frequencies by team

	Boston		Chicago		Cleveland		Dallas		Miami		New Orleans		Oklahoma City		San Antonio	
	f	%	f	%	f	%	f	%	f	%	f	%	f	%	f	%
Original Tweet	146	97	143	95	125	83	94	63	148	99	93	62	141	94	147	98
Retweet	13	9	8	5	25	17	56	37	9	6	58	39	10	7	4	3
Direct reply	10	7	20	13	0	0	7	5	19	13	11	7	2	1	45	30
@ mention	39	26	49	33	69	46	83	55	125	83	41	27	72	48	64	43
Hashtag	54	36	111	74	73	49	50	33	105	70	42	28	25	17	69	46
Link	17	11	34	23	95	63	30	20	16	11	18	12	71	47	2	1
Video	0	0	0	0	1	1	1	1	2	1	0	0	3	2	5	3
Picture	14	9	3	2	2	1	43	29	4	3	5	3	24	16	15	10

Note: f = frequency.

(n = 82, 55%). The New Orleans Hornets utilized the accountable level more frequently (n = 60, 40%) and the Boston Celtics utilized the basic level more frequently (n = 83, 55%). The Dallas Mavericks were fairly even in their use of the reactive level (n = 51, 34%) and the accountable level (n = 55, 37%). Table 2.4 summarizes the findings of the relationship levels for the sample and by team.

The proactive level, which represents the fourth highest level of relationship building, was defined by user interaction in this study. The proactive level was operationalized as the number of times a brand's tweet was retweeted or marked as a favorite by consumers using Twitter. Incorporating user interaction into the relationship building levels provides more insight into how consumers respond to the brand's relationship building efforts via Twitter. The number of times a user retweeted posts from each team or marked the tweet as a favorite were added together to generate a value for the proactive level.

Independent sample t-tests were used to analyze the relationship between the other relationship levels and user interaction (proactive level). A significant difference was found between the proactive level (M = 89.74, SD = 199.24) and the reactive level (M = 110.07, SD = 227.32), t (df) = 4.07, p < .05; the accountable level (M = 28.67, SD = 78.53), t (df) = –4.284, p < .05; and the partnership level (M = 10.71, SD = 39.18), t = (df) = –3.790, p < .05. The reactive level was significantly higher than any other level in the analysis, which in this context is to be expected. Teams that posted original information on Twitter with options for users to interact (e.g., join the conversation with a hashtag) are more likely to have users respond to those messages by retweeting it to their followers or by indicating that the tweet is one of their favorites. These findings indicate that engaging consumers to interact with a brand on Twitter does not necessarily require interaction at higher relationship building levels such as the partnership level. Studying the reactive level and how users interact with those types of messages has potential to provide further insights into how relationships are formed between brands and consumers.

Message Orientation

The message orientation indicated the type of message broadcast by the brand through Twitter. Each tweet was coded according to whether the objective of the tweet was to give opinion, give suggestion, give information, ask opinion, ask suggestion, or ask information. The most frequently utilized message orientation in the overall sample, as well as for each individual team, was to give information (n = 866, 72%).

Table 2.4 Relationship level

	Sample		Boston		Chicago		Cleveland		Dallas		Miami		New Orleans		Oklahoma City		San Antonio	
	f	%	f	%	f	%	f	%	f	%	f	%	f	%	f	%	f	%
Basic	270	23	83	55	7	5	12	8	37	25	19	13	30	20	55	37	27	18
Reactive	680	57	53	35	116	77	113	75	51	34	110	73	49	33	82	55	106	71
Accountable	166	14	4	3	7	5	25	17	55	37	2	1	60	40	11	7	2	1
Partnership	84	7	10	7	20	13	0	0	7	5	19	13	11	7	2	1	15	10
Total	1200	100	150	100	150	100	150	100	150	100	150	100	150	100	150	100	150	100

Note: f = frequency.

Table 2.5 Message orientation

	Sample		Boston		Chicago		Cleveland		Dallas		Miami		New Orleans		Oklahoma City		San Antonio	
	f	%	f	%	f	%	f	%	f	%	f	%	f	%	f	%	f	%
Ask for opinion	15	1	0	0	4	3	1	1	4	3	1	1	3	2	2	1	0	0
Ask for suggestion	0	0	0	0	0	0	0	0	0	0	0	0	0	0	0	0	0	0
Ask for information	21	2	2	1	1	1	1	1	3	2	4	3	1	1	1	1	8	5
Give opinion	105	9	3	2	21	14	2	1	29	19	7	5	31	21	8	5	4	3
Give suggestion	193	16	33	22	7	5	50	33	6	4	28	19	8	5	38	25	23	15
Give information	866	72	112	75	117	78	96	64	108	72	110	73	107	71	101	67	115	77
Total	1200	100	150	100	150	100	150	100	150	100	150	100	150	100	150	100	150	100
promotional Event	112	9	25	17	2	1	25	17	6	4	17	11	4	3	17	11	16	11

Note: f = frequency.

All other message orientations, except those that ask suggestion, were recorded in the sample. Tweets from the New Orleans Hornets had the highest frequency of giving opinion (n = 31, 21%) and the Cleveland Cavaliers had the most tweets that gave suggestions (n = 50, 33%). For ask information, the San Antonio Spurs used this message orientation more frequently than other teams in the sample (n = 8, 5%) and both the Chicago Bulls (n = 4, 3%) and Dallas Mavericks (n = 4, 3%) used the ask opinion orientation most frequently. However, the ask information and ask opinion categories have much smaller values than the other message orientation categories, indicating that even by the teams that use them the most, they are still not used very frequently. Table 2.5 summarizes the findings of the message orientation analysis.

Including a measure for message orientation accounts for more meaningful information about the specific types of messages that brands communicate using Twitter. Understanding the relationship level is important, but knowing what those tweets say is also important in identifying the potential variables that precede relationship building. These findings indicate that most of the teams use Twitter to give information to their followers. This can include information about promotional events sponsored by the teams. In this sample of NBA teams, 112 tweets (9%) were about promotional events. Based on the findings in this analysis, teams looking to improve communication about promotional events with fans could utilize the reactive level of relationship building by posting an original tweet with opportunities for users to follow up for additional information. In this analysis it was the reactive level that proved to have the highest levels of user interaction, so if a team wants to share information about upcoming promotions, then using Twitter would be a logical tool to meet communication goals.

Discussion

The content analysis method provides largely descriptive information about an area of study, in this case the tweets of a sample of NBA teams. While this method is often limited by its descriptive nature, the authors argue that findings from content analysis provide a starting point for understanding the strategies brands use for social media interaction. The findings from the current study indicate that, while the reactive relationship level is the most commonly used by NBA teams in the sample, the other levels are also represented and in some cases (the Dallas Mavericks) the tweets represent a fairly even mix of relationship building levels. Results of the current study also revealed that the reactive level had a significant influence on user interaction (defined as the proactive relationship building level). Additionally, incorporating information about the message orientation provided more insight into the types of messages produced by brands. The current sample revealed that the majority of tweets for all NBA teams in the sample gave information to users.

The most frequently occurring relationship level in this sample of tweets was the reactive level. The reactive level was operationalized as an original tweet with the presence of a link to an external website and/ or hashtag. The original definition indicated that at the reactive level the consumer is encouraged to initiate post-sell communication with the brand. In this instance, the consumer is encouraged to continue communication initiated by the brand (i.e., the tweet). The external link allows consumers to follow up on information presented in the tweet at a different website; the hashtag allows the consumer to join the conversation as hashtags are a way to categorize tweets. Brands that include hashtags in tweets allow consumers to respond by including the same hashtag in their tweet, which can be considered a form of consumer follow-up. In the present study, 44% of the sample used hashtags in their tweets and 29% of the sample included links to external websites. The inclusion of brand-specific hashtags in a tweet provides brands with a way to encourage consumers to respond to the brand through social media.

These findings indicate that the reactive level, specifically the presence of hashtags, can provide a starting point for initiating a consumer–brand relationship using Twitter. The proactive and partnership level indicates higher levels of interaction among brands and followers, but the reactive level has potential to be the catalyst that leads to those higher levels of interaction. By identifying brand-specific hashtags, consumers can interact with both the brand and other consumers of that brand, thus leading to the possible development of a brand community using social media. One of the objectives of the current research was to identify the potential starting level of relationship building between consumers and brands. This is not to say that there is not a potential benefit of higher levels of consumer–brand interaction (i.e., at the accountable or partnership level). Content analysis research can provide insights into what information is present but research should also consider the consumer perspective; such as, at what point do consumers respond to relationship building efforts of brands or consumer attitudes toward brand relationships at different levels. This type of research is necessary before making generalizations about the reactive level as a starting point in relationship building.

Building on previous research conducted by the authors, the current study incorporates the role of consumer feedback to brand interaction on Twitter. Incorporating user feedback (retweeting and marking a brand's tweets as favorites by consumers) allows for a more accurate picture of the two-way communication that occurs between brands and consumers through Twitter. This is an important step in developing a model of relationship marketing using social media and in identifying what initiates a consumer–brand relationship. In the current study, combining the number of times a tweet was retweeted and marked as a favorite by another user represented the proactive level. Significant differences were found between the proactive level (user interaction) and the reactive level (brands encourage consumers to initiate communication), as well as between the accountable level (the brand retweeting an original tweet from another user) and the partnership level (continual conversation between the brand and the user); the reactive level was found to have the highest difference ($M = 110.07$). Therefore, the assumption can be made that users are more likely to respond to tweets classified at the reactive level than the other levels. These findings support the assumption that at the reactive level, consumer–brand relationships through social media can be developed.

Additionally, support was found for a relationship between proactive level tweets and accountable and partnership level tweets. At the accountable level, consumers retweeted tweets that the brand had retweeted from other users and at the partnership level, users would retweet or favorite a conversational tweet between themselves and the brand. Conversely, the basic level did not indicate significant results. These findings indicated that consumers engaged in interaction with the brand via Twitter at the higher levels of consumer–brand interaction (reactive, accountable, and partnership).

Incorporating user interaction into the five levels of relationship building allowed for a more comprehensive view of consumer–brand interaction via Twitter. The findings of this study demonstrated that consumers responded more to brands that tweet on a reactive level. Previous research conducted by the authors only examined communication by the brand, but the very nature of relationship marketing indicates that the relationship is mutually beneficial for both the brand and the consumer; therefore, it is important to study how the consumer responds to a brand's communication efforts. Incorporating consumer response into the model provides an efficient way to do that.

The message orientation construct was developed from previous research into the specific types of messages communicated by brands through Twitter. Types of messages examined in the current study were ones that asked for information, suggestions, or opinions and gave information, suggestions, or opinions. The most commonly used message orientation in the current study was to give information (72%). Based on findings in this study, brands in the sample used Twitter to give information at the reactive level (encouraging consumers to initiate further communication) and consumers in turn responded more to reactive level tweets.

Message orientation provided an additional variable to be considered when determining the antecedents of consumer–brand relationships. This research attempted not only to determine the level at which NBA teams in the sample relate with consumers but also to determine the content and instrumental purposes of tweets. Knowing not only how brands use the features of Twitter (retweeting, including multimedia, replying directly to consumers) but also the specific types of messages (giving information or opinions) can provide more information about the total experience of communicating and establishing a relationship with a brand via Twitter. Results of this study revealed that the majority of tweets in the sample were oriented toward giving information to consumers, which indicates that messages are being broadcast to a mass audience. These initial categories (give information, suggestion, opinion and ask information, suggestion, and opinion) should be further refined to more context-specific categories; for example, in this study the informational messages communicated through "give information" tweets could be recoded into more specific categories, such as injury reports or score updates.

The current research can be viewed as another step in developing a more comprehensive model of relationship marketing that includes the antecedents to building consumer–brand relationships. The results of this study demonstrated that the reactive level and tweets providing information could provide a starting point for the future development of such a model. Definitions for relationship levels in Twitter were refined in this study to incorporate user interaction and more specific attributes of Twitter to distinguish between relationship building levels. Continued research on social media branding and Twitter should continue refining these operational levels until a more generalizable model can be presented. Using content analysis to study existing practices allows for adjustments to be made to these practices rather than creating new strategies.

References

Apostolopoulou, A., & Biggers, M. (2010). Positioning the New Orleans Hornets in the "who dat" city. *Sports Marketing Quarterly, 19,* 229–234. Retrieved from http://www.fitinfotech.com

Ashworth, L., Dacin, P. T., & Thomson, M. (2009). Why on earth do consumers have relationships with marketers. In D. J. MacInnis, C. W. Park, & J. R. Priester (Eds.), *Handbook of brand relationships* (pp. 82–106). Armonk, NY: M.E. Sharpe.

Bee, C. C., & Kahle, L. R. (2006). Relationship marketing in sports: A functional approach. *Sports Marketing Quarterly, 15,* 102–110. Retrieved from http://www.fitinfotech.com

Berry, L. (1995). Relationship marketing of services – Growing interest, emerging perspectives. *Journal of the Academy of Marketing Science, 23*(4), 236–245. doi: 10.1177/009207039502300402

Berry, L. (2000). Cultivating service brand equity. *Journal of the Academy of Marketing Science, 28*(1), 128–137. doi: 10.1177/0092070300281012

Berry, L. (2002). Relationship marketing of services perspectives from 1983 and 2000. *Journal of Relationship Marketing, 1*(1), 59–77. doi: 10.1300/J366v01n01_05

Bhattacharya, C. B., & Bolton, R. N. (2000). Relationship marketing in mass markets. In J. N. Sheth & A. Parvatiyar (Eds.), *Handbook of relationship marketing* (pp. 327–354). Thousand Oaks, CA: Sage Publications.

Bhattacharya, C. B., & Sen, S. (2002). Consumer-company identification: A framework for understanding consumers' relationships with companies. *Journal of Marketing, 67,* 76–88. doi: 10.1509/jmkg.67.2.76/18609

Fournier, S. (1998). Consumers and their brands: Developing relationship theory in consumer research. *Journal of Consumer Research, 24*(4), 343–353. Retrieved from http://ejcr.org/

Gronroos, C. (1994). From marketing mix to relationship marketing: Toward a paradigm shift in marketing. *Management Decision, 32*(2), 4–20. doi: 10.1108/00251749410054774

Gronroos, C. (2004). The relationship marketing process: Communication, interaction, dialogue, value. *The Journal of Business & Industrial Marketing, 19*(2), 99–113. doi: 10.1108/08858620410523981

Gwinner, K. P., Gremier, D. D., & Bitner, M. J. (1998). Relational benefits in services industries: The customer's perspective. *Journal of the Academy of Marketing Science, 26*(2), 101–114. doi: 10.1177/0092070398262002

Hambrick, M. E., Simmons, J. M., Greenhalgh, G. P., & Greenwell, T. C. (2010). Understanding professional athletes' use of twitter: A content analysis of athlete tweets. *International Journal of Sport Communication, 3,* 454–471. Retrieved from http://www.humankinetics.com/IJSC/journalAbout.cfm

Java, A., Song, Z., Finin, T., & Tseng, B. (2007). Why we twitter: Understanding microblogging usage and communities. *Proceedings of the Joint 9th WEBKDD and 1st SNA-KDD Workshop '07* (pp. 56–65). San Jose, CA. Retrieved from http://aisl.umbc.edu/resources/369.pdf

Kaplan, A. M., & Haenlein, M. (2010). Users of the world, unite! The challenges and opportunities of social media. *Business Horizons, 53,* 59–68. doi: 10.1016/j.bushor.2009.09.003

Kittle, B., & Ciba, D. (2001). Using college web sites for student recruitment: A relationship marketing study. *Journal of Marketing for Higher Education, 11*(3), 17–37. doi: 10.1300/J050v11n03_02

Kotler, P. (1992). Marketing's new paradigms: What's really happening out there. *Strategy & Leadership, 20*(5), 50–52. doi: 10.1108/eb054382

Kwon, E. S., & Sung, Y. (2011). Follow me! Global marketers' twitter use. *Journal of Interactive Advertising, 12*(1), 4–16. Retrieved from http://jiad.org/

Lin, J., & Pena, J. (2011). Are you following me? A content analysis of TV network brand communication on Twitter. *Journal of Interactive Advertising, 12*(1), 17–29. Retrieved from http://jiad.org

Parvatiyar, A., & Sheth, J. N. (2000). The domain and conceptual foundations of relationship marketing. In J. N. Sheth & A. Parvatiyar (Eds.), *Handbook of relationship marketing* (pp. 3–38). Thousand Oaks, CA: Sage Publications.

Ross, S. D. (2006). A conceptual framework for understanding spectator-based brand equity. *Journal of Sport Management, 20*, 22–38. Retrieved from http://journals.humankinetics.com.libdata.lib.ua.edu/jsm

Sheth, J. N., & Parvatiyar, A. (2000). The evolution of relationship marketing. In J. N. Sheth & A. Parvatiyar (Eds.), *Handbook of relationship marketing* (pp. 119–148). Thousand Oaks, CA: Sage Publications.

Twitter (2012). Retrieved March 12, 2012, from About Twitter: www.twitter.com

Underwood, R., Bond, E., & Baer, R. (2001). Building service brands via social identity: Lessons from the sports marketplace. *Journal of Marketing Theory and Practice, 9*(1), 1–13. Retrieved from http://www.jmtp-online.org/

Wallace, L., Wilson, J., & Miloch, K. (2011). Sporting Facebook: A content analysis of NCAA organizational sport pages and Big 12 Conference Athletic department pages. *International Journal of Sport Communication, 4*, 422–444. Retrieved from http://www.humankinetics.com/IJSC/journalAbout.cfm

Watkins, B. (2012). *Building a relationship on Twitter: A content analysis of university Twitter accounts.* Paper presented at the meeting of the Association for Education in Journalism and Mass Communication, Chicago, IL.

Williams, J., & Chinn, S. J. (2010). Meeting relationship-marketing goals through social media: A conceptual model for sport marketers. *International Journal of Sport Communication, 3*, 422–437. Retrieved from http://www.humankinetics.com/IJSC/journalAbout.cfm

3
Marketing Techniques and Strategies: Using Social Media as a Revenue-Generating Vehicle

Casey Hart, John Allen Hendricks and Linda Thorsen Bond

Strategically targeting specific demographics with information to persuade an individual or individuals to take action is not new. This could range from propaganda to advance a government's agenda or advertising to sell useless products or services that are not particularly needed by consumers. Advances in technology have required strategies to evolve and adapt to an ever-changing media landscape. Specifically, the advertising industry has had to focus its attention on the social media juggernaut that continued its growth through 2012. One study revealed that in 2011, Facebook acquired 200 million new users bringing the total number of users to 800 million, while Twitter had 100 million users, and LinkedIn had 64 million users (Bennett, 2011). In 2011, another study indicated there were a trillion video playbacks on YouTube and more than 200 billion videos viewed per month on average (Internet 2011 in numbers, 2012). Thus, Choi (2011) asserted: "it is no secret that social media is at the top of many businesses' agenda and that its effective utilization can enhance the businesses' competitive advantage in the marketplace" (p. 11).

Moreover, what makes social media so appealing to businesses, including advertisers, is that it allows advertisers to strategically target consumers using the demographic information, such as gender, ethnicity, education, and political and religious affiliations, that they voluntarily provided on their social media profiles (Steel & Fowler, 2011). Considering social media's prominent role in the lives of so many technologically savvy consumers and its wide appeal to such a large and diverse demographic, it is a crucial subject to examine in relation to how the advertising industry is utilizing social media to generate revenue.

Hence, this chapter examines the highly effective social media advertising campaign created and used by Old Spice from January 2012 to June 2012. *Forbes* magazine declared the Old Spice social media advertising campaign as one of the best ever (Taylor, 2010).

Literature Review

In 2012, many consumers utilized social media such as Facebook, Twitter, and YouTube to communicate and network with friends and share information. A Pew Study revealed that, in 2011, 65% of online users were accessing social networking, or social media, sites (Madden & Zickuhr, 2011). Madden and Zickuhr (2011) stated: "Overall, positive responses far outweighed the negative and neutral words that were associated with social networking sites (more than half of the respondents used positive terms)" (para. 3). Another Pew Study revealed why consumers were attracted to social media:

> Roughly two thirds of social media users say that staying in touch with current friends and family members is a major reason they use these sites, while half say that connecting with old friends they've lost touch with is a major reason behind their use of these technologies. (Smith, 2011, para. 1)

While users of social media have connected with friends, advertisers have seized the opportunity to communicate with specific demographics. Warren (2009) observed: "social networks offer advertisers several key advantages over regular sites. They can target users based on location, age and relationship-status by virtue of having accessible profile information. Companies can also communicate directly with potential customers using social media channels" (para. 3). Also, the coveted 18- to 34-year old demographic is highly involved with social media platforms; thus, they are easily accessible to advertisers (Taylor, Lewin, & Strutton, 2011).

In 2011, a study revealed that advertisers recognized the key advantages of strategically targeting their messages to the point that it was estimated that spending on Facebook, Twitter, and other social media by advertisers would reach $4.4 billion, or 7% of online advertising spending, by 2016 (Hof, 2011). Davis (2011) estimated that by 2013, advertising revenue spent on social media networks worldwide would reach a staggering $10 billion. Further, Davis (2011) asserted: "Facebook will 'draw the bulk of these dollars' while LinkedIn gets 3% or a little less than $250 million" (para. 3). That is partly because advertisers were able to set up Facebook pages at one time with relatively little ongoing cost, and partly because Facebook, Twitter, YouTube, and other social media sites did not offer much in the way of advertising formats at the time (Hof, 2011).

Despite the impressive advertising expenditures predicted on social media such as Facebook, YouTube, and Twitter, it is more important to advertisers to have effective marketing techniques and strategies to motivate consumers to purchase products and services. Determining effective social media advertising techniques is not an easy task especially when consumers view advertising on social media as intrusive and culturally unacceptable (Taylor et al., 2011). For example, the introduction of Twitter's QuickBar – designed to place Twitter advertisements on tweets – was dubbed "#d**kbar" by users and was quickly removed by Twitter executives (Slutsky, 2011a, para. 2). As a result of the interactive nature of social media, Wheaton (2009) asserted: "the order of the day now is not to inflict creative notions on consumers with mere repetition but to enter into a two-way conversation with them and talk about the issues they want to talk about" (para. 3).

It took businesses a while to realize that social media marketing could indeed be beneficial to their bottom line. Despite an expected spending increase in advertising dollars on social media, the effectiveness of advertising on social media was relatively unknown by the advertising industry (van Noort, Antheunis, & van Reijmersdal, 2012). Dugan (2010) found that nonprofit organizations were more likely to use and monitor social media outlets than businesses that were profit driven. Interestingly, for-profit businesses were not as keen on social media as nonprofit organizations. In 2010, Facebook received the majority of advertising dollars spent on social media, with Twitter predicted to eventually emerge as a strong competitor to Facebook for advertising dollars (Dugan, 2010). During the first half of 2011, Facebook's advertising revenue was $1.6 billion (Steel & Fowler, 2011). Facebook, YouTube, and Twitter appealed to advertisers because word of mouth campaigns could be started on its pages at a minimal cost. Specifically, when consumers see something on social media that appeals to them they pass it along to friends who, in turn, pass it along to their friends. Most importantly, advertisers know they must engage consumers "with branded content and interactive advertising that is good enough to make people want to share it with their network of friends" (Taylor, 2010, para. 2).

The interactivity that occurs within social media among friends is very important to advertisers. Facebook's vice president for global sales, underscores the importance of the interactive experience on social media by stating "...people are 68% more likely to remember seeing the ad if their friend has recommended it and twice as likely to remember the message of the ad [that was recommended by their friend]" (Slutsky, 2011b, para. 13). One social media expert found that "90% of consumers trust peer recommendations and only 14% trust advertisements" (Qualman, 2012, para. 31–32). Also, it was predicted that social media technology would create an environment where products and services would find consumers rather than consumers having to search for them (Qualman, 2012).

The advertising industry remained strong with $151 billion spent by advertisers in 2010 to reach 308 million citizens in the United States (Lee, 2011). To ensure those dollars were spent effectively, the advertising industry recognized the need to transition advertising dollars to where the consumers were located on social media. Data revealed that advertisers were indeed using social media to reach consumers. In 2010, "71% of the top-500 companies used Facebook, 59% used Twitter and 50% used blogging" (van Noort et al., 2012, p. 39). The key for advertisers is learning what makes an effective marketing campaign.

Old Spice. While many companies and organizations have attempted to utilize for profit the new and varied tools afforded them by the proliferation of social media technology, few have achieved the measure of success of Old Spice. Boasting record sales and market visibility, numerous observers have speculated as to why and how the brand has achieved such success so quickly. Many analysts (Jaffe, 2010; Neff, 2010, 2011; Taylor, 2010) acknowledged that Old Spice was exercising a new strategy that made heavy use of social media vehicles like YouTube, Twitter, and Facebook. However, the analysts were hesitant to give social media the lion's share of credit for the brand's revitalization. Predominantly attributing the couponing campaign, along with other media launches, for the over 106% increase in sales that Old Spice enjoyed in June 2010 (Neff, 2010), some analysts (Baskin, 2011a, 2011b; Jaffe, 2010) downplayed the social media aspect of the campaign as self-serving, brash, silly, or as nothing more than a novelty. But, it was hard to ignore that in the months after the launch of the *Man Your Man Could Smell Like* campaign in February 2010, social media activity on Old Spice's Twitter and Facebook pages skyrocketed and product sales increased drastically over a five-month period. Neff (2010) cited metrics from market research firm SymphonyIRI indicating that Old Spice experienced a 95% growth in sales, Twitter feed @OldSpice blossomed to over 80,000 followers and the brand's Facebook fan base grew to over 630,000. This was an increase in social media activity for the brand of over 800% (Neff, 2010).

Through social media, Old Spice was making use of an innovative advertising and marketing strategy to generate new revenue. By taking advantage of the intrinsically interactive nature of social media, Old Spice was starting a conversation with its consumers. Importantly, Old Spice was building a new relationship with a new consumer base. Accordingly, this study explored the techniques Old Spice used in shaping social media messages to build a dialogue with its target audience. The purpose of this study was to examine what techniques led to a sustained overall growth in sales and social media activity during the first six months of 2012 when two new social media advertising campaigns were introduced titled, *Smell is Power* and *Believe in your Smellf.* The following research questions were formulated to determine which advertising techniques and strategies were successful for social media networks:

RQ1: What techniques did Old Spice use to achieve success in social media marketing in 2012?

RQ2: What differences existed between the techniques or strategies implemented in the highly successful *Smell is Power* campaign versus the less successful *Believe in your Smellf* campaign?

Method

This study was a textual analysis that examined the activity of Old Spice across social media networks as popular texts and analyzed the potential symbolic interpretation of themes including hypermasculinity, hyperbole, humor, imagery, product claims, and usage across a large, heterogeneous audience (Burns & Thompson, 1989). Particularly, this study sought to determine what social media techniques Old Spice used to maintain a steady stream of market visibility through the first half of 2012. This study examined the social media activity of Old Spice across Twitter, Facebook, and YouTube to advertise its products, build interest, and stimulate growth within its consumer base. Using videos (YouTube), tweets (Twitter), and status posts (Facebook) as text, this study analyzed how the different social media were used in concert with one another to create a dialogue with the consumer. The analyses were conducted within the context of the basic uses and gratifications communication theory (Severin & Tankard, 2001), which argues that consumers are active participants in media and generally seek out content that may either be incorporated into their lives in a utilitarian manner such as news or information, or provide some form of psychological payoff such as entertainment, status, comfort, or support of preconceived social notions. When considering the viral nature of social media marketing, which relies on media consumers finding enough value in the content to then share it with other consumers, the uses and gratification theory is germane.

Sample and Operationalization

This study examined the advertising activity of Old Spice across the social media networks of Twitter, Facebook, and YouTube from January 1, 2012, to June 30, 2012. Old Spice, similar to many other brands, has established a dedicated presence on each site. On Facebook, Old Spice has a dedicated brand *page*. A page is the basic unit of virtual presence on Facebook and allows users to communicate with *friends* or *fans*. The term *friend* usually applies to private users who subscribe to view and interact with each other's pages. *Fan,* on the other hand, is the term for individuals who express they *like* and are interested in following the activity not of a private individual, but of a brand, company, or public figure. A private page and a brand page differ in the amount of access other Facebook users may have to the pages and how the pages are listed in searches and metrics. Old Spice, for example, is listed under the sub-category of health/beauty rather than people. With regard to how interactions occur on the site, there is no appreciable difference between private users and brands like Old Spice. Users may post *status updates* as often as they wish, which are then visible to all other users who are friends or fans. These updates may be images, videos, hyperlinks, or simply text. These status updates are often used as catalysts to spur on conversations and dialogues with friends or fans who may then *like* the comments and/or respond to them for other users to see. Many brands use these to push new products or call attention to new promotions.

Twitter, although similar to Facebook in some ways, is quite different in most respects. Twitter allows users, private or otherwise – to create an account. Through Twitter, users are capable of posting short comments, or observations, called *tweets* limited to 140 characters. Tweets are generally text-based, but often include hyperlinks to other forms of media (like videos hosted on YouTube) or other social media sites like Facebook. Users on Twitter may *follow* other individuals or entities, meaning they will be notified whenever that entity posts a new tweet. For brands and corporate entities, this process can be helpful in allowing for quick notification of new promotions and products to their loyal consumer base. Twitter has also gained notoriety as a social media vehicle for people on the move as the character restrictions and overall format make it especially friendly for smartphone users. Therefore, brevity is particularly valued on Twitter.

YouTube is a video-hosting, social media network. In simple terms, it allows users to upload videos that may then be embedded in websites, distributed quickly via email, or hyperlinked through most other social media sites. While the individual video is the basic unit of media on YouTube, users may create a *channel* within which their videos are collected and displayed for viewing. These channels can be organized in a variety of ways depending on user preferences and can include corporate or brand logos or designs. However, in 2010, Old Spice began creating content specifically for YouTube and then relying on private *subscribers* (i.e., individuals who request interaction with a particular YouTube channel) to enjoy and distribute the media content. This concept of letting private online users *be* the vehicles for the distribution of videos and media content is referred to as *viral marketing*. Viral marketing, however, is dependent upon content being of a kind and quality that will motivate viewers to share the content with other users via social media. Some companies have struggled with this process, while others have enjoyed great success.

User Statistics

This study asked two central questions. The first question, relating to what techniques Old Spice used to achieve success in social media marketing, was addressed by analyzing the content of *Smell is Power* from a uses and gratification perspective, since it was the most successful of the two campaigns that were introduced in 2012. The second question, concerning the differences between the *Smell is Power* and the *Believe in your Smellf* campaigns, required more quantitative data. In order to assert that certain techniques were more effective than others, it was important to carefully track the number of users interacting with the various sites during the sample period. When available, this study used metrics pulled directly from Facebook, Twitter, and YouTube, but accurate information is extremely limited directly from the sites. For this reason, this study used data gathered by Socialbakers.com (Facebook Statistics, 2012; Twitter Statistics, 2012) and Socialblade.com (YouTube Statistics, 2012); each website tracks and archives day-to-day activity metrics on social media sites. The tracking data were the pure statistics concerning activity across the social media networks examined in this study, generally used as signposts to show periods during the sample time frame where activity spiked. By being able to quantitatively track day-to-day changes, this study was able to more accurately determine and demonstrate when an increase occurred on social media networks during certain Old Spice campaigns and not during others.

Analysis

From January 2012 through June 2012, Old Spice released two major social media campaigns, during two different, distinct periods during which Old Spice marketed its brand heavily through social media using two unique brand themes. The two campaigns were referred to as *Smell is Power*, which ran from January 2012 through the end of April 2012, and *Believe in your Smellf*, which ran from April 2012 through June 2012. Each social media campaign was launched with the release of a short promotional advertisement on the brand's YouTube channel, that was then embedded and hyperlinked to and from both Twitter and Facebook. In this way, Old Spice utilized a multi-network social media strategy wherein the three major social media were interconnected with one another and online traffic was controlled through links and embedded material. Cleverly, with the launch of each social media marketing campaign, both the look and personality of each channel changed to reflect the new theme of the campaign. More about this will be explained in the analyses, but it is important to understand that on both occasions the social media page design as well as the *voice* of Old Spice (i.e., the tone in which tweets or status updates were delivered and conversations with other users were conducted) changed to reflect the new theme.

Smell is Power

Data in Figures 3.1 (Twitter followers), 3.2 (YouTube subscribers), and 3.3 (Facebook fans) reveal that the *Smell is Power* social media advertising campaign garnered a more powerful response from and interest among consumers than the *Believe in your Smellf* campaign. Therefore, when analyzing the two campaigns, special attention was given to what social media techniques the *Smell is Power* campaign utilized that the *Believe in your Smellf* did not.

In answering Research Question 1 (what techniques did Old Spice use to achieve success in social media advertising in 2012?), this study examined the *Smell is Power* campaign launched on January 12, 2012 with the release of the *Old Spice | Mind Blown* (2012) YouTube advertisement. The campaign itself was composed of five video advertisements, released on YouTube, featuring professional football player and actor Terry Crew. These advertisements were: *Old Spice | Mind Blown* (2012),

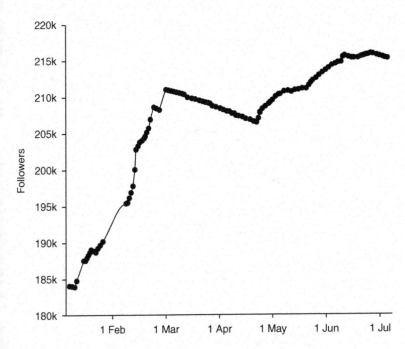

Figure 3.1   Old Spice Twitter metrics, 2012

Source: Twitter Statistics (2012). *Socialbakers.com*. Retrieved from http://www.socialbakers. com. Reprinted with permission.

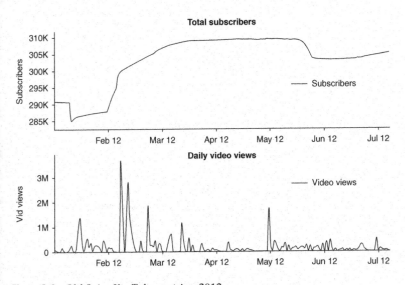

Figure 3.2   Old Spice YouTube metrics, 2012

Source: YouTube Statistics (2012). *Socialblade.com*. Retrieved from http://socialblade.com /youtube/user/Old%20Spice. Reprinted with permission.

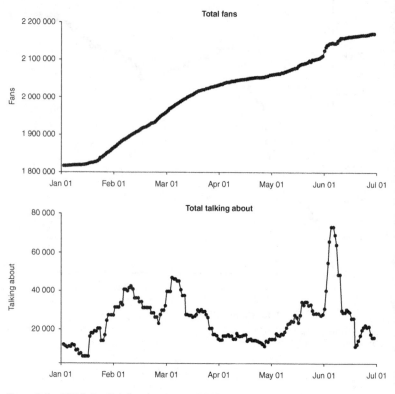

Figure 3.3   Old Spice Facebook metrics, 2012

Source: Facebook Statistics (2012). *Socialbakers.com*. Retrieved from http:\\www.socialbakers.com. Reprinted with permission.

Old Spice | Charmin (2012), *Old Spice | Bounce* (2012), *Old Spice | Vending Machine* (2012), and *Old Spice | Bowling* (2012). They incorporated a great deal of hyperbole and an in-your-face attitude of hypermasculinity. In each of the 2012 videos Crews would literally burst on the scene (usually in an explosion) humorously yelling at the viewer about how powerful Old Spice products were. Each advertisement used a great deal of over the top imagery and larger than life claims, usually accompanied by the claim coming true on screen via visual effects, such as Crews' mind actually leaving his head and exploding in front of him in the *Blown Mind* advertisement.

This kind of exaggerated pitch was repeated on both Facebook and Twitter posts since both channels, throughout the duration of the campaign, operated as if Crews (in character from the YouTube advertisements) was in control of the status updates and tweets. Each weekday during the campaign, tweets would appear on @OldSpice (Twitter), often in all capital letters indicating a raised voice, repeating lines from the YouTube advertisements, making wild comments or asking followers to respond to outlandish scenarios. These would simultaneously appear on Facebook. The posts on both sites would often contain links either to other Old Spice YouTube advertisements, or to other entertaining items, like doctored photos showing Old Spice products in a variety of strange or interesting situations. These included a stick of deodorant swimming with dolphins or a bottle of body wash slalom waterskiing. These advertising strategies and humorous approaches appealed to a new, younger consumer. Many posts on both Twitter and Facebook even hyperlinked to, or featured, user-created content like music videos composed of montages of Crews' Old Spice advertisements on YouTube.

There were three trends that stood out about this campaign. First, from the perspective of either being useful to consumers or providing some form of psychological payoff, the advertisements released through YouTube were entertaining. The use of hyperbole and fast-paced visual satire kept the ads unpredictable and kept viewers wondering what Crews was going to do next because literally anything was possible. Additionally, each of the advertisements was 30 seconds or less in duration, meaning that viewers could easily watch them multiple times without becoming fatigued or occupying a great deal of time. The advertisements also took advantage of one of the great strengths of YouTube in that they were easily copied, downloaded, or posted on other social media channels. These qualities made the videos prime media packages for viral marketing to generate revenue. Furthermore, on Twitter and Facebook, Old Spice regularly offered users helpful or interesting content, or features like themed desktop backgrounds or promotional deals.

Second, although it was through YouTube that Old Spice released the videos that essentially set the theme, it was through Facebook and Twitter that the thematic elements became ubiquitous and user-oriented. That is to say, through social media like Facebook and Twitter, Old Spice was able to keep its theme and brand front of mind, actually creating a personal interactive relationship with its consumers. For example, consumers could see the entertaining Terry Crews advertisements, which were often reposted on both sites, but could then ask questions or make comments to which Crews himself would supposedly respond. It was personal; the campaign had a figurehead and a distinct personality to which consumers could relate.

Finally, the *Smell is Power* campaign was constantly fresh and utilitarian. This is to say that through the lifespan of the campaign Old Spice released new statements, questions, photos, or other material on a daily basis via social media. Every weekday users would be sent some new bit of user-created content or a variety of other things designed to keep consumers coming back for more. In much the same way as the spontaneous, exaggerated videos were designed to keep viewers wondering what Crews might do next, the Facebook and Twitter posts were designed to keep fans/followers wondering what Crews or Old Spice would post next.

By referring to Figures 3.1, 3.2, and 3.3, the tremendous success of the *Smell is Power* campaign is clear. Figure 3.2 shows that on YouTube subscribers to Old Spice's brand channel grew from approximately 285,000 to almost 310,000 through the life of the campaign (YouTube Statistics, 2012). Moreover, in mid-February, after the release of the fifth advertisement, *Old Spice | Bowling* (2012), and the subsequent promotion through Twitter and Facebook, subscribers and daily video views on YouTube increased substantially.

Figure 3.1 also indicates that the campaign was highly successful in boosting a growth from 184,673 Twitter followers in January 2012, at the launch of the campaign, to over 211,000 in March 2012 (Twitter Statistics, 2012); this is a growth of over 87% in just over one month. Similar growth was also experienced on Facebook as Figure 3.3 indicates, fans of Old Spice jumped from over 1.8 million in January 2012 to over two million in March 2012 (Facebook Statistics, 2012). Additionally, Figure 3.3 shows that users *talking about* Old Spice on Facebook spiked in February with the release and promotion of the *Smell is Power* YouTube advertisements (Facebook Statistics, 2012). However, throughout March 2012 and into April 2012, social media activity fizzled out across all three sites. No new YouTube videos had been released by Old Spice since February 2012, and fans and followers appear to have grown bored, as Figure 3.2 shows, subscribing plateaued to indicate no new interest in the YouTube channel and daily video views became negligible (YouTube Statistics, 2012). Figure 3.1 also shows that Twitter followers began to drop off through March 2012 and into April 2012 (Twitter Statistics, 2012).

Believe in your Smellf

The second campaign, titled *Believe in your Smellf* and launched in April 2012, was examined in response to Research Question 2 in order to determine what differences existed in this campaign that might have led to a weaker social media reaction among consumers. Launching with a YouTube video titled, *Old Spice | I Can Do Anything* (2012), showing a man listening to an Old Spice self-help tape and repeating increasingly exaggerated and farcical mantras. While the visual and scripted elements of the video were characteristically exaggerated and hypermasculine, the advertisement did not directly relate to consumers and was rather lax compared to those featured in the *Smell is Power* campaign.

Similarly, neither the lead advertisement, nor the two that followed via YouTube, translated well into a comprehensive and relatable Facebook and Twitter dialogue with consumers. This was in sharp contrast to the *Smell is Power* campaign. What was particularly telling in this regard was that throughout the *Believe in your Smellf* campaign the amount of interaction between Old Spice and users on both Facebook and Twitter was significantly lower. Whereas during the *Smell is Power* campaign, Old Spice regularly interacted with consumers via retweets on Twitter and dialogues on Facebook, this interactive relationship was much less prevalent during the span of the *Believe in your Smellf* campaign. Moreover, while many users during the first campaign regularly parroted Crew's over-the-top remarks in their social media comments and responses, during the second campaign very few consumers parroted the campaign's new mantra. Old Spice itself did not appear to fully embrace *Believe in your Smellf,* only posting sporadic tweets acknowledging the new campaign. The disparity between the proliferation and ubiquitous nature of the messages in the first and second campaign was clear.

The format and execution of the advertisements in the *Believe in your Smellf* campaign were quite different from those of the more successful *Smell is Power* campaign. Figure 3.3 shows that Facebook experienced only a mild growth in the fan base and discussions of the brand stagnated through April 2012 and into May 2012 where only modest growth was seen through the life of the campaign (Facebook Statistics, 2012). Figure 3.2 shows that growth in subscribers to Old Spice's YouTube channel was tepid indicating that while no subscribers were lost, no new subscribers were gained (YouTube Statistics, 2012). Additionally, Figure 3.2 indicates that daily views were comparatively low during the life of this campaign, which could be characterized as a somewhat apathetic response to the new advertisements and social media techniques (YouTube Statistics, 2012). Figure 3.1 does show that there was growth in Twitter followers during this time, but not in the same dramatic way as during the *Smell is Power* advertising campaign (Twitter Statistics, 2012). In fact, during this campaign which ran from April 2012 to early June 2012, growth was only sufficient to regain the followers lost during March and April.

Discussion

This study examined two major research questions when analyzing the Old Spice campaigns of early 2012. The first research question asked what techniques Old Spice used to achieve success in social media advertising and used the *Smell is Power* campaign as an example of what success looks like. The second asked what differences existed between the techniques or strategies used in the *Smell is Power* campaign and the quantifiably less successful *Believe in your Smellf* campaign. On examination – three major differences appear in the analysis. First, in order for social media advertising and viral marketing to be successful, media content must be fresh and useful to consumers either from a utilitarian or psychological perspective. While both campaigns used videos that were at very least entertaining, during the *Smell is Power* campaign Old Spice appeared to make a concerted effort to keep content fresh, energetic and of a kind and quality that would appeal to a youthful consumer base. Essentially, Old Spice provided content that could easily be disseminated among consumers and which consumers would want to share with others.

Second, personality cannot be dismissed within social media marketing. One of the most obvious differences between the first and second campaigns was the presence of a spokesman/figurehead. The use of a highly energetic, charismatic, almost archetypal embodiment of the brand's theme or image, in essence, provides consumers with a face with which to relate. This is even more important when it comes to social media since consumers are not just talking with a faceless brand or a corporate entity (like parent company Procter & Gamble), they are interacting with Terry Crews, the in-your-face, hypermasculine pitchman who bursts through walls and makes claims that would be considered humorous among the targeted, young male social media demographic.

Finally, this study discovered that what separated the highly successful *Smell is Power* campaign from the less impressive *Believe in your Smellf* campaign was the pure utilization of that which makes social media marketing both unique and potentially difficult, interaction with consumers. Within the *Smell is Power* campaign, interaction with consumers or user comments was regular and, to a degree, personal. The perception was that Crews would comment directly on user comments on Twitter, and a great deal of user-generated content was acknowledged and posted on Facebook. This interactive relationship between brand and consumer appears to have been very successful based on the metrics in Figures 3.1, 3.2, and 3.3 as well as the number of retweets on Twitter and likes on Facebook posts. During the *Believe in your Smellf* campaign there were fewer interactions between the brand and the consumer. While consumers did regularly comment on both the Facebook and Twitter pages, Old Spice rarely responded and almost never acknowledged user-generated content.

Ultimately, in response to the questions this study set out to examine, what led to the tremendous consumer response to the Old Spice *Smell is Power* campaign (RQ1) and the less impressive response to the *Believe in your Smellf* campaign (RQ2) were varying degrees of dedication to simple social media strategies. First, provide users with content that is fresh, accessible, and useful to them where they are. Second, relate to user consumers in a personal, direct way. Social media is most effective when it is personal. Finally, create an interactive relationship with users. The theory of uses and gratifications argues that consumers are active members of the media process and through social media this cannot be ignored. For social media advertising campaigns to be successful, a dialogue must be created where the company and the consumer interact with each other, rather than the traditional role of companies talking at consumers hoping to sell them products or services. These three basic techniques are what Old Spice did very well in the *Smell is Power* campaign, which generated a powerful user response across social media, and they are also what Old Spice did not do as well during the *Believe in your Smellf* campaign, which may have contributed to a less enthusiastic consumer reaction.

Only time will reveal whether this social mediacentric strategy truly has legs, but in 2012 it proved effective for Old Spice. Perhaps what one should take from this study above all else is that, for a product or brand that desires to reinvigorate itself in a younger marketplace, social media appears to be an excellent vehicle. Provided, that is, that the product or brand understands the needs, desires, and expectations of social media users. Old Spice's success was not predicated on forcing itself into someone's personal (virtual) space and constantly nagging them to buy, but rather understanding what it takes to be invited into a consumer's virtual world as an interesting or funny friend who always has a story to tell. The ability to build this kind of relationship is the true power of social media in advertising (Agresta, Bough, & Miletsky, 2010). This study showed that the trajectory of success increased exponentially as Old Spice escalated its use of social media and built an interactive relationship with consumers via social media. Future studies examining the growing use of social media by businesses to generate revenue by using social media effectively remains a topic ripe for additional research.

References

Agresta, S., Bough, B. B., & Miletsky, J. I. (2010). *Perspectives on social media marketing*. Boston, MA: Muska/Lipman.

Baskin, J. S. (2011a, July 27). Old Spice's love affair with itself serves no sales purpose. *AdAge CMO Strategy*. Retrieved from http://adage.com/article/cmo-strategy/spice-s-love-affair-serves-sales-purpose/228943/

Baskin, J. S. (2011b, August 10). Is P&G's biggest innovation old-fashioned functionality? *AdAge CMO Strategy*. Retrieved from http://adage.com/article/cmo-strategy/p-g-s-biggest-innovation-fashioned-functionality/229179/

Bennett, S. (2011). Facebook, Twitter, LinkedIn: The social media statistics of today. *Mediabistro.com*. Retrieved from http://www.mediabistro.com/alltwitter/social-media-statistics_b17188

Burns, G., & Thompson, R. J. (1989). Introduction. In G. Burns (Ed.), *Television studies: Textual analysis* (pp. 1–6). New York, NY: Praegar Publishers.

Choi, S. M. (2011). Advertising and social media. *International Journal of Advertising, 31*(1), 11–12. doi: 10.2501/IJA-30–1-011–012

Davis, N. (2011, October 5). Social media ads will be a $10 billion business in 2013. *BusinessInsider.com*. Retrieved from http://articles.businessinsider.com/2011–10–05/tech/30246178_1_emarketer-online-ads-linkedin

Dugan, L. (2010, August 16). Ad spending on social networks to reach $2 billion by 2011; But is it enough? *Socialtimes.com*. Retrieved from http://socialtimes.com/ad-spending-on-social-networks-to-reach-2-billion-by-2011-but-is-it-enough_b20322

Facebook Statistics. (2012). *Socialbakers.com*. Retrieved from http:\\www.socialbakers.com

Hof, R. (2011, August 26). Online ad spend to overtake TV by 2016. *Forbes.com*. Retrieved from http://www.forbes.com/fdc/welcome_mjx.shtml

Internet 2011 in numbers. (2012, January 17). *Pingdom.com*. Retrieved from http://royal.pingdom.com/2012/01/17/internet-2011-in-numbers/

Jaffe, J. (2010, July 27). Sugar and Old Spice. *Adweek*. Retrieved from http://www.adweek.com/news/advertising-branding/sugar-and-old-spice-102903

Lee, E. (2011). How social media stole your mind, took advertising with it. *Advertising Age, 82*(9), 2–57. Retrieved from http://adage.com/article/digital/social-media-stole-mind-advertising/149120/

Madden, M., & Zickuhr, K. (2011, August 26). *65% of online adults use social networking sites*. Washington, DC: Pew Internet and American Life Project. Retrieved from http://pewinternet.org/Reports/2011/Social-Networking-Sites.aspx

Neff, J. (2010, July 26). How much Old Spice body wash has the Old Spice guy sold? *Advertising Age*. Retrieved from http://adage.com/article/news/spice-body-wash-spice-guy-sold/145096/

Neff, J. (2011, August 4). Old Spice is killing it on YouTube again, but sales are down double-digits. *Advertising Age*. Retrieved from http://adage.com/article/the-viral-video-chart/spice-killing-youtube-sales/229080/

Old Spice | Blown Mind. (2012, January 11). *YouTube.com*. Retrieved from http://www.youtube.com/watch?v=BNbMvlPc_7U

Old Spice | Bounce. (2012, February 01). *YouTube.com*. Retrieved from http://www.youtube.com/watch?v=PvYP_d2S1Pg

Old Spice | Bowling. (2012, February 05). *YouTube.com*. Retrieved from http://www.youtube.com/watch?v=_fNYFp1VCX8

Old Spice | Charmin. (2012, February 01). *YouTube.com*. Retrieved from http://www.youtube.com/watch?v=WxnSBEkk3Ms

Old Spice | I Can Do Anything. (2012, April 23). *YouTube.com*. Retrieved from http://www.youtube.com/watch?v=dOFj9toF4Ho

Old Spice | Vending Machine. (2012, February 01). *YouTube.com*. Retrieved from http://www.youtube.com/watch?v=5Ziwz5Ltn-w

Qualman, E. (2012, January 4). 39 social media statistics to start 2012. *Socialnomics.com*. Retrieved from http://www.socialnomics.net/2012/01/04/39-social-media-statistics-to-start-2012/

Severin, W. J., & Tankard, J. W. (2001). *Communication theories: Origins, methods, and uses in the mass media.* 5th ed. New York, NY: Addison Wesley Longman.

Slutsky, I. (2011a, April 4). Ad growing pains for Twitter. *Advertising Age, 82*(14). Retrieved from http://adage.com/article/digital/ad-growing-pains-twitter/152883/

Slutsky, I. (2011b, May 2). Facebook's sales chief: Madison Avenue doesn't understand us yet. *Advertising Age, 82*(18). Retrieved from http://adage.com/article/digital/facebook-s-sales-chief-mad-ave-understand/227314/

Smith, A. (2011, November 15). *Why Americans use social media.* Washington, DC: Pew Internet and American Life Project. Retrieved from http://pewinternet.org/Reports/2011/Why-Americans-Use-Social-Media.aspx

Steel, E., & Fowler, G. A. (2011, November 2). Big brands like Facebook, but they don't like to pay. *The Wall Street Journal.* Retrieved from http://online.wsj.com/article/SB10001424052970204294504576613232804554362.html

Taylor, D. G., Lewin, J. E., & Strutton, D. (2011, March). Friends, fans, and followers: Do ads work on social networks? How gender and age shape receptivity. *Journal of Advertising Research, 51*(1), 258–275. doi: 10.2501/JAR-51-1-258-275

Taylor, V. (2010, August 17). The best-ever social media campaigns. *Forbes.com*. Retrieved from http://www.forbes.com/2010/08/17/facebook-old-spice-farmville-pepsi-forbes-viral-marketing-cmo-network-social-media.html

Twitter Statistics. (2012). *Socialbakers.com*. Retrieved from http://www.socialbakers.com

van Noort, G., Antheunis, M. L., & van Reijmersdal, E. A. (2012). Social connections and the persuasiveness of viral campaigns in social network sites: Persuasive intent as the underlying mechanism. *Journal of Marketing Communication, 18*(1), 39–53. doi: 10.1080/13527266.62011.620764

Warren, C. (2009, September 25). Study: Time spent on social networks has tripled. *Mashable.com*. Retrieved from http://mashable.com/2009/09/25/social-networking-triple/

Wheaton, K. (2009, April 13). Big agencies face challenge from social-media upstarts. *Advertising Age, 80*(3), 12. Retrieved from http://adage.com/article/print-edition/big-agencies-face-challenge-social-media-upstarts/135900/

YouTube Statistics. (2012). *Socialblade.com*. Retrieved from http://socialblade.com/youtube/user/Old%20Spice

4

The Current Trends in Social Media Usage at Corporations: Analysis of Facebook Fan Pages of Fortune 500 Companies

Jae-Hwa Shin, Heather Carithers, Seungae Lee, Meghan Graham and Nicole Hendricks

From its humble beginnings on the campus of Harvard University in 2004, Facebook has become a multi-billion dollar enterprise, the most successful of the social media. College students were the first users, followed by high school students and others with access to the Internet. By 2007 many businesses, nonprofits, and other organizations had a Facebook presence, and by 2010 a majority of U.S. Fortune 500 companies were using Facebook fan pages. Facebook has helped corporations maintain relationships with their customers through various forms of contact.

With refinements over the years, social media have become a useful tool for organizations of all kinds to communicate with their public since the Internet has become a way for users to exchange information with those in a global community at a rapid pace. Nearly half of all Americans go online with a laptop, mobile broadband card, and a mobile phone to participate in online communication. Fifteen years ago, Parks and Floyd (1996) demonstrated that online communication had become a very large part of socializing and entertaining.

Facebook, as one of the most popular social media, had about 900 million users in February 2012, and was expected to surpass one billion active accounts by the end of that year (Goldman, 2012). The popularity of Facebook is not only limited to personal users. It has also become essential for many organizations. Approximately 69% of Fortune 2000 companies use social media. Thirty-seven percent of those companies have plans to increase their social media usage over the next five years

(McCorkindale, 2010). Currently, many organizations are conducting research on social media to help them implement this new technology and recognize its effectiveness (Paine, 2009). Considering its popularity among a large segment of the public, Facebook has a significant potential for organizations to mediate disputes, communicate with the public, and strengthen relationships. Companies are able to keep track of audience perceptions and approval by how many likes their Facebook fan page has. Companies are also able to track the interactions that they have with consumers by using the organizational features that Facebook offers. These features are instrumental in facilitating interaction with existing or potential consumers.

Although there have been many studies examining how organizations are utilizing their websites and company blogs to improve customer relationships, research is not voluminous regarding the use of Facebook in daily practice. The purpose of this study was (a) to examine how Fortune 500 companies utilize Facebook to disclose company information, disseminate company/product information, and interact with consumers, and (b) to provide important insights into the adoption of Facebook fan pages for companies seeking to increase their brand awareness and essentially improve the relationship with their public.

Literature Review

For-profit vs. Nonprofit Use of Facebook

Waters, Burnett, Lamm and Lucas (2009) supported the observation that for-profit organizations tend to use social media to advertise new products and validate their existing brands. They posited that social media have had a positive effect on issues regarding for-profit organizations, nonprofit organizations, and government sectors. Social media have enabled organizations to achieve greater transparency. Organizations without clear statements about their accountability and a sense of responsiveness are often not well-received by consumers. One of the benefits of organizations using Facebook is that it facilitates and encourages transparent and open communication (Waters et al., 2009). This type of two-way communication fosters and promotes consumer–company relationships. According to Vorvoreanu (2009), research has confirmed that transparent and mutually beneficial relationships between organizations and the public lead to positive outcomes.

On the other hand, the use of social media by nonprofit organizations continues to grow. Greenberg and MacAulay (2009) stated that nonprofit organizations were among the first to adopt new electronic technologies. Charity and volunteer-based groups use the Internet as a major means to increase their social efforts. Butcher (2009) also indicated that nonprofits have adopted social media at a much faster rate than Fortune 500 companies and academic institutions.

Yet, for-profit organizations have a large stake in social media. Vorvoreanu (2009) stated, "Companies wishing to engage in public relations and marketing efforts on Facebook have to be mindful of Facebook culture, and their communication with the public" (p. 77). Organizations attempt to establish and maintain a relationship with Facebook users, cultivating existing relationships and seeking to reach potential customers or constituents. For-profits like Wal-Mart and Starbucks strive to establish and maintain consumer–company relationships to increase brand awareness and customer loyalty.

Dialogic Communication and Relationship Cultivation

Social media have revealed the benefits of two-way communication. Phillips (2008) noted that the two-way communication presented by social media allows providers to offer a large amount of content tailored to personal interests and affords the individual user new ways to act out a wide variety of self-expression. Phillips (2008) suggested this difference in the way one expresses himself/herself provides a more beneficial relationship when compared to a face-to-face relationship. An individual's need to belong to a group, or more than one group, can be satisfied in his/her involvement in social media. Facebook users are rewarded for a sense of belonging through the interaction.

Many studies have examined the online effectiveness of three relationship cultivation strategies, these are disclosure, information dissemination, and interaction. In describing disclosure, Berman, Abraham, Battino, Shipnuck, and Neus (2007) noted the importance of providing a detailed organizational description along with information about the company's history. They recommended logos and hyperlinks to connect consumers to organizational websites. Berman et al. (2007) also recommended that companies list the individuals who are responsible for maintaining the social networking profile, even though this is not commonly found on Facebook. One of the main reasons for companies to use social networking sites is to distribute information (Crespo, 2007). Posting links to external news items, photographs, video, and audio files are often used to distribute information about the organization. Also, message boards or discussion walls to post announcements and press releases are used to disseminate information. Jo and Kim (2003) suggested that listing email addresses and a calendar of events helps increase interactivity online, and interactivity is necessary to create relationships with consumers.

Framing

For Sieff (2003), analysis of framing is useful to researchers because it allows insight into how media communicate news stories, how audiences interpret news, and the interactions between media and audience. He understands media framing both in terms of how it is presented and how it contributes to the "internal mental structures" used by news consumers to "lighten the burden of information processing" (p. 263). How a topic is framed is directly related to how it is perceived or understood. According to Entman (1993), "to frame is to select some aspects of a perceived reality and make them more salient in a communicating text" (p. 52).

Iyengar (1991) distinguished between episodic and thematic framing. Episodic framing examines the center of an issue and does not incorporate outside factors. Thematic framing, conversely, focuses on context and a background story. Thematic framing looks at the big picture, whereas episodic framing incorporates a case-by-case method. Pan and Kosicki (1993) categorized frames into four categories:

> Fact-based frames are those that contain statements that cannot be disproved and are accepted as absolute truths. Interest-based frames deal with wants or goals that can be beneficial in the future. Value-based frames deal with issues of opinion and are personal in nature. Value-based frames cannot be universal. Relational frames are those that involve the feelings of the individuals involved. Relational frames are not logical or rational in nature. (Pan & Kosicki, 1993, p. 8)

On the other hand, Druckman and McDermott (2008) acknowledged that there is a direct link between the emotional state a person is in and how a specific frame affects him or her. They noted:

> people tend to become more involved and interested when they feel positive emotions such as enthusiasm, but actually become more attentive to external stimuli, information-seeking, and open to attitude change when they are experiencing negative emotions that generate anxiety (e.g., distress). (p. 302)

Druckman and McDermott (2008) also noted that emotions which are negative in nature will have an adverse effect on people's reaction to specific frames: "aversive emotions like anger, then, trigger the disposition rather than the surveillance system; the disposition system leads people to be less attuned to the external environment" (p. 302). So, an emotion like anger will cause a person to stop their thought processes and avoid exposure to a specific frame.

Alhabash, Littau, Wise, Eckler, and Kononova (2009) suggested the uses and gratifications theory played a role in the emotional aspect of Facebook use. This is evident because studies show that Facebook and other social media are used to fulfill the gratifications of an individual's needs (Alhabash et al., 2009). They suggested using the surveillance function of Facebook to determine whether the user is utilizing social browsing and social searching, which they defined as:

> Social browsing is conceptualized as the selections of general pages, when participants were not looking at information of a particular person, but rather browsing through a pool of information that involved more than one person or one type of information (e.g., the newsfeed page, all events page, all events, all friends page, etc…). On the other hand, social searching is more concerned with goal-oriented surveillance, where participants moved from the general content to the pages belonging to a particular person. (p. 7)

From these definitions, one can assume that individuals using Facebook for social browsing are not in a state likely to result in an emotional post. However, if individuals engage in social searching, they are more likely to post an emotional response.

Research Questions

The first set of research questions looks at the dominance of disclosure strategies, information dissemination tools, and involvement strategies to help to provide a clear picture of how Fortune 500 companies use Facebook to disclose company information, disseminate important information, and promote interaction.

RQ1: What is the dominant disclosure strategy of Fortune 500 companies on Facebook?

RQ2: What is the dominant information dissemination strategy of Fortune 500 companies on Facebook?

RQ3: What is the dominant involvement strategy of Fortune 500 companies on Facebook?

Eight different functions were coded including: (a) text, (b) tags, (c) photos, (d) links to products, (e) links to audio or video, (f) links to traditional media, (g) links to other websites, or (h) mixed media links. The dominant function was also looked at in terms of company posts, comments, others' posts and others' comments.

RQ4a: What is the dominant function of Facebook fan page wall posts?

RQ4b: Is there any difference between company posts and comments, and others posts and comments on Facebook fan page wall posts in terms of dominant functions?

Five different themes were coded and looked at in terms of dominance. The themes coded were: (a) fact-based, (b) interest-based, (c) value-based, (d) relational, or (e) other. Themes were also looked at in terms of (a) company post, (b) comments, and (c) others' posts and comments.

RQ5a: What is the dominant theme of Facebook fan page wall posts?

RQ5b: Is there any difference between company posts and comments, and others posts and comments on Facebook fan pages wall posts in terms of dominant themes?

Messages in company posts were coded as: (a) product/brand promotion, (b) event promotion, (c) news, (d) public service announcements, or (e) other. Frames for company responses were coded as: (a) showing gratitude, (b) apologizing, and (c) providing information for further interaction, such as links to contact information. Others posts and responses were coded as: (a) facts, (b) questions, (c) comments about product/brand, (d) compliments/appreciation/gratitude, and (e) complaints.

RQ6: What is the dominant message used in Facebook fan page wall posts?

The frame was coded as episodic or thematic; where episodic framing examines the center of an issue and does not incorporate outside factors, while thematic framing utilizes context and a background story is used. Frame was also examined in terms of (a) company posts, (b) company responses, (c) others posts, and (d) others responses to see if there was a difference in frames.

RQ7a: What is the dominant frame used in Facebook fan page wall posts?

RQ7b: Is there any difference between company posts and comments, and others posts and comments on Facebook fan pages wall posts in terms of dominant frames?

Emotions were coded as: (a) positive, (b) negative, and (c) neutral, and were also looked at in terms of (a) company posts, (b) company responses, (c) others posts and (d) others responses. Emotions were also compared in terms of (a) company posts, (b) company responses, (c) others posts and (d) others responses, to see if there was any difference in dominance.

RQ8a: What is the dominant emotion of Facebook fan pages wall posts?

RQ8b: Is there any difference between company posts and comments, and others posts and comments on Facebook fan pages wall posts in terms of dominant emotions?

Responses were coded based on the question of whether or not there was a response to the post. Also, types of responses were examined in terms of positive, negative or neutral statements, or questions.

RQ9a: If there was a response, what was the dominant type?

RQ9b: Is there any difference between company comments and others comments on Facebook fan pages wall posts in terms of response types?

The rank of the Fortune 500 companies was examined to see (a) if there was any link between rank and how many likes a company's Facebook fan page had and (b) if there is any association between the company's ranking, and themes, frames and emotions of their Facebook posts.

RQ10: Is the Fortune 500 company's ranking associated with the number of likes on Facebook fan pages, themes, frames and emotions of the posts?

Method

This study used content analysis to examine how Fortune 500 companies use their Facebook fan pages to disclose company information, disseminate information, and create interactions with their fan base and conversely how the audiences are using the fan pages. The 2010 Fortune 500 company list was retrieved from Forbes.com. The sample consisted of every tenth company posted on the list of the Forbes Fortune 500 companies (*n* = 50). They included Wal-Mart Stores, Hewlett Packard, Procter & Gamble, Target, Lowes, Pepsi Co., Intel, Morgan Stanley, Ingram Micro, Hartford Financial Services, Amazon. com, Motorola, American Airlines (AMR), AFLAC, United Airlines (UAL), Colgate-Palmolive, Progressive, Toys 'R' Us, Continental Airlines, Office Depot, DISH Network, AutoNation, Texas Instruments, BJ's Wholesale Club, Starbucks, Tenet Healthcare, NRG Energy, Nordstrom, Ashland, Chesapeake Energy, C.H. Robinson Worldwide, OfficeMax, CarMax, Dole Food, Thrivent Financial for Lutherans, Symantec, McGraw-Hill, Harris, SunGard Data Systems, PetSmart, Mutual of Omaha Insurance, MasterCard, Atmos Energy, Harley-Davidson, Travel Centers of America, NCR, Charles Schwab, Kelly Services, Radio Shack, and Live Nation Entertainment. Companies without a Facebook fan page were not included. Companies that did not allow fans to post on their fan page were also not considered. The sample consisted of wall posts of selected companies that were posted every other day starting February 1, 2011, through February 13, 2011.

All posts were divided into four categories: company's posts, company's responses, others' posts and others' responses. The term others refers to the posters who post a comment or response on the fan pages and who are not affiliated with the Fortune 500 company. The sample was a total of 8,442 posts on Facebook fan pages. Others posts were the most dominant type of wall post found on Fortune 500 company walls, with a total of 4,361 (51.7%). Others responses were found to be the second most dominant type of posts with 2,791 (33.1%) posts coded. Company posts and company responses had the least amount of posts with 1,007 (11.9%) company responses, and 283 (3.4%) company posts.

Fortune 500 companies were categorized by industry, such as arts/ humanities, education, healthcare, human services, public/society benefit, religious, or other. For example, the publishing company, McGraw-Hill, was coded as education. To evaluate functionality, the profiles of companies were coded for each item displaying company disclosure, information dissemination, and involvement (Muralidharan, Rasmussen, Patterson, & Shin, 2011; Waters et al., 2009). For disclosure strategies these items were included: (a) company description, (b) history or founding, (c) mission statements, (d) URL, (e) logos, (f) administrators listed, and (g) others. Information dissemination strategies were coded to understand the types of links and files disseminated via posts.

These strategies were evaluated by the presence of the following items: news link, photos, video files, audio files, discussion wall, boxes, and others. Lastly, involvement strategies were coded, including organization email address, phone number, calendar of events, sweepstakes or contests, e-commerce store, and others. The rank of 2010 Fortune 500 companies and the number of like clicks were also coded for company information.

The dominant function of each post and response was coded to see whether they included text, tags, photos, links to products, links to audio or video, links to traditional media, links to other websites, or mixed media links. The dominant theme of each post was also coded as fact-based, interest-based, value-based, relational, or other. The classification and definition for the typology was based on Knight (1999). The dominant frame was coded as episodic or thematic, and the dominant emotion was categorized as positive, negative, and neutral for each post (Muralidharan et al., 2011).

The dominant message frames were coded separately in terms of company posts, company responses, others posts and others responses. The message frames for each were developed through initial coding. Company wall posts were coded as product/brand promotion, event promotion, news, public service announcements, or other. The message frames were defined as:

a) *Product/brand promotion:* Information about incentives, contests, and other activities;
b) *Event promotion:* Information about sponsorships, conferences, and other events;
c) *News:* Information about awards, financial situations, or other general information;
d) *Public service announcement:* Information about weather, health awareness, and other issues of public concern.

On the other hand, company responses were coded as gratitude, apologizing, and providing information for further interaction, such as a link to contact information. Others posts and responses were coded as facts, questions and comments about product/brand, compliments/appreciation/gratitude, or complaints in terms of the dominant message. Each post was coded in terms of function, themes, frames, emotions and messages. The same coding categories are applied to analyze all four post types. However, the coding categories for messages were developed separately for (1) company posts, (2) company responses, (3) others posts, and (4) others responses. Collectively, the responses by both companies and consumers were coded for receiving positive, negative, neutral comments or by posing questions to the sampled companies. This reveals the type of responses: positive, neutral, negative or question, that was used to respond to the post or response originally posted. To explore consumer responses to posts, the number of likes a company received was also noted.

Intercoder reliability was established by the initial coding. Based on the percentage of agreement and calculation of Holsti's method, intercoder reliability ranged from a low of .87 to 1.0 (disclosure, information dissemination and involvement strategies). The intercoder reliability for other variables were: .87 (emotion), .89 (theme), .90 (message) and .92 (frame). The initial coding process was completed with several training sessions among coders.

Results

The results for RQ1 demonstrated that logo (n = 47; 94%), URL (n = 47; 94%), history (n = 28; 56%) and description (n = 27; 52%) were most commonly found on the Facebook profile pages of the fifty selected Fortune 500 companies. Other disclosure strategies commonly found on Facebook profile pages were mission statement, administrators, company overview and pages that the company liked to link to. It is important to note that administrator and mission statement were rarely found on any Facebook fan pages. There was no significant association between the industry type and the disclosure strategies on the Fortune 500 Facebook profile pages.

The findings for RQ2 indicated that photos (n = 45; 90%), videos (n = 36; 72%), and discussion wall (n = 34; 68%) were most commonly found on the Facebook profile pages of the fifty selected Fortune 500 companies. News links (n = 15; 30%) were used sometimes, but boxes (n = 7; 14%) and audio (n = 2; 4%) were used least as a strategy for information dissemination. Links to a company's YouTube or Twitter account were found as other strategies. There were significant associations between the type of industry, photos (χ^2 = 16.1, df = 5, p < .05) and discussion wall (χ^2 = 12.1, df = 5, p < .05).

The results of RQ3 suggested that a discussion board (n = 35; 70%) and calendar of events (n = 24; 48%) were most commonly found on the Facebook fan pages of the fifty selected Fortune 500 companies as displayed in Table 4.1. Phone number (n = 11; 21.4%), sweepstake (n = 10; 20%), e-commerce stores (n = 7; 14%) or email to the company

Table 4.1 Dominant function of Facebook fan page wall posts

Function	Company posts	Company responses	Others posts	Others responses	Total
Text	67	596	3,353	2,777	6,793
Tag	1	1	155	2	159
Photo	16	1	325	2	344
Link to product	11	1	3	1	16
Link to audio/video	12	0	30	0	42
Link to traditional media	30	0	28	7	65
Link to other website	128	408	415	2	953
Mixed media	18	0	52	0	70
Total	283	1,007	4,361	2,791	8,442

($n = 4$; 8%) were the least used strategies for involvement. Other involvement strategies commonly found on Facebook fan pages were polls and games ($n = 15$; 30%). There was a significant relationship between the type of industry and one of the items listed as involvement strategies. Discussion board ($\chi^2 = 11.8$, $df = 5$, $p < .05$) has a statistically significant relationship with the company industry. Text posts ($n = 6,793$; 80.4%) were the most dominant functions among the 8,442 messages analyzed in this study, followed by a link to another website ($n = 953$; 11.3%) or photo ($n = 344$; 4%). There was then a big gap with tag ($n = 159$; 1.8%), mixed media ($n = 70$; 0.8), link to traditional media ($n = 65$; 0.7), link to audio/video ($n = 42$; 0.5) also used. A link to products ($n = 16$; 0.19%) was the least dominant function used by Fortune 500 companies.

The findings of RQ4 revealed that text-post was also the most dominant for all four types: company posts ($n = 67$; 24% out of 283 total company posts), company responses ($n = 596$; 59% out of 1,007 total company responses), others posts ($n = 3,353$; 76% out of 4,361 total others posts), and others responses ($n = 2,777$; 99.4% out of 2, 791 others responses). Links to other websites were also frequently used by company posts ($n = 129$; 49%) and company responses ($n = 408$; 41%). There was a significant relationship among company posts and responses, and others posts and responses in terms of dominant function ($\chi^2 = 2,912$, $df = 21$, $p < .05$).

The results of RQ5 showed that the dominant theme was interest-based ($n = 4,296$; 50.9%), while the least used theme was value-based ($n = 108$; 1.27%) across the 8,442 posts and responses of company and others. Interestingly, while the dominant themes for company posts ($n = 184$; 65%), others posts ($n = 2,718$; 62%), and others responses

(n = 1,307; 47%) were consistently interest-based, the dominant theme for company responses was relational (n = 757; 75%). This could explain the purpose of company responses to posts. While others write posts or responses to pursue their own interests, company responses were mostly used to build or create a relationship. There was a significant association between post types and theme (χ^2 = 1,332.1, df = 12, p < .05).

The findings of RQ6 showed that the dominant message used in company posts was product/brand promotion (n = 130; 45.6%), followed by news (n = 57; 20%), event promotion (n = 52; 18.2%) and public service (n = 9; 3%). The dominant message in company responses was information for further interaction (n = 649; 63.3%), gratitude (n = 266; 25.9%) and apology (n = 65; 6.3%) among the 1,007 company responses analyzed. The most dominant message for others posts and responses was neutral comments about the company's products (n = 2,740; 38.1%). Compliment and/or appreciation posts (n = 1,891; 26.2%) were the second most dominant message, but complaints (n = 648; 9%) did not appear frequently.

The results of RQ7 revealed that the dominant frame is episodic (n = 4,507; 97.2%), while thematic frame is used least (n = 129; 2.8%). Company posts had 86.5% (n = 245) episodic frames and others posts had 97.9% (n = 4,262) (χ^2 = 126.2, df = 1, p < .05). It was interesting to note that both company and others posts had few thematic frames. This may be due to the nature of Facebook comments, which are relatively short and direct.

The findings of RQ8 indicated that the dominant emotion types were neutral (n = 3,513; 41.6%) and positive (n = 3,349; 39.7%), while negative emotions (n = 1,580; 18.7%) occupied the least. Consistently, neutral emotion was found most in company posts (n = 146; 51%), company responses (n = 595; 60%), and others posts (n = 1,887; 44%). Positive emotion was found second most in company posts (n = 135; 48%), company responses (n = 407; 40%), and others posts (n = 1,846; 42%). However, others responses were evenly distributed among positive (n = 950; 34%), negative (n = 945; 34%), and neutral (n = 896; 32%) emotions. The posts by others also have a relatively higher percentage of negative emotion (n = 628; 14%) than company posts (n = 2; 0.7%) and company responses (n = 5; 0.4%). Between the post types and emotions, there was a significant association (χ^2 = 793.3, df = 6, p < .05). When a negative post is updated, the companies respond with positive and neutral emotions to console, designed to maintain and improve the relationship. However, others often respond negatively if the posts are negative. Since a company's response is targeting most of the people who visit the company's fan pages rather than random individuals, the company would be more likely to deliver messages that arouse affirmative, constructive and encouraging tones and reflect the positive images of the company such as responsibility and morality.

The results of RQ9 indicated that only 35.3% (n = 2,981) of posts received responses, which means more than half (n = 5,461; 64.7%) of posts did not receive responses from either the company or others who responded on the fan pages but were not affiliated with the Fortune 500 companies. Table 4.2 shows that most company posts (n = 225; 80% out of 283 total company posts) received responses, indicating that others visiting their fan pages were very attentive to the company's message. However, company responses (n = 202; 20% out of 1,007 total company responses) did not receive as many following responses as their posts. Others posts (n = 2,332; 47% out of total 4,361 others posts) and others responses (n = 2,276; 35% out of 4,361 total others responses) also created reasonable numbers of responses.

As exhibited in Table 4.3, the dominant type of response, was neutral (n = 1,597; 54%), followed by positive (n = 1,016; 34%) then negative (n = 359; 12%). Company posts (n = 162; 73%) or company responses (n = 80; 40%) were more positive, while others posts (n = 1,173; 58%) and others responses (n = 298; 57%) were more neutral (χ^2 = 7,949, df = 3, $p < .05$).

Table 4.2   Responses to posts

Response	Company posts	Company responses	Others posts	Others responses	Total
Yes	225	202	2,039	515	2,981
No	58	805	2,322	2,276	5,461
Total	283	1,007	4,361	4,361	8,442

Table 4.3   Type of responses

Type	Company posts	Company responses	Others posts	Others responses	Total
Positive	162	80	677	97	1,016
Negative	5	49	189	116	359
Neutral	57	69	1,173	298	1,597
Question	1	4	0	4	9
Total	225	202	2,039	515	2,981

In Table 4.3, the findings of RQ10 suggested that there was a positive correlation between the companies' ranking in Fortune 500 and the number of likes on Facebook fan pages ($r = .13$; $p < .05$). Also, statistically significant relationships between the company's categorical ranking in Fortune 500, and theme ($\chi^2 = 1,849$, $df = 16$, $p < .05$), frame ($\chi^2 = 104.6$, $df = 4$, $p < .05$), or emotion ($\chi^2 = 1,001.1$, $df = 8$, $p < .05$) were observed. In the posts of more highly ranked companies, more interest-based or relational themes were found; more episodic frames are noticeable, and more positive emotional expressions were posted.

Discussion

Social media have become a valuable tool for a number of Fortune 500 companies in recent years. Despite their benefits, the findings of this study suggest that companies are not using social media to best effect. Corporations are now able to respond to various customer service issues in a fast and efficient way using social media, but the usage is limited to certain purposes. There is also a wide variance among the companies in their uses of social media. For example, some companies frequently update posts and actively respond to customer comments. Others rarely or never respond to customer comments, and some of them even have sites that are inactive or contain very few posts, as if they were created just to have a presence on Facebook. Also, the number of posts on a company's fan page varies drastically (i.e., Starbucks 18.3% and McGraw-Hill 0%). Based on the fact that others posts and responses make up 83% of posts on Fortune 500 Facebook fan pages, it can be implied that Facebook fan pages are customer-oriented, participatory and open-ended in terms of the amount of content, which suggest the nature and trend of social media. Yet, the potential has not been fully explored and developed by most corporations.

There has been a swift change during the last several years. According to McCorkindale (2010), more than three-quarters of Facebook fan pages of Fortune 500 Companies in 2008 did not have updated posts or recent news. An analysis of their Facebook fan pages in 2011 showed that an increasing number of corporations were using social media to build positive relationships with their customers. The results of the functionality of the profile pages confirmed striking changes in the use of Facebook fan pages by Fortune 500 from 2008 to 2011. Only a small number of corporations included disclosure, and most of the companies didn't use information dissemination in 2008 (McCorkindale, 2010). However, the results of this study indicated that within the space of a few years, more than half of the sampled companies used Facebook for both disclosure and information dissemination purposes. This implies that corporations are now using Facebook profile pages more actively than before and operating diverse platforms, such as links to other media such as Twitter and YouTube, to deliver their messages. Interestingly, only a few items like discussion and calendar of events were utilized as involvement strategies, and most companies did not take advantage of Facebook's key features.

Interestingly, company posts and responses often used links to another website or other types of media. Companies may use this type of function in order to induce further involvement and interaction with the customers. Social media are being used to make further contacts and support the goal of audience interaction and participation. Corporations seem to be exploring social media as a means of interacting with their customers.

In terms of dominant themes, company posts, others posts and others responses were dominated by interest-based posts. However, a majority of company responses were relational and informational, revealing that the company's goal is to inform consumers and try to achieve further interaction. Companies are most likely to respond in an effort to satisfy others' interest, and build or improve upon external relationships. The dominant message used in company posts and company responses was product/brand promotion and information for further interaction. On the other hand, the dominant message in others posts and others responses was comments about products. Overall, companies and customers are mainly exchanging information and opinions about products on Facebook fan pages. The result is not a surprise considering the fact that the sites are commercial and profit-making. The purpose of company posts may be to offer more information regarding their own products and services to their existing or potential customers, and researching, or taking feedback from them.

In all types of post, the dominant frame was episodic. The episodic frame was used predominantly by both companies and customers. Only small numbers of thematic frames were present. This may be because most posts on Facebook fan pages consist of short messages or casual notes. This is most likely due to the features of Facebook that limit the length of a post.

Neutral posts show a slightly greater presence on fan pages than positive or negative posts. In comparison between company and others, companies posted more positive posts, but others posted more negative posts. The way in which the company responded to a negative post often resulted in a neutral or positive response from consumers. For example, if the company responded to a negative wall post with a neutral or positive tone, the consumer's subsequent response was positive or neutral. It may be that a consumer's complaint was acknowledged by the company on Facebook and possibly resolved using another channel. This type of circular communication holds promise for satisfying consumer needs, and contributes to the ongoing process of relationship-building from the company's perspective.

As earlier stated, interactive communication, which seems to be an essential relationship-building tool, was not yet highly evident on the Facebook fan pages. The fan pages were mostly occupied by customers who left posts without any further responses or ongoing interactions. Considering the significant difference between the corporations and Facebook users in the amount of the posts, it is too soon to conclude a lack of active two-way communication. A majority of companies who receive responses from customers should consider how to interact with these customers more actively and utilize the key features of Facebook.

Fortune 500 company rankings were associated with the number of likes on Facebook fan pages. A positive correlation implies that the companies who are successful in profit-making may also have corresponding support from customers who hit a like button, which suggests a Facebook user's positive attitude to the companies and may translate into higher profits. Certain frames and themes seem to be used more prominently by more highly ranked companies, and this finding offers some insight into a Facebook fan page management strategy for corporations.

Overall, most of the corporations do not seem to be fully utilizing the majority of their Facebook wall pages. On the other hand, the majority interaction that is taking place on the fan pages is from the customers. The small percentage of company posts and responses to customers could imply that the companies may use the new medium mostly for the purpose of tracking or monitoring the public without a fully-fledged usage. Despite the caveats, Facebook has the potential as an effective vehicle for communication with their consumers.

One of the limitations of this study is the sampling frame during a short time period, which included wall posts that were posted every other day for a two-week time frame, starting February 1, 2011, and ending February 13, 2011. Also, it is important to note that wall posts can be deleted at any time so that the number of posts can vary from day to day. This does not happen often, but is possible. It is one of the weaknesses of content analysis of Facebook and other social media.

Customers posted on the fan pages to satisfy their own interests, while organizations mostly responded to customer posts to offer further information about services and products, mediate issues and build relationships. A majority of the complaints on Facebook seemed to be resolved by companies responding with an attempt at further contact with the consumer. The resolutions and strengthened connection between corporations and customers can lead to more fans and returning visitors to the fan page. Future research should investigate the way in which corporations effectively resolve customer complaints and respond to customer opinions.

The dominant emotion of posts or responses on Facebook was either positive or neutral. It seems that some companies censor the posts, considering the variance in the number of posts per day. This is evidenced by the fact that more recent posts contain more emotionally negative content.

References

Alhabash, S., Littau, J., Wise, K., Eckler, P., & Kononova, A. (2009). *The "face" of Facebook: Emotional responses during social networking.* Paper presented at the annual meeting of the International Communication Association, Chicago, IL.

Berman, S. J., Abraham, S., Battino, B., Shipnuck, L., & Neus, A. (2007). New business models for the new media world. *Strategy & Leadership, 35*(4), 23–30.

Butcher, L. (2009). Nonprofit organizations outpace businesses in use of social media. *Oncology Times, 31,* 39–40.

Crespo, R. (2007). Virtual community health promotion. *Prevention Chronicles, 4*(3), 75.

Druckman, J. N., & McDermott, R. (2008). Emotion and the framing of risky choice. *Political Behavior, 30,* 297–321.

Entman, R. M. (1993). Framing: Toward a clarification of a fractured paradigm. *Journal of Communication, 43,* 51–58.

Goldman, D. (2012, April 23). Facebook tops 900 million users. *CNNMoney.* Retrieved from http://money.cnn.com/2012/04/23/technology/facebook-q1/index.htm

Greenberg, J., & MacAulay, M. (2009). NPO 2.0? Exploring the web presence of environmental nonprofit organizations in Canada. *Global Media Journal: Canadian Edition, 2*(1), 63–88.

Iyengar, S. (1991). *Is anyone responsible? How television frames political issues.* Chicago, IL: The University of Chicago Press.

Jo, S., & Kim, Y. (2003). The effect of web characteristics on relationship building. *Journal of Public Relations Research, 15*(3), 199–223.

Knight, M. G. (1999). Getting past the impasse: Framing as a tool for public relations. *Public Relations Review, 25*(3), 381–398.

McCorkindale, T. (2010). Can you see the writing on my wall? A content analysis of the Fortune 500's Facebook social networking sites. *Public Relations Journal,* 4(3).

Muralidharan, S., Rasmussen, L., Patterson, D., & Shin, J. H. (2011). Hope for Haiti: An analysis of Facebook and Twitter usage during the earthquake relief efforts. *Public Relations Review, 37*(2), 175–177.

Paine, K. D. (2009, March). *How to set benchmarks in social media: Exploratory research for social media.* Paper presented at the annual meeting of the International Public Relations Research Conference, Miami, FL.

Pan, Z., & Kosicki, G. M. (1993). Framing analysis: An approach to discourse. *Political Communication, 10,* 55–75.

Parks, M. R., & Floyd, K. (1996). Making friends in cyberspace. *Journal of Communication, 46*(1), 80–98.

Phillips, D. (2008). The psychology of social media. *Journal of New Communications Research, 3*(1), 79–85.

Sieff, E. M. (2003). Media frames of mental illness: The potential impact of negative frames. *Journal of Mental Health, 12*(3), 259–269.

Vorvoreanu, M. (2009). Perceptions of corporations on Facebook: An analysis of Facebook social norms. *Journal of New Communications Research, 4*(1), 67–86.

Waters, R. D., Burnett, E., Lamm, A., & Lucas, J. (2009). Engaging stakeholders through social networking: How nonprofit organizations are using Facebook. *Public Relations Review, 35*(2), 102–106.

Part II

Social Media and Public Relations

5

Convergence of Digital Negotiation and Risk Challenges: Strategic Implications of Social Media for Risk and Crisis Communications

Karen Freberg and Michael J. Palenchar

Strategic risk and crisis communication amalgamation with social media is one of the considerable growth areas of communication research and practice. Individuals and organizations can use social media to engage in dialogue with a wide range of stakeholders while sharing information (textual and visual) on various social media platforms; transforming how crisis professionals are targeting risk bearers, who are often their consumers before, during, and after a crisis.

The use of non-traditional, emerging media communication channels, such as social media, also raises the possibility that unconfirmed, word-of-mouth information can reach and influence individuals in addition to information via traditional or legacy media channels. Individuals are then directly experiencing a crisis through instantaneous updates and sharing through various social media platforms, transforming them into digital risk bearers. The use of authenticity embedded into social media platforms is also establishing a community based on collective knowledge, dialogue, and storytelling.

This chapter discusses emerging issues and best practices within social media from the public relations and crisis communication literature including: (1) issues and challenges associated with authenticity and trustworthiness of the messages emerging from social media, (2) perception of apology strategy and relationship management in a crisis, and (3) convergence of digital negotiation with best practices for effective crisis preparedness in social media. The three case studies used as the context for this discussion include the 2011 Japanese earthquakes and tsunami, Kenneth Cole Twitter crisis during the 2011 Egyptian riots, and Hurricane Irene in 2011. These exploratory case studies highlight the insufficiently studied issues that arise in dealing with new forms of communication technology in crisis situations. The case studies were structured to focus on specific details such as background information on the issue, current status of the industry in light of the situation, overview of the problem or issue being studied, primary message strategies and responses that are being implemented by the key parties involved, and important concepts related to social media.

Crisis Communications

Crises come in various forms and can impact an organization or individual at any time. In other words, crises are significant, disruptive events that often feature a rapid onset. An event precipitating a crisis has been described as "big trouble that arises suddenly" (Lerbinger, 1997, p. 6). Pearson and Clair (1998) stated that a crisis usually results from "a low-probability, high-impact event" (p. 60), while Fearn-Banks (2001) portrayed a crisis as a "major occurrence with a potentially negative outcome" that "interrupts normal business transactions" (p. 480).

A crisis can be the perception of an event rather than the event itself, which suggests that individual reactions to a perceived crisis can be quite diverse (Penrose, 2000). Several factors that contribute to the overall perception of a crisis situation include the severity and magnitude of the event (Burnett, 1998), perceived control (Coombs & Holladay, 1996), and the likelihood that an event will actually occur (Wrigley, Salmon, & Park, 2003). There may be differences between how one person identifies a crisis compared to another depending on how much involvement and investment people have with that organization or issue, and the perceived role that the particular situation has in their daily lives.

Crisis events occur in various forms and can be categorized into different types, which helps crisis communicators select an appropriate course of action. Examples of these events include natural disasters, faux pas, terrorism, transgressions, accidents, workplace violence, rumors, malevolence, challenges, technical errors, and human errors (Coombs, 2007). Ultimately, risk bearers need to be guided through a crisis (Sandman, 2006) because it typically produces a high level of uncertainty, which communicators can reduce by providing needed information in the form of crisis communication messages (Seeger, Sellnow, & Ulmer, 1998). Ultimately, crisis communication professionals work to identify stakeholders impacted by a crisis so as to be prepared to communicate and disseminate information to key audience members (Heath, Lee, & Ni, 2009).

Crisis Communication Message Strategies

Crisis communication refers to the provision of effective, efficient messages to relevant audiences during the course of a crisis. Reynolds and Seeger (2005) stated that crisis communication "seeks to explain the specific event, identify likely consequences and outcomes, and provide specific harm-reducing information to affected communities in an honest, candid, prompt, accurate, and complete manner" (p. 46). Crisis communication can direct the course of a crisis process in a positive direction when done well or in a negative direction if done poorly.

As crisis communication message strategies have evolved so have the efforts of researchers to describe and form theories that lead to best practices. Crises can appear in various forms and are attributed with different perceptions and attributes based on the type of crisis being discussed, level of responsibility of the main party involved in the crisis, and the message strategies implemented before, during, and after a crisis.

Coombs' (2007) situational crisis communication theory (SCCT) identified 10 crisis types or frames: natural disaster, rumor, product tampering, workplace violence, challenges, technical error product recall, technical error accident, human error product recall, human error accident, and organizational misdeed. SCCT also combines corporate apologia, image restoration theory, and attribution theory (Coombs, 2002). Put simply, SCCT uses these elements to help determine the most appropriate message responses to particular types of crises. Attribution theory, first introduced to social psychology by Heider (1958), attempts to explain how people attribute, or assign, causality to internal, personality factors or external, situational factors. Incorporating attributions into SCCT enhanced its ability to predict how audience perceptions of an organization's role in a crisis will affect its outcome in terms of reputation and associations. Coombs' (2007) model also provides crisis communicators with strategies and responses that focus on changing perceptions of a crisis or the organization in crisis.

Social Media

Social media initiates innovation with communication technology platforms that enable knowledge sharing, digital storytelling, collaboration, and relationship building among a community with common interests and needs. According to Mangold and Faulds (2009), social media is defined as being "a wide range of online, word-of-mouth forums including blogs, company sponsored discussion boards and chat rooms, consumer-to-consumer e-mail, consumer product or service ratings websites and forums, Internet discussion boards and forums, microblogs" (p. 358). Social media have provided an innovative communication platform used by businesses and agencies to promote a positive reputation (Prentice & Huffman, 2008), an unfiltered view of consumer perceptions based on digital word-of-mouth communications (Marken, 2007), convergence of social and technological networks (Kleinberg, 2008), and the establishment of social media influencers (Freberg, Graham, McGaughey, & Freberg, 2011).

Digital communication platforms are used to connect groups of people using social networking sites like Facebook and Google+, microblogs like Twitter, photosharing sites like Instagram and Pinterest, and video sharing sites like YouTube and Vimeo. All these platforms enable social media users to engage in real-time conversations, enhanced with multimedia, through computer, tablet, or smartphone. Crisis communication professionals need to be prepared to engage in the dialogue, on behalf of the organization or agency they represent, and on the various platforms used by their key stakeholders (Bruns, Burgess, Crawford, & Shaw, 2012).

With social media the individual user can create and curate information in multiple contexts to be shared via one-to-one, one-to-many, or many-to-many communications. With social media, individuals not only receive information through these platforms but they can also create their own content or forward content to others. By doing so, individuals can contribute directly to the media by providing eyewitness perspectives of an event, often bypassing the professional reporters on the scene, and providing unfiltered views of what is happening around them (Gordon, 2007).

One of the innovations relevant to crisis communication provided by social media is crowdsourcing. Crowdsourcing is a strategic action taken on behalf of an organization, agency, or individual to organize and curate visual real-time data in a centralized location. Crowdsourcing is a form of outsourcing not directed to other companies but to the crowd or general public by means of an open call, which typically occurs via an Internet platform (Schenk & Guittard, 2011). Crowdsourcing not only provides opportunities to share knowledge and information, but it has accelerated the speed of innovation and creativity among a diverse global audience. Various items can be uploaded and shared with audience members including news articles, blog posts, videos, citizen reporting activities, pictures, and other types of user-generated content.

Crowdsourcing capabilities have been used in various campaigns and initiatives such as crisis communications and disaster responses (e.g., Haiti earthquake in 2010 and Ushahidi in 2010) and radiation warnings and readings (e.g., Japanese earthquakes and tsunami in 2011) in an effort related to fundraising, volunteering, and sharing knowledge to address risk and crises locally, nationally, or globally.

Social Media and Crisis Communications

Social media can benefit individual stakeholders and involved organizations during a highly tense situation, which has allowed people to feel they have more control over a crisis as well as more connection to the community (Shklovski, Burke, Kiesler, & Kraut, 2010). Increased empowerment of the individual stakeholder leads to greater feelings of control over the situation and a willingness to help others in the community, feelings which could be mobilized by crisis responders.

Social media provides stakeholders with an opportunity to discuss issues that they deem salient to them in an online community, bypassing the traditional gatekeepers (e.g., media, emergency management agencies, hospitals) during a crisis. At the same time, stakeholders expect tailored and personalized, rather than prepared, statements and messages from organizations. Organizations are expected to listen and respond to stakeholder concerns. Recognizing the influence of social media allows public relations professionals to use this technology strategically to scan and monitor for potential issues, prepare for crises, and implement online communication (González-Herrero & Smith, 2008).

The role of emerging technologies during crises continues to grow, and more community members and risk bearers rely on these communication platforms for information relevant to a crisis situation (Palen, Anderson, Mark, Martin, Sicker, Palmer & Grunwald, 2010). In addition, crisis communicators are challenged by the rapid dissemination of information shared via social media. Kleinberg (2008) noted the dangers of "a rumor, a political message, or a link to an online video – these are all examples of information that can spread from person to person, contagiously, in the style of an epidemic" (p. 69).

Researchers recognize the need to evaluate the impact of social media on crisis communications (Coombs, 2007; Palen, Hiltz, & Liu, 2007; Veil, Buehner, & Palenchar, 2011). More recent research has explored the use of social media in crisis situations in general (Shklovski, Palen, & Sutton, 2008), and in specific crisis events including the 2007 Virginia Tech Shootings (Liu, Palen, Sutton, Hughes, & Vieweg, 2008) and the 2008 Tennessee Valley Authority (TVA) ash spill (Sutton, 2010).

Specifically, Shklovski et al. (2008) reviewed how emergency center operators, police, military, and medical personnel have actively used new forms of technology in communicating remotely in a disaster or crisis situation. Sutton (2010) analyzed Twitter updates and conversations in regards to the TVA ash spill crisis and highlighted the fact that they received messages on Twitter before traditional media. Vieweg, Palen, Liu, Hughes, and Sutton (2008) identified possible risks for organizations that inadvertently provide false information to stakeholders in a time of crisis.

Effective theories exist for guiding the responses of organizations responsible for a crisis, such as SCCT, and a modification of SCCT that incorporates social media, the social-mediated crisis communication model (SMCC) (Liu, Austin, & Jin, 2011). However, the primary focus of most crisis models appears to be reputation management, as opposed to predicting audience compliance with crisis safety messages. Freberg (2012) investigated audience response to a food recall message presented by a professional source (the CDC official website) versus a user-generated source (a non-expert blog linked to a Facebook page) and found that intent to comply was higher in response to the professional source than to the user-generated source, but only for respondents in older age cohorts (those born before 1964).

Method

Case study as a methodology is well positioned to explore real-world functioning of organizations in context (such as a crisis), it stimulates reflection, and serves as a motivation for future action (May, 2006). Traditional and application-oriented disciplines such as strategic communication have used case studies to analyze specific issues that influence the operations and practices of a corporation (Yin, 1994). Case studies are structured to focus on specific details that involve the corporation and the issue being examined. Specific details for a case study should include (a) background information on the issue, (b) current status of the industry in light of the situation, (c) overview of the problem or issue being studied, (d) key message strategies and responses that are being implemented by the key parties involved, (e) discuss the key concepts involved in the phenomenon, and (f) make recommendations for future campaigns and research.

These case studies were analyzed as exploratory case studies. In exploratory case studies, analysis may be undertaken as a prelude to further social science research (Yin, 1989). Stake (1995) recommended that the selection of exploratory case studies offers the opportunity to maximize what can be learned. Exploratory case studies can help to discuss the insufficiently studied issues that arise in dealing with new forms of communication technology, such as social media and mobile technologies used in crisis situations. These case studies are also structured as explanatory since they are looking at how global audiences and domestic residents reacted to the proposed social media strategies in each case from a historical and post-hoc perspective.

Results

Case Study 1: Japanese Tsunami 2011

The earthquakes and tsunami that hit Japan in March 2011 provide useful illustrations of the nexus of crisis communication and emerging communication and information technologies. On March 11, 2011, at 2:46 PM, an 8.9 magnitude earthquake hit the coast of Japan about 231 miles north of Tokyo. This crisis became a story that was shared not only in the traditional media but also across user-generated content sites. The Pew Research Center (2011) reported that the Japanese quake and tsunami events that took place during the week of March 7–11, 2011, accounted for 20% of the top hyperlinks shared among international stories on Twitter.

Both professional and lay sources via social media were used to communicate messages in this crisis. Twitter was used to discuss various opinions about the multiple issues associated with the tsunami and earthquakes, and related food safety crises, as well as to share information about where people could donate to relief efforts (Amid Tweeted, 2011). Within Twitter, users were assigning hashtags, which are tags that allow updates to be easily searchable by others interested in the same information. Some of the hashtags that were used during this crisis included #Japan, #JPQuake, #JapanQuake, and #PrayForJapan (Twitter Hope, n.d.). Mixi, a user-generated social media popular in Japan, also played a prominent role during this crisis. A user's description of Mixi emphasized its importance as a source of information, as people "rely on this for everything, how else are you supposed to get this kind of information?" (Industry Securities, 2011, para. 14).

Other social media platforms used during the Japanese earthquakes and tsunami crisis included crowdsourcing websites, which allowed users to upload information about radiation testing in Japan (RDTN. org), video sharing websites that allowed users to communicate with victims of the tsunami and earthquakes (YouTube), and social games on Facebook (Zynga games like FarmVille and FrontierVille) that provided means to donate to specific charities relevant to the crisis. The RDTN.org site allowed users on the ground to share information and updates about radiation with others. One of the risks associated with this type of information is the possibility that individuals on the ground are not properly trained in radiation technology. The RDTN.org site did follow a good practice of tagging a reading as "unofficial information" to distinguish that post from information from an established professional source also on the ground.

Case Study 2: Kenneth Cole's Twitter Failure

Organizations and businesses have their own distinct personality characteristics, but there are times when one individual disproportionately represents the overall reputation of the brand. Compared to situations in which individuals are strongly identified with brands, less personalized organizations and corporations may have an advantage in crisis situations because they have a more general brand personality. Fashion designer Kenneth Cole is an example of an individual who also serves as a brand. In these cases, a crisis involving the individual can have a devastating effect on the entire brand.

One of the risks associated with crisis situations for brands solely tied to one strong personality is that the individual's comments and actions can open a window into their true selves. The timing and tone of their responses, actions taken before, during, and after a crisis, and their previous interactions with the media are all examples of how this can illuminate their true personality to their stakeholders.

During the Cairo uprising in Egypt in 2011, Cole initiated an organizational crisis by tweeting the following: "Millions are in uproar in #Cairo. Rumor is they heard our new spring collection is now available online at http://bit.ly/KCairo -KC" (Kenneth Cole's #Cairo, 2011, para. 3). This particular tweet was controversial due to its use of the assigned hashtag for the Cairo uprising. As mentioned previously, hashtags provide a mechanism for others to follow a particular topic on Twitter. Given the highly emotional and somber nature of the political situation in Egypt, the public was not amused by Cole's apparently frivolous message promoting his spring fashion collection (Fashion Brand, 2011). Even worse, anger about Cole's tweet led to the establishment of false Twitter accounts purportedly representing Cole, such as KennethColePR. This fake account was used to release mocking tweets from the fashion designer (Learning From, 2011).

One of Cole's signature marketing traits established over his years in the fashion industry is the use of controversial and shocking slogans, but in this particular situation, many believed he may have gone too far (Kenneth Cole, 2011). Cole did eventually initiate an apology tweet reflecting on the circumstances surrounding the controversy: "Re Egypt tweet: we weren't intending to make light of a serious situation. We understand the sensitivity of this historic moment -KC" (Kenneth Cole's #Cairo, 2011, para. 5). Cole further submitted an apology statement on his Facebook page:

> I apologize to everyone who was offended by my insensitive tweet about the situation in Egypt. I've dedicated my life to raising aware-ness about serious social issues, and in hindsight my attempt at humor regarding a nation liberating themselves against oppression was poorly timed and absolutely inappropriate. (Kenneth Cole's #Cairo, 2011, para. 1)

While the efforts made by Cole, and the staff behind the Kenneth Cole brand, were apparently well-considered and appropriate, the case provides important reminders of the need to understand the impact of real-time commentary and its consequences for a brand's reputation. While Cole apologized both on Facebook and Twitter, the actions and behaviors displayed in a single 140 character statement will not be forgotten that easily in the minds of his global followers (Kenneth Cole's Twitter, 2011).

Case Study 3: Hurricane Irene

Hurricane Irene, which hit the East Coast of the United States during the hurricane season of 2011, turned out to be one of the most destruc-tive hurricanes of the last three decades, killing at least 27 people. The last hurricane that produced this amount of impact on the East Coast was Hurricane Wilma, which hit Florida in 2005 (Associated Press, 2011). Even before Hurricane Irene landed on the East Coast, fear and levels of uncertainty escalated across states from Vermont to Florida (Fountain, 2011). The significance of this natural disaster prompted President Obama, on August 26, 2011, to give a formalized statement to residents of locations of potential impact:

> I cannot stress this highly enough: If you are in the projected path of this hurricane, take precautions now. The federal government has spent the better part of last week working...to see to it that we're

prepared. All indications point to this being a historic hurricane. (Obama Says, 2011, August 26, para. 4)

Ushahidi, a geolocation and crisis-mapping site, established an Irene Recovery Map for those impacted by the natural disaster to help organize clean-up efforts. One of the messages communicated by Ushahidi was the need for ordinary people to help other ordinary people to build a community recovery effort (Irene Recovery, n.d.). The goals of the recovery effort were to update information, based on location, through the site, and publicize information relevant to the key cities, communities, and states involved in Hurricane Irene. Figure 5.1 below shows a screen shot of the Ushahidi page during the Hurricane Irene disaster.

Crowdsourcing played an important role in the Hurricane Irene crisis. In particular, two sites (Esri and Kyoo) presented a different picture of what was being discussed, shared, and commented on from users regarding this particular natural disaster. Kyoo allowed users to see Twitter, Facebook, YouTube, and blog posts tagged with the key term "Hurricane Irene" in a centralized location. Esri, on the other hand, showcased a geolocation map (similar to Google Maps) and pinpointed specific locations on the East Coast where people were updating via Twitter, YouTube, and Flickr. However, there was some confusion over

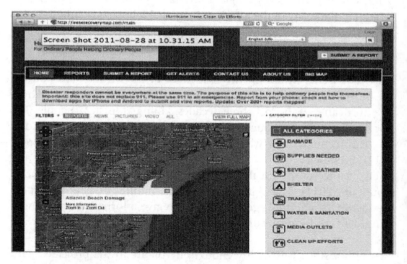

Figure 5.1   Hurricane Irene recovery map from Ushahidi

Note: Retrieved from http://blog.ushahidi.com/index.php/2011/08/28/irene-recovery-map/.

which hashtag to use regarding this natural disaster hitting the East Coast of the United States. Solis (2011) mentioned that hashtags are considered to be the tool to help organize conversations based on tagged key words and help index these conversations for businesses and professionals in social media to monitor.

Discussion

Authenticity and Trustworthiness

Several themes emerged from reviewing the messaging, strategies, and crisis communication practices among these three exploratory case studies. The issue of message effectiveness as a function of source credibility was one of the key components shared by all three case studies. During the Japanese earthquakes and tsunami crisis, government agencies and media respondents were updating the public in multiple languages through Twitter, Mixi, YouTube, and other social media platforms. Cole and his staff addressed the emotional criticism stimulated by his controversial Twitter update during the Egyptian riots in February 2011. The Hurricane Irene case study showcased the need for multiple agencies and weather professionals to establish source credibility.

Message effectiveness is influenced by source credibility (Rohr, Luddecke, Drusch, Mueller, & Alvensleben 2005), which can be defined as "the amount of credibility (believability) attributed to a source of information (either a medium or an individual) by the receivers" (Bracken, 2006, p. 724). The main parties involved in these case studies had a sense of authority and credibility when communicating via social media during their respective crises.

Audiences are more likely to perceive organizations as trustworthy when communication is two-way (Ropeik, 2006; Sandman, 2006). Individuals want information that reduces their uncertainty and gives them action steps to take that they can personally control, and the organizations and agencies that have been able to do this effectively are more likely to be viewed as trustworthy. Another lesson emerging from these case studies is the need to provide networks with reliable information from credible sources. In the cases involving the Japanese earthquakes and tsunami and Hurricane Irene, individuals came together at a centralized site to share information to provide others with real-time information in various formats. Social media is about a dynamic line of communication that allows users to engage in dialogue and respond to textual and visual commentary shared and created by others virtually. Ideal crisis communication messages include information about process and policy approaches, listening to the public's concerns and better understanding the audience, providing messages of self-efficacy, and demonstrating honesty, candor, and openness (Venette, 2006).

In these three case studies, some of these approaches were practiced while others were not. For example, the Kenneth Cole crisis showed that the brand reacted to the concerns regarding the outrage emerging from their tweet regarding the Egypt crisis, but the situation may have been too open and over sensitive due to the existing international political crisis. For Hurricane Irene, the mixed messages and different hashtags made it difficult for people to locate the information they needed. The Japanese disaster followed these best practices by incorporating messages of self-efficacy (where to go for information and how to find out about radiation and water contamination) as well as being transparent with real-time information.

Perception of Apology Strategy and Relationship Management

Crisis communication scholars have illuminated features of messages that are most effective in reaching the public during a crisis situation. For example, information presented to the audience should be clear, concise, and presented in a manner that is appropriate for the situation. One challenge faced by strategic communicators practising crisis communication is the multiplicity of voices and messages emerging online that are communicated at a rapid speed, breaking down barriers of time and location.

All three case studies showcased crisis communication message strategies, but the Kenneth Cole case study in particular featured the apology message, used to acknowledge that the organization in question is at fault, and to state its intent to move forward in its business operations. In previous crises, the "apology strategy had the strongest positive effect on perceptions of an organization's reputation" (Coombs & Holladay, 2008, p. 253). Crisis communication message strategies and apologies coexist in most crisis situations. Individuals using apology to respond in these intense periods are being proactive by working to "shape attributions of the crisis and/or perceptions of the organization itself" (Coombs, 2004, p. 267).

The apology concept can be described in various ways. According to Hearit (2005), an apology is a "broad term to respond to organizational criticism by offering a vigorous and compelling defense" (p. 4) while Weyeneth (2001) viewed an apology more as a symbolic action. The sincerity of an apology message can be doubtful, with the strategy being "sometimes compared to responses such as denial or excuse that do little, if anything to address the concerns of victims" (Coombs & Holladay, 2008, pp. 252–253). By issuing an apology to key audiences an organization can focus attention on the crisis as a public relations issue as opposed to an issue for the entire organization, which would not be in the best interests of the organization in resolving the crisis success-fully (Hearit, 2005).

The apology message strategy reflects on the organization's level of responsibility in a crisis situation and how it is perceived by the stake-holders (Coombs, 2004). Crises should first be evaluated in terms of the organization's responsibility, and the interpretation of apology messages depends on an individual's personal experience and the involvement that they have with the organization, as well as the level of responsibility they attribute to the organization in crisis. In regards to the Kenneth Cole crisis, people familiar with Cole's tendency to issue shocking messages would be more content with his apology than those who were unfamiliar with him.

Digital Negotiation for Effective Crisis Preparedness

The last theme emerging from these three case studies is the conver-gence of digital negotiation within best practice for crisis commu-nication and preparedness with social media. According to a report by Shandwick (2009), communicating during a crisis should not be separated into traditional and social media communications, but conceptualized as inline communications. Inline communication is an integrated approach of digital storytelling, communication, and negotiation within a communications plan that is not confined to one medium. All three situations involved in the case studies under review illustrate efforts to treat traditional and social media channels differ-ently – which raises the question of whether there would have been different results if the parties involved had implemented inline crisis communications. By viewing crisis communication universally across these channels, organizations could have anticipated the risk of poten-tial issues, such as the dissemination of false information in the case of Hurricane Irene.

One of the ways digital negotiation and dialogue emerged was by bringing in the digital community to help upload and share informa-tion through crowdsourcing practices. One of the fundamental prin-ciples within crowdsourcing is the role of collaboration among users within the digital community (Gao, Barbier, & Goolsby, 2011). They defined collaboration as the ability to share information and resources, and cooperation among various organizations. The use of crowdsourcing promotes the dissemination of important information and the reduction of uncertainty.

One of the features that makes crowdsourcing capabilities for crisis communications compelling is the use of photography and videos, which provides crisis communicators with a rapid eyewitness account on the ground (Liu et al., 2008). This allows users to create information that is disseminated through the rest of the community from a centralized location (Starbird & Palen, 2011). In addition, crowdsourcing provides a way for individuals responding in a crisis situation to share their story with a global audience in a centralized location in various contexts.

As the use of technology increases and mobile technologies become integrated into daily social and business practices, these emerging tools need to become a focus of discussion and research within risk and crisis communications. These tools should be incorporated into crisis communication training, education, and simulation exercises for practitioners and researchers. While these emerging technologies are important, they do not replace the theoretical and historical foundation of crisis communication practices, which includes transmitting risk messages to the public, engaging risk bearers before and throughout a crisis, and disseminating messages to the media about updates during a crisis situation. Instead, they should be incorporated into these and all other best practices.

Even though social media are becoming more mainstream in society and communications practices, it does not mean that everyone involved in the crisis communications, or the stakeholders within a specific community, know or understand these forms of technology. Lack of education and training, along with the limited amount of technology resources available, are other potential challenges and risks that may plague crisis communication professionals in this new area.

Emerging technologies such as mobile devices and applications within crisis communication need to be explored further to review best practice and the application of these communication platforms in a crisis or disaster situation. Research into social media is being done in various disciplines such as systems engineering, computer science, and computer engineering and the strategic communications academic community needs to review these findings and integrate this literature into the theoretical and applied perspectives of crisis communication practices.

References

Amid tweeted frustration, Japan may take control of TEPCO. (2011, April 1). 4VF-News Channel. Retrieved from http://www.time.com/time/world/article /0,8599,2062591,00.html

Associated Press. (2011, August 23). Hurricane Irene strengthens on path to Carolinas. *USA Today*. Retrieved from http://www.usatoday.com/weather /storms/hurricanes/story/2011–08–23/Hurricane-Irene-strengthens-on-path-to-Carolinas/50106650/1

Bracken, C. C. (2006). Perceived source credibility of local television news: The impact of television form and presence. *Journal of Broadcasting & Electronic Media, 50*, 723–741.

Bruns, A., Burgess, J., Crawford, K., & Shaw, F. (2012, January). *#qldfloods and @ QPSMedia: Crisis communication on Twitter in the 2011 South East Queensland Flood*. ARC Centre of Excellence for Creative Industries & Innovation (CCI) Media Ecologies Project. Retrieved from http://snurb.info/files/2012/qldfloods and QPSMedia.pdf

Burnett, J. J. (1998). A strategic approach to managing crises. *Public Relations Review, 24*(4), 475–488.

Coombs, W. T. (2002). Deep and surface threats: Conceptual and practical implications for "crisis" vs. "problem." *Public Relations Review, 28*(4), 339–345.

Coombs, W. T. (2004). Impact of past crises on current crisis communications. *Journal of Business Communication, 41*(3), 265–289. doi: 10.1177/0021943604265607

Coombs, W. T. (2007). *Ongoing crisis communication: Planning, managing, and responding* (2nd ed.). Thousand Oaks, CA: Sage.

Coombs, W. T., & Holladay, S. J. (1996). Communication and attributions in a crisis: An experimental study in crisis communication. *Journal of Public Relations Research, 8*(4), 279–295.

Coombs, W. T., & Holladay, S. J. (2008). Comparing apology to equivalent crisis response strategies: Clarifying apology's role and value in crisis communication. *Public Relations Review, 34*, 252–257.

Fashion brand Kenneth Cole highjacks Egypt hashtag to promote its new collection. (2011, February 3). Retrieved from http://thenextweb.com /socialmedia/2011/02/03/fashion-brand-kenneth-cole-hijacks-egypt-hashtag-to-promote-its-new-collection/

Fearn-Banks, K. (2001). Crisis communication: A review of some best practices. In R. L. Heath & G. Vasquez (Eds.), *Handbook of public relations* (pp. 479–486). Thousand Oaks, CA: Sage.

Freberg, K. (2012). Intention to comply with crisis messages communicated via social media. *Public Relations Review, 38*(3), 416–421.

Freberg, K., Graham, K., McGaughey, K., & Freberg, L. (2011). Who are the social media influencers? A study of public perceptions of personality. *Public Relations Review, 37*(1), 90–92.

Fountain, H. (2011, August 29). Storm's worst deluge swamped the mountains in the northeast. *The New York Times*. Retrieved from http://www.nytimes. com/2011/08/30/ us/30inland.html?_r=1

Gao, H., Barbier, G., & Goolsby, R. (2011). Harnessing the crowdsourcing of social media disaster relief. *The IEEE Computer Society*, 10–14.

González-Herrero, A., & Smith, S. (2008). Crisis communications management on the web: How internet-based technologies are changing the way public relations professionals handle business crises. *Journal of Contingencies & Crisis Management, 16,* 143–153.

Gordon, J. (2007). The mobile phone and the public sphere: Mobile phone usage in three critical situations. *Convergence, 13,* 307–319.

Hearit, K. (2005). *Crisis management by apology: Corporate response to allegations of wrongdoing.* New York, NY: Routledge.

Heath, R. L., Lee, J., & Ni, L. (2009). Crisis and risk approaches to emergency management planning and communication: The role of similarity and sensitivity. *Journal of Public Relations Research, 21*(2), 123–141.

Heider, F. (1958). *The psychology of interpersonal relations.* New York, NY: Wiley.

Industry Securities. (2011, March 28). *IPhone versus Soviet subterfuge make Fukushima no Chernobyl.* Retrieved from http://news.isc.vn/en/gl/others/iphone-versus-soviet-subterfuge-make-fukushima-no-chernobyl.html

Irene Recovery. (n.d.). Retrieved from http://irenerecoverymap.com/main

Kenneth Cole's #Cairo Tweet angers the Internet. (2011, February 3). Retrieved from http://mashable.com/2011/02/03/kenneth-cole-egypt/

Kenneth Cole causes outrage online by using the crisis in Egypt to sell clothes. (2011, February 4). Retrieved from http://fashion.telegraph.co.uk/news-features /TMG8302261/   Kenneth-Cole-causes-outrage-online-by-using-the-crisis-in-Egypt-to-sell-clothes.html

Kenneth Cole's Twitter Fail. (2011, February 3). Retrieved from http://www.mediabistro.com/prnewser/kenneth-coles-twitter-fail_b14367

Kleinberg, J. (2008). The convergence of social and technological networks. *Communications of the ACM, 51*(11), 66–72.

Learning from Kenneth Cole's Social Media Mistake. (2011, February 4). Retrieved from http://blog.hubspot.com/blog/tabid/6307/bid/9286/Learning-From-Kenneth-Cole-s-Social-Media-Mistake.aspx

Lerbinger, O. (1997). *The crisis manager: Facing risk and responsibility.* Mahwah, NJ: Lawrence Erlbaum.

Liu, B. F., Austin, L., & Jin, Y. (2011). How publics respond to crisis communication strategies: The interplay of information form and source. *Public Relations Review, 37,* 345–353.

Liu, S., Palen, L., Sutton, J., Hughes, A., & Vieweg, S. (2008). *In search of the bigger picture: The emergent role of on-line photo-sharing in times of disaster.* Paper presented at the annual meeting of the International ISCRAM Conference, Washington, DC.

Mangold, W. G., & Faulds, D. J. (2009). Social media: The new hybrid element of the promotion mix. *Business Horizons, 52,* 357–365.

Marken, G. A. (2007). Social media…The hunted can become the hunter. *Public Relations Quarterly, 52*(4), 9–12.

May, S. (2006). Ethical challenges and dilemmas in organizations: A case study approach. In S. May (Ed.), *Case studies in organizational communication: Ethical perspectives and practices* (pp. 1–18). Thousand Oaks, CA: Sage.

Obama says Hurricane Irene "extremely dangerous." (2011, August 26). Retrieved from http://www.reuters.com/article/2011/08/26/us-storm-irene-obama-idUST RE77P4IM20110826

Palen, L., Anderson, K. M., Mark, G., Martin, J., Sicker, D., Palmer, M., & Grunwald, D. (2010). A vision for technology-mediated support for public participation and assistance in mass emergencies and disasters. *Proceedings of ACM-BCS Visions of Computer Science.*

Palen, L., Hiltz, R., & Liu, S. (2007). Online forums supporting grassroots participation in emergency preparedness and response. *Communications of the ACM, 50*(3), 54–58.

Pearson, C. M., & Clair, J. A. (1998). Reframing crisis management. *Academy of Management Review, 23*(1), 59–76.

Penrose, J. M. (2000). The role of perception in crisis planning. *Public Relations Review, 26*(2), 155–171.

Pew Research Center. (2011, March 17). *Twitter responds to Japan's disaster.* Pew Research Center Publications. Retrieved from http://pewresearch.org /pubs/1933/twitter-response-japan-earthquake-breaking-news-eyewitness-bulletin-board-fund-raising

Prentice, S., & Huffman, E. (March 2008). Social media's new role in emergency management. *Idaho National Laboratory.* Retrieved from http://www.inl.gov /technicalpublications/ Documents/3931947.pdf

Reynolds, B., & Seeger, M. W. (2005). Crisis and emergency risk communication as an integrative model. *Journal of Health Communication, 10,* 43–55.

Rohr, A., Luddecke, K., Drusch, S., Mueller, M. J., & Alvensleben, R. (2005). Food quality and safety – consumer perception and public health concern. *Food Control, 16,* 649–655.

Ropeik, D. (2006). Best practices response. *Journal of Applied Communication Research, 34*(3), 253–256.

Sandman, P. M. (2006). Crisis communication best practices: Some quibbles and additions. *Journal of Applied Communication Research, 34*(3), 257–262.

Schenk, E., & Guittard, C. (2011). Towards a characterization of crowdsourcing practices. *Journal of Innovation Economics, 1,* 93–107.

Seeger, M. W., Sellnow, T. L., & Ulmer, R. R. (1998). Communication, organization, and crisis. In M. Roloff (Ed.), *Communication yearbook* (Vol. 21, pp. 230–275). Thousand Oaks, CA: Sage.

Shandwick, W. (2009). *Weber Shandwick inline communications report.* Retrieved from http://www.webershandwick.co.uk/filelibrary/Inline-Report.pdf

Shklovski, I., Burke, M., Kiesler, S., & Kraut, R. (2010). Technology adoption and use in the aftermath of Hurricane Katrina in New Orleans. *American Behavioral Scientist, 53,* 1228–1246.

Shklovski, I., Palen, L., & Sutton, J. (2008). *Finding community through information and communication technology in disaster events.* Paper presented at the annual meeting of the ACM Proceedings of Computer Supported Cooperative Work Conference, San Diego, CA.

Solis, B. (2011, June 16). *The hashtag economy.* Retrieved from http://www. briansolis.com/ 2011/06/ hashtag-this-the-culture-of-social-media-is/

Stake, R. (1995). *The art of case research.* Thousand Oaks, CA: Sage.

Starbird, K., & Palen, L. (2011). "Voluntweeters": Organizing by digital volunteers in times of crisis. Paper presented at the annual meeting of the *CHI 2011* Conference, Vancouver, Canada.

Sutton, J. N. (2010). *Twittering Tennessee: Distributed networks and collaboration following a technological disaster.* Paper presented at the annual meeting of the International ISCRAM Conference, Seattle, WA.

Twitter Hope 140 Blog – Japan Tsunami Hashtags. (n.d.). Retrieved from http://hope140.org/blog/

Veil, S., Buehner, T., & Palenchar, M. J. (2011). A work-in-process literature review: Incorporating social media in risk and crisis communication. *Journal of Contingencies and Crisis Management, 19*(2), 110–122.

Venette, S. J. (2006). Special section introduction: Best practices in risk and crisis communication. *Journal of Applied Communication Research, 34*(3), 229–231.

Vieweg, S., Palen, L., Liu, S., Hughes, A., & Sutton, J. (2008). Collective intelligence in disaster: An examination of the phenomenon in the aftermath of the 2007 Virginia Tech Shootings. *Proceedings of the Information Systems for Crisis Response and Management Conference* (ISCRAM 2008).

Weyeneth, R. R. (2001). The power of apology and the process of historical reconciliation. *The Public Historian, 23*(3), 9–38.

Wrigley, B. J., Salmon, C. T., & Park, H. S. (2003). Crisis management planning and the threat of bioterrorism. *Public Relations Review, 29,* 281–290.

Yin, R. (1989). *Case study research: Design and methods* (Rev. ed.). Beverly Hills, CA: Sage.

Yin, R. (1994). *Case study design research: Design and methods* (2nd ed.). Thousand Oaks, CA: Sage.

6

Exploring Social Media Empowerment of Public Relations: A Case Study of Health Communication Practitioner Roles and the Use of Social Media

Brian G. Smith

Much has been written on the influence of digital media on public relations. Scholarship purports that an investment in digital media (including online communication and social media) stands to improve public relations practitioners' power and management responsibilities (Porter, Sweetser, & Chung, 2009). And yet, the context of digital media innovation – Integrated Marketing Communication (IMC) – may limit the role of public relations in management, rendering it a marketing support function (Hallahan, 2007). Exploratory research is necessary to reconcile this dichotomy: the empowerment of public relations via use of digital communication on the one hand, and the potential subservience of public relations to marketing in an IMC structure on the other.

The health industry represents a particularly fertile research ground – health information is the most commonly researched topic on the Internet for people of all ages (Pew, 2006). This research, a case study of a nationally-recognized hospital, examines the public relations role of health communication practitioners in digital communication within the context of IMC. This report outlines the dichotomy of public relations empowerment vs. scholarly concerns about the subservience of public relations to marketing in IMC.

Literature Review

Defining public relations roles in management over non-professional technical and promotional roles has been an ongoing purpose of public relations research (Pasadeos, Renfro, & Hanily, 1999). Innovation in the digital communication landscape, as well as the increasing use of integrated marketing communication (IMC) by organizations, color the public relations role debate in a new hue, as environmental changes stand to alter role considerations. On the one hand, digital communication technology has been linked to increased influence of the public relations function in organizations, but on the other hand, IMC has increased scholarly concerns over a structure that could confine public relations to marketing support.

Public Relations Roles

Managerial roles, which are considered critical for the professionalization of the public relations industry (Dozier & Lauzen, 2000), consider public relations practitioners as experts (Diga & Kelleher, 2009) and include organizational advisory and counseling, influence and access to the dominant coalition with a proverbial seat at the executive table, and interpreting and analyzing public opinion (Dozier & Broom, 2006; Hutton, 1999). Technician roles limit public relations to communication tactics, including writing, marketing support, and publicity (Dozier & Broom, 2006; Hutton, 1999).

The management mandate of the public relations function is the cultivation and maintenance of relationships with the public upon whom organizational legitimacy, success, and failure depend (Broom, Casey, & Ritchey, 2000; Broom, 2009). In fact, scholars consider relationship management as the key differentiating role for the public relations function (Ferguson, 1984; Hutton, 1999; Ledingham, 2006) because it replaces technician-based promotion with the organization–public relationship as the unit of analysis (Sallot, Lyon, Acosta-Alzuru, & Jones, 2003).

Public relations roles and digital communication

Digital communication, defined as computer-mediated communication featuring multiple-media forms including sound, video, and motion (Arens, Weigold, & Arens, 2010), includes Internet and web-based communication. Social media, a subset of digital communication, can be defined as "a mechanism for an audience to connect, communicate, and interact with each other and their mutual friends through instant messaging or social networking sites" (Correa, Hinsley, & de Zúñiga, 2010, pp. 247–248).

Digital communication has been linked to managerial roles for public relations (Diga & Kelleher, 2009; Porter & Sallot, 2005). Blog use, for example, increases practitioner power through its direct access to engage the public in two-way communication (Porter, Sweetser Trammell, Chung, & Kim, 2007). Practitioners who use digital communication also hold greater expert power and prestige, and those in public relations management are also more likely to use blogs for engaging the public than are public relations technicians (Porter & Sallot, 2005).

Digital communication and relationship cultivation

Public relations practitioners use digital communication for relationship cultivation (Yang & Lim, 2009; Park & Reber, 2008; Cho & Huh, 2007; Seltzer & Mitrook, 2007; Vorvoreanu, 2006). Kent, Taylor, and White (2003) have identified five dialogic principles that influence relationship cultivation online, including: (a) usefulness of website information, (b) dialogic feedback loops, (c) ease of interface, (d) conservation of visitors and (e) generation of return visits.

Other variables considered for relationship cultivation via digital media include communicated commitment and conversational human voice. Through communicated commitment, practitioners engage the public openly to build organizational legitimacy (Kelleher & Miller, 2006). Through the conversational human voice, practitioners connect personally with the public (Searls & Weinberger, 2001). Research has shown that communicated commitment and conversational human voice are effective for communicating during a crisis (Sweetser & Metzgar, 2007) and correlate positively with public relations relationship outcomes (Kelleher, 2009).

IMC and Digital Communication

The development of digital technology has also influenced the communication structure within which public relations operates. In particular, digital communication has led to the integration of marketing communication (IMC) activities for communication impact (Kerr, Schultz, Patti, & Kim, 2008; Gurau, 2008). IMC, considered a marketing initiative that involves the strategic coordination of messages, media channels, and targets the public (Groom, 2008; Kliatchko, 2008), is the organizational response to a consumer-dominant society that now chooses media context and messaging (Hanlon & Hawkins, 2008). Through IMC, practitioners first consider the gamut of sources through which consumers receive and act on a message, and then they seek to build relationships based on message consistency.

IMC builds on the interactive capacity granted by communication technology (Mulhern, 2009). However, few studies have considered the interplay of digital communication with traditional efforts. Most research explores the basic notions of communication impact through message consistency (Stokes, 2009; Schultz & Patti, 2009; Mulhern, 2009; Gurau, 2008). Perhaps for this reason, Schultz (2007) identified the convergence of digital and traditional media as the next frontier in IMC research.

IMC Concerns and Solutions

IMC as a messaging and channel blitzkrieg, initiated and conducted as a process of marketing planning (Kerr et al., 2008), may fuel public relations scholar fears of marketing as the dominant communication function (Grunig, Grunig, & Dozier, 2002). In a review of public relations literature, Hallahan (2007) found that the common concern about IMC is marketing's potential encroachment on public relations as a management function. Though research has failed to corroborate these concerns (Hallahan, 2007), IMC scholarship has done little to assuage them. IMC studies often consider public relations under the context of marketing, including media relations, promotion, and publicity (Hendrix, 2004; Kerr et al., 2008; Stammerjohan, Wood, Chang, & Thorson, 2005; Kitchen, Brignell, Li, & Spickett, 2004; Lawler & Tourelle, 2002).

Concerns notwithstanding, the link between public relations and IMC may be IMC's purpose: public-first mindset toward relationship cultivation (Groom, 2008; Gurau, 2008). Hallahan (2007) has argued that integration's focus on relationships gives public relations and marketing a shared language. At the same time, however, differences persist – marketing emphasizes customer loyalty (Groom, 2008); public relations, mutual benefit (Broom et al., 2000).

Scope of the Research

The dichotomy of public relations empowerment via digital communication, and, simultaneously, the function's potential limitation by IMC needs evaluation. Considering the shared focus on relationship cultivation between IMC and public relations, and the relational capacity of digital communication, public relations' roles in relationships are central to this evaluation. This study follows other public relations research in considering relationship roles in digital communication (Yang & Lim, 2009; Sweetser & Metzgar, 2007; Seltzer & Mitrook, 2007).

Research Questions

The following research questions guided data collection:

RQ 1: How is digital communication integrated with traditional communication? Digital communication includes online and digital distribution of communication (i.e., Internet, social media, web-based and cell phone technology). Traditional communication includes print and broadcast forms not considered web-based, including print publications, and television and radio broadcasts.

RQ 2: What roles do public relations practitioners fulfill in the integration of digital and traditional communication? The general framework for this research question positions technician roles against managerial responsibilities. The principle difference in consideration during analysis was based on the opportunity for decision-making responsibilities for the organization or the communication department, with managerial roles exhibiting these responsibilities and technician roles devoid of such responsibilities.

RQ 3: How do public relations practitioners use digital communication to cultivate relationships with the public? The act of cultivating relationships, in this study, is considered as efforts that produce a mutual orientation between the organization and its public. The public includes, but was not limited to, consumers, physicians, employees, donors, board members, decision-makers, opinion leaders, and business partners.

Method

This study is a qualitative case analysis of public relations at a nationally-ranked hospital that integrates digital and traditional communication. Case studies are commonly used to examine organizational phenomena, and are useful for the evaluation of theory in the context of a single organization (Yin, 2003).

Data Collection

Data collection comprised ten in-depth interviews, in person and over the phone, with three public relations professionals (including the public relations director), three marketing professionals (including the marketing director), the social media manager (who works under public relations), the director of web and information technology, and the organization's two designated professionals who split responsibilities between public relations and marketing. Interviews lasted 45 to 75 minutes, and were loosely structured, based on an interview guide developed from the literature to allow respondent experiences to be the subject of study rather than researcher agendas (Rubin & Rubin, 2005). Topics of discussion included respondent roles, communication integration, and use of digital media in campaigns. Sample questions included: "How do you conduct integrated communication from your role?" and "How do you use digital communication with your traditional print and broadcast efforts?" Data collection emphasized depth and was considered complete when new ideas and answers appeared exhausted (Denzin & Lincoln, 2007).

Sample

Qualitative research considers sample size relevant to the objectives of complete understanding (McCracken, 1993, p. 71) and this study's sample was purposive and theory-driven (Miles & Huberman, 1994). Preliminary phone conversations with the public relations director confirmed that the participating organization strategically coordinates messages and media channels for consistency, which is consistent with the definition of IMC (Kliatchko, 2008). Respondents were selected based on their role and ability to discuss as many categorical concepts as possible (Glaser & Strauss, 1967), as well as their availability. In the end, most of the public relations and marketing practitioners were interviewed, and others (the web manager, sports marketing manager, and social media manager) were added based on interviews that revealed their involvement in the integration of digital and traditional communication. Respondent sampling involved a snowball method of requesting referrals, beginning with the public relations and marketing directors and moving through communication staff. Sampling was considered complete when a saturation of responses was reached, consistent with the standards of theoretical sampling (Glaser & Strauss, 1967).

Data analysis

Structured analysis (Miles & Huberman, 1994) with a grounded theory style (Glaser & Strauss, 1967) was used to identify all possible themes. General coding themes were developed from the literature, and included aspects of integration (messages, media channels, and the public), practitioner roles (technician vs. manager) and relationship cultivation principles. Themes were left open and broad to identify depth.

Following data collection, transcripts were analyzed based on the constant comparative method, as transcripts were reviewed one at a time, each subsequent transcript was analyzed for added depth from the previous review (Glaser & Strauss, 1967). Each interview was then summarized, noting individual contributions to themes and depth of understanding. Interpretation efforts were designed to tell the story of integration, and involved keeping a running narrative through a reflexive process of memo writing (Miles & Huberman, 1994, p. 86).

The validity of this study follows Kvale's (1995) three concepts of validity. Craftsmanship validity was employed through the development of a flexible interview guide, based on concepts in the literature. Communicative validity was achieved by establishing this study's claims through discourse in open-ended interviews. This study also demonstrates pragmatic validity, as its results are beneficial in helping professionals navigate the integrated communication environment. Validity in this study is also based on the confirmation of interpretations through a theoretical fit of the findings (Glaser & Strauss, 1967).

Case Organization: Park Hospital

Park Hospital – whose name has been changed for confidentiality – is a nationally-ranked hospital in the southeastern United States. The hospital integrates public relations and marketing together into one communication department. Each function houses a small team of four to six practitioners, led by a director, and each practitioner is assigned to one or two hospital service lines, reflecting a newsroom beat system. Formal processes of integration are carried out on this service line level, where public relations and marketing practitioners strategize with service line doctors and administrators for consistent communication through coordination meetings. Additional integration efforts occur at the department level, as the directors of each department work to ensure that each service line is in harmony with the organization's broad communication objectives.

Marketing and public relations roles are divided based on skill and audience. Marketers fulfill roles in business relationship management and coordinate events and advertising endeavors. Their primary audiences are consumers, businesses, and media advertisers. Public relations professionals work primarily in media relations, but also spearhead crisis communication efforts. Their primary audiences are media professionals, doctors, and donors. Overlaps exist between public relations and marketing, and in response to recent economic constraints, the public relations and marketing directors created a new cross-functional position with a dual role in marketing and public relations. Currently, two practitioners fulfill this role.

RQ 1: How is digital communication integrated with traditional communication?

The hospital began integrating online and traditional communication activity in response to a recent economic downturn requiring efficiency. Integration has led to changes in messaging, traditional print media, and communicator activities online.

Ad hoc integration

Many communication efforts are spontaneous, as communicators explore the creative avenues of emerging online media tools. The social media manager explained how communication efforts changed based on a sudden spike in the hospital's Facebook page visits. When research showed that the spike was due to recently posted job openings, a new Facebook campaign on job openings was initiated. As this demonstrates, integrating online and traditional communication is conducted on a trial, case-by-case basis. One public relations practitioner explained it this way:

> I think in the past, we were more, "This is marketing. This is PR", but as media changes and the hospital changes, it's becoming, "Here's this event or we need to increase referrals here," then we just figure out how to do it and get it done.

Message finessing

Online communication tools are often used as an extension to extant print and broadcast efforts – in some instances messages are copied over from one medium to an online counterpart. Some communicators consider online tools for efficiency and resonance with the public. A marketing communicator explained, "In a brochure, people get verbose and it's hard to rein in the doctors to get them to be concise, but really, [Twitter] is a call to action to 'click here' and learn more."

Online communication tools are used for their enhanced message creation. Communicators transform press releases into online videos featuring the hospital's doctors talking about topics which are then sent to media professionals. The social media manager explained: "The words aren't the main thing anymore, it's the pictures, it's the video.

I can foresee a time when I can't put together a story without thinking how it's going to look on video." Communicators report few standards for message integration. One communicator said, "There's no formal way we say we use [online and offline] messages, we just know what our themes are."

Online communication may be replacing traditional efforts, particularly print. The social media manager reported, "We dismantled all of our internal print communications, now we're exclusively communicating with our employees through email, blogs, and e-newsletters." He went on to explain that in other communication efforts, "the print stuff has almost become a secondary." The public relations director said, "I can't think of one thing public relations does that isn't [online]."

Targeting the public

Communicators integrate digital and traditional communication to target specific sectors of the public. The marketing director described the hospital's formula for communication as "who we're trying to reach, what's our budget, what are our key messages, and what vehicles position us the best." Another communicator confirmed, "We try to reach all audiences with all different vehicles" and respondents value the way Twitter and Facebook "drive people to your desired sites and also get your desired audience," as the sports marketing manager remarked. Some of these desired audiences include reporters, donors, and even employees. One public relations practitioner said, "Even if there's something going on in our lobby, employees may not pick that up on their email, but they'll pick it up on Facebook."

Online tools are also used to craft action-oriented messages (i.e., calls to action), while traditional media, like print and broadcast, are reportedly informational. In this way, the two communication forms work in tandem, one informing, the other toward action. "I don't think we've ever gotten a call just because they saw our billboard," the marketing director explained. "But it's a nice reminder and it serves as an umbrella…so that when we do have an Internet sidebar ad, they already know us." Virtual facility tours, Twitter chats with doctors, and online registration further highlight the way the hospital seeks to build interactivity via online tools. The web director explained, "The goal is to create that long term relationship with the patient."

Distributing responsibility

One purpose in integrating communication is to foster responsibility and self-initiative for internal groups to create their own content.

The web director spoke of "distributed authorship roles" for communicators within each of the service lines in the hospital and the director of public relations said, "Integration is on the people level... We rely on the other pieces and they rely on us." The web director summarized this distributed responsibility:

> For the web you have very technical people, you have creative people, you have server people. You could have very creative marketing people but they don't have anything to do with creating a web page, they know what the message needs to be. So we (the Web department) know how to get the web page done correctly. Then you have the service line people who know what their goal is.

> RQ 2: What roles do public relations practitioners fulfill in the integration of digital and traditional communication?

In the ongoing integration of digital and traditional communication, public relations fills a social role to marketing's website management. Public relations practitioners cultivate connections, create content, and innovate strategy.

Public relations as social connection

The public relations department is the recognized leader of social media initiatives. The public relations director designated one of her tenured staff members as a full-time social media manager and the two work in tandem to strategize social media efforts. Other public relations practitioners follow suit, serving as the lead voices on social media within their service lines. Social media management may grant public relations strategic orientation. A practitioner who splits time between marketing and public relations said that strategy is usually handled by marketing, "except, if you bring in the social media. Then it's done by PR for sure."

Managing social media is considered a natural role for public relations because of the function's emphasis on relationships. The social media manager explained that social media affords him an opportunity to build relationships the way he prefers because "you're not just trying to cram your PR messages down their throat... you get them information in a form that is going to be valuable for them, [which is] the best way to develop a relationship with them." Communicators recognize the division between public relations and marketing in relationships. One public relations practitioner complained that marketers work impersonally to send out mass communication material, which he calls "a waste."

Public relations as content creator

Practitioner roles in digital communication are also based on their recognized acumen in writing. Whereas marketers focus on the design of the hospital's websites, public relations professionals are called upon to produce content for their online presence, including the hospital's website and its social media presence. The public relations director said, "My staff gets pulled into marketing projects because [marketers] can't write."

Marketers are dedicated to one project at a time, and are relied upon to "see a project through," said one dual marketing-public relations practitioner; public relations practitioners, on the other hand, address the full range of hospital activities, and focus on the art of the story. Public relations writing roles translate online into "getting the right story out" (as one practitioner said) and practitioners are counted on to know the best way to tell the story to the hospital's public in a variety of online and traditional communication media. A by-product of this emphasis on writing and storytelling is that public relations fulfills earned media roles in online (as well as traditional) communication venues, including pitching bloggers and promoting Twitter chats.

Part of the reason that social media has been assimilated into the public relations function is because so much of it is free. The marketing director explained that social media is a vehicle for the public relations office because, "they're the ones responsible for our free messaging, and anything we control out there, whether it's a tweet or a Facebook page."

Public relations as innovator

Public relations practitioners are active in exploring new venues for communicating, and have taken the lead in social media efforts, assessing opportunities and seeking system-wide acceptance of social media tools. This innovation began with the public relations director's decision to dedicate one staff member to full-time social media management. This individual manages the social media sphere for the hospital, pushing the hospital into new territory for the health industry. While other hospitals have been shutting down access to social media because of privacy concerns, the social media manager has convinced administrators to relax the boundaries. Efforts include Twitter chats and Facebook as a vehicle for communicating with employees during a crisis.

Practitioners also assume watchdog, advisory and educational roles to ensure proper use of digital communication. The social media manager said he often has to remove comments from employees and patients that may have been in violation of HIPPA privacy rules. "I know what's appropriate to put on. An employee may not. That's why the important thing is education about patient privacy and the potential and immediate impact of this."

RQ 3: How do public relations practitioners use digital communication to cultivate relationships with the public?

Practitioners unanimously consider their responsibilities in terms of cultivating relationships with the gamut of Park Hospital's stackholders, including patients, employees, doctors, donors, the media and others. In cultivating relationships online, practitioners emphasize dialogue and becoming part of the lives of the public through information and engagement, while working within the privacy constraints of HIPPA regulations.

Online relationships through dialogue

"Most of our audiences are passive – the real challenge of social media is to get that conversation going," the social media manager explained. "I spend a lot of time looking at Twitter, looking at who's looking at us, and if there's an opportunity to jump in and have a conversation, we do it." Common platforms for dialogue include responding to Facebook and Twitter posts, and friending the online public to "send them the message that we're part of the conversation," the social media manager continued. Through dialogue, practitioners hope to create an emotional connection. The social media manager explained:

> There's this veil when you're writing for a magazine, you want to reach out through that veil and touch people. That's what social media gives you. You don't have that disconnection with social media. It's immediate. Even Facebook, within 35 seconds of posting something, somebody gives you a thumbs up. So you know immediately you're reaching somebody, even if it's one person.

Practitioners use social media to increase interaction and public response. The public relations director said, "We've been so focused on getting people to follow us, but the key is, what are they saying about us? That's really what we're focusing on now." To that end, practitioners use online tools to conduct chats with doctors and other knowledge experts in the medical field. One practitioner, for example, said she hosted an online chat by partnering with a popular tech blogger to reach his readers exclusively.

Online relationships through life connection

Practitioners use online tools to connect the public with the hospital and its physicians around topics that relate to their lives. The social media manager said. "You want to be in their minds, but you also want to be part of their lives as well."

To this end, practitioners use digital communication to talk about the variety of personal issues that the hospital can address, including nutrition, athletics, and lifestyle, giving messaging an educational focus. Some areas of education include healthcare reform and ways to manage the flu season. The marketing director explained the need to provide educational value to the public:

> To click on [a site], you've got to have a reason to do it. I mean, click here to learn more about us? Who's going to do that? It's got to be "Click here to attend a free seminar on a healthier heart." Offer them something.

Some consider the hospital's online patient-portal, through which patients can schedule an appointment or make a reservation, as a mini-relationship engine because it provides patient value. By giving patients direct access to their own health information held at the hospital, a relationship is created via return visits and the utility of the information itself (according to the web director).

Discussion

A single case study is insufficient to prove whether public relations gains or loses managerial orientation in IMC. Rather, case studies serve to develop or expand theory. In that context, this study shows social media involvement may be a variable for public relations management in IMC. The validity of this variable may be found in IMC's theoretical foundation on relationships. Integrated marketing communication represents a recognized redirection of focus from internal marketing objectives to external public needs (Schultz & Patti, 2009). It may be natural then, that in a structure that is oriented toward strategic relationships, communication functions similarly oriented toward realizing such relationships would maintain managerial roles. In this sense, public relations roles may be tied to relationship management in IMC.

A general theory for public relations roles in IMC may be as follows: *Public relations gains managerial responsibilities in IMC as it fulfills roles in relationship management.*

From this theoretical proposition, digital communication and its capacity to connect public relations practitioners with a variety of stakeholders, facilitates public relations' roles in relationship management, and thus grants greater managerial responsibilities. At Park Hospital, public relations is recognized as the function with more relationship acumen, and both marketing and public relations practitioners consider it the responsibility of public relations to cultivate the internal and external relationships that will benefit the hospital. Because practitioners are innovating social media use, they are both fulfilling relationship responsibilities for the organization and building strategic management roles.

Relationship acumen, or the ability to cultivate relationships for the hospital, may be tied to the fulfillment of priorities in the dialogic communication model proposed by Kent et al. (2003). Dialogic feedback, through practitioners' use of Facebook and Twitter, and practitioner emphasis on useful information, via efforts to educate the public online about health issues, are two variables that may be tied to practitioner managerial roles. Other efforts proposed in the dialogic communication model (i.e., visitor recruitment, retention, and ease of use) were not as widely considered by practitioners, perhaps because they are more promotional in nature, and may not feature the relational capacity of dialogic feedback and useful information.

This study also introduces the notions of control and limitation as key considerations in online relationship cultivation. That is, the dichotomy between practitioner desire for control over the information communicated and public desire to maintain control over the social media platform through which the interactions take place. Though this study only considered practitioner viewpoints, future research should consider this dichotomy by examining public perspectives. This is particularly relevant considering that relational interactions between an organization and its public may not occur on an organization-sponsored and controlled platform, like the organization's own website. That public relations practitioners may not control the platform through which the online relationship occurs, may place more importance on a conversational human voice and communicated commitment (Kelleher & Miller, 2006), rather than on the technical aspects listed by Kent et al. (2003), like visitor retention and ease of use.

On Digital and Traditional Communication Integration

Though much of the research in IMC has established it as a branding and messaging initiative (Kliatchko, 2008), this study demonstrates how the integration of digital communication with traditional print and broadcast efforts may assist practitioners to fulfill the purpose of integration: to cultivate relationships through an audience-first orientation (Hallahan, 2007). As organizations expand the coordination of digital and traditional communication, the realization grows that this initiative must be more than coordinated messaging – it is a feedback-based communication approach that builds from the perspectives of the public and seeks consistency from the vantage point of the public need rather than the public dollar.

Messaging and one-look, one-voice considerations of IMC, which have defined the discipline (Kliatchko, 2008), are only tactical considerations in the early stages of IMC. Early on, Duncan and Caywood (1996) proposed that higher levels of IMC involve the evaluation of points of interaction between an organization and its public, toward strategic orientation to stakeholder needs, with relationships as the outcome.

Practical Implications

If IMC is a response to changing user interests and a need to connect directly with the public (and meet their needs), then the integration of digital and traditional communication activities should be based on user needs, not consistency. Far too many IMC efforts are considered from the one-look, one-voice perspective that promotes carbon-copying messages across media. This represents basic considerations of IMC at best. Integrating communication requires consideration of the needs of the public based on the medium or point of contact, not message and image consistency, putting emphasis on a public-defined value of information rather than on messaging. In this way, communication integration is, and should be, considered a relational process, not a branding or message-matching initiative.

The Social Media Link between Public Relations and IMC

Defining the relationship between marketing and public relations is public relations' greatest challenge (Hutton, 2010). In detailing the practice of public relations within an integrated structure, this study provides the context for developing that relationship: social media. Digital communication tools grant greater capacity for interaction, and it is possible, a greater capacity for public relations to fulfill managerial roles in relationship cultivation.

References

Arens, W. F., Weigold, M. F., & Arens, C. (2010). *Contemporary advertising & integrated marketing communications* (13th ed.). New York, NY: McGraw-Hill.

Broom, G. M. (2009). *Cutlip & Center's effective public relations*. Upper Saddle River, NJ: Pearson.

Broom, G. M., Casey, S., & Ritchey, J. (2000). Concept and theory of organization-public relationships. In J. A. Ledingham & S. D. Bruning (Eds.), *Public relations as relationship management: A relational approach to the study and practice of public relations* (pp. 3–22). Mahwah, NJ: Lawrence Erlbaum.

Cho, S., & Huh, J. (2007). *Corporate blogs as a public relations tool: A content analysis applying the relational maintenance framework.* Paper presented at the annual meeting of the International Communication Association, San Francisco, CA.

Correa, T., Hinsley, A. W., & de Zúñiga, H. G. (2010). Who interacts on the web?: The intersection of users' personality and social media use. *Computers in Human Behavior, 26,* 247–253.

Denzin, N. K., & Lincoln, Y. S. (2007). Introduction: The discipline and practice of qualitative research. In N. K. Denzin & Y. S. Lincoln (Eds.), *Collecting and Interpreting Qualitative Materials* (2nd ed.) (pp. 1–44). Thousand Oaks, CA: Sage.

Diga, M., & Kelleher, T. (2009). Social media use, perceptions of decision-making power, and public relations roles. *Public Relations Review, 35,* 440–442.

Dozier, D. M., & Broom, G. M. (2006). The centrality of practitioner roles to public relations theory. In C. H. Botan & V. Hazleton (Eds.), *Public relations theory II* (pp. 137–170). Mahwah, NJ: Lawrence Erlbaum Associates.

Dozier, D. M., & Lauzen, M. M. (2000). Liberating the intellectual domain from the practice: Public relations, activism, and the role of the scholar. *Journal of Public Relations Research, 12,* 3–22.

Duncan, T., & Caywood, C. (1996). The concept, process, and evolution of integrated communication. In E. Thorson & J. Moore (Eds.), *Integrated communication: Synergy of persuasive voices* (pp. 13–34). Mahwah, NJ: Lawrence Erlbaum Associates.

Ferguson, M. A. (1984, August). *Building theory in public relations: Interorganizational relationships as a public relations paradigm.* Paper presented at the annual meeting of the Association for Education in Journalism and Mass Communication, Gainesville, FL.

Glaser, B. G., & Strauss, A. L. (1967). *The discovery of grounded theory: Strategies of qualitative research.* New York, NY: Aldine de Gruyter.

Groom, S. A. (2008). Integrated marketing communication: Anticipating the "age of engage." *Communication Research Trends, 27*(4), 3–19.

Grunig, L. A., Grunig, J. E., & Dozier, D. M. (2002). *Excellent public relations and effective organizations: A study of communication management in three countries.* Mahwah, NJ: Lawrence Erlbaum Associates, Inc.

Gurau, C. (2008). Integrated online marketing communication: Implementation and management. *Journal of Communication Management, 12*(2), 169–184.

Hallahan, K. (2007). Integrated communication: Implications for public relations beyond excellence. In E. L. Toth (Ed.), *The future of excellence in public relations and communication management* (pp. 299–336). Mahwah, NJ: Lawrence Erlbaum Associates.

Hanlon, P., & Hawkins, J. (2008). Expand your brand community online. *Advertising Age, 79*(1), 14–15.

Hendrix, J. A. (2004). *Public relations cases.* Belmont, CA: Thomson/Wadsworth.

Hutton, J. G. (1999). The definition, dimensions, and domain of public relations. *Public Relations Review, 25,* 199–214.

Hutton, J. G. (2010). Defining the relationship between public relations and marketing: Public relations' most important challenge. In R. L. Heath (Ed.), *The Sage handbook of public relations* (pp. 509–522). Thousand Oaks, CA: Sage.

Kelleher, T. (2009). Conversational voice, communicated commitment, and public relations outcomes in interactive online communication. *Journal of Communication, 59,* 172–188.

Kelleher, T., & Miller, B. M. (2006). Organizational blogs and the human voice: Relational strategies and relational outcomes. *Journal of Computer-Mediated Communication, 11*(2), article 1.

Kent, M. L., Taylor, M., & White, W. J. (2003). The relationship between web site design and organizational responsiveness to stakeholders. *Public Relations Review, 29,* 63–77.

Kerr, G., Schultz, D., Patti, C., & Kim, I. (2008). An inside-out approach to integrated marketing communication: An international analysis. *International Journal of Advertising, 27*(4), 511–548.

Kitchen, P. J., Brignell, J., Li, T., & Spickett, G. (2004). The emergence of IMC: A theoretical perspective. *Journal of Advertising Research, 44*(3), 19–30.

Kliatchko, J. (2008). Revisiting the IMC construct: A revised definition and four pillars. *International Journal of Advertising, 27*(1), 133–160.

Kvale, S. (1995). The social construction of validity. *Qualitative Inquiry, 1,* 19–40.

Lawler, A., & Tourelle, G. (2002). Public relations: The integrated communication tool in the launch of a new software operating system – A case study. *Journal of Communication Management, 7(2),* 156–159.

Ledingham, J. A. (2006). Relationship management: A general theory of public relations. In C. H. Botan & V. Hazleton (Eds.), *Public relations theory II* (pp. 465–484). Mahwah, NJ: Lawrence Erlbaum Associates.

McCracken, G. (1993). *The long interview.* Newbury Park, CA: Sage.

Miles, M. B., & Huberman, A. M. (1994). *Qualitative data analysis* (2nd ed.). Thousand Oaks, CA: Sage.

Mulhern, F. (2009). Integrated marketing communications: From media channels to digital connectivity. *Journal of Marketing Communications, 15*(2) 85–101.

Park, H., & Reber, B. H. (2008). Relationship building and the use of web sites: How Fortune 500 corporations use their web sites to build relationships. *Public Relations Review, 34,* 409–411.

Pasadeos, Y., Renfro, R. B., & Hanily, M. L. (1999). Influential authors and works of the public relations scholarly literature: A network of recent research. *Journal of Public Relations Research, 11,* 29–52.

Pew Research Center. (2006). *Online health search 2006.* Retrieved from http://www.pewinternet.org/~/media//Files/Reports/2006/PIP_Online_Health_2006.pdf

Porter, L. V., & Sallot, L. M. (2005). Web power: A survey of practitioners' worldwide web use and their perception of its effects on their decision-making power. *Public Relations Review, 31,* 111–119.

Porter, L., Sweetser, K. D., & Chung, D. (2009). The blogosphere and public relations: Exploring practitioner's roles and blog use. *Journal of Communication, 13*(3), 250–267.

Porter, L. V., Sweetser Trammell, K. D., Chung, D., & Kim, E. (2007). Blog power: Examining the effects of practitioner blog use on power in public relations. *Public Relations Review, 33*, 92–95.

Rubin, H. J., & Rubin, I. S. (2005). *Qualitative interviewing: The art of hearing data* (2nd ed.). Thousand Oaks, CA: Sage.

Sallot, L. M., Lyon, L. J., Acosta-Alzuru, C., & Jones, K. O. (2003). From aardvark to zebra: A new millennium analysis of theory development in public relations academic journals. *Journal of Public Relations Research, 15*, 27–90.

Schultz, D. (2007). Northwestern University's Don Schultz, the "father of integrated marketing communications." Retrieved from http://www.medill-imc.podomatic.com

Schultz, D. E., & Patti, C. H. (2009). The evolution of IMC: IMC in a customer-driven marketplace. *Journal of Marketing Communications, 15*(2/3), 75–84.

Searls, D., & Weinberger, D. (2001). Markets as conversations. In R. Levine, C. Locke, D. Searls, & D. Weinberger (Eds.), *The cluetrain manifesto: The end of business as usual* (pp. 75–114). New York, NY: Perseus.

Seltzer, T., & Mitrook, M. A. (2007). The dialogic potential of weblogs in relationship building. *Public Relations Review, 33*, 227–229.

Stammerjohan, C., Wood, C. W., Chang, Y., & Thorson, E. (2005). An empirical investigation of the interaction between publicity and advertising, and previous brand attitudes and knowledge. *Journal of Advertising, 34*(4), 55–67.

Stokes, A. Q. (2009). Living the sweet (d)Life! Public relations, IMC, and diabetes. *Journal of Communication Management, 13*(4), 343–361.

Sweetser, K. D., & Metzgar, E. (2007). Communicating during crisis: Use of *blogs* as a relationship management tool. *Public Relations Review, 33*, 340–342.

Vorvoreanu, M. (2006). Online organization–public relationships: An experience-centered approach. *Public Relations Review, 32*, 395–401.

Yang, S-U., & Lim, S. (2009). The effects of blog-mediated public relations (BMPR) on relational trust. *Journal of Public Relations Research, 21*, 341–359.

Yin, R. K. (2003). *Case study research: Design and methods* (3rd edn). Thousand Oaks, CA: Sage.

7

140 Characters for Better Health: An Exploration of the Twitter Engagement of Leading Nonprofit Organizations

Marcus Messner, Yan Jin, Vivian Medina-Messner, Shana Meganck, Scott C. Quarforth and Sally K. Norton

The nonprofit sector is one of the fastest growing in the U.S. economy. Making up roughly 10% of the overall economy, it employs 13 million people and generates annual revenues of $300 billion (Kanter & Fine, 2010). Nonprofit organizations play an important role in nearly every aspect of American society, especially in the health sector which, until recently, there was a lack of universal access to healthcare (Forbes, 2011). Due to their great impact on public life, it is essential for nonprofits to communicate effectively with their public and develop new media strategies for their public relations practice. The emergence of social media platforms such as Twitter allows nonprofits to directly engage with their audiences and build communities around their causes (Kanter & Fine, 2010).

Today, online users across the generations are actively looking online for health information. According to Zickuhr (2010), "searching for health information, an activity that was once the primary domain of older adults, is now the third most popular online activity for all internet users 18 and older" (p. 3). Lenhart, Purcell, Smith, and Zickuhr (2010) also noted that 60% of all adults search for health topics online, with a larger percentage growth among teens. Among the teens 31% get health, dieting, or physical fitness information online and 17% look for information on health topics such as drug use and sexual health. Fox (2010) reported that there are also over 250,000 apps related to health for the iPhone and over 30,000 for the Android platform, connecting social and mobile media for health communication.

Not only has the multi-generational use of social media increased over the last few years, but the way that health information is retrieved and shared through these new platforms has also changed. Fox (2011) found that 11% of the 62% of adults who use social media have followed a friend's health experience, while 15% have gotten health information from others through social media. Additional trends demonstrate that adults use social media to raise money or awareness for a particular health issue, post comments about a particular health question, and/or join health-related groups (Fox, 2011). While these numbers translate into a small percentage of the adult population as a whole, the data demonstrate a shift in the regularity with which adults access health information online from anywhere. Therefore, it is important to examine how nonprofit organizations use social media as public relations tools to reach online audiences by targeting their specific health concerns.

Of particular interest to the social media activities of nonprofit organizations is the microblogging platform Twitter, which is one of the largest social media networks in the world (Alexa.com, 2012). The purpose of this study was to explore Twitter engagement and thereby an increasingly important part of the public relations strategies of leading U.S. nonprofit organizations in the health sector and to analyze their practices. The overall engagement of nonprofit organizations with social media has an impact on their ability not only to reach their clients, supporters, and sponsors, but also to build online communities and networks and increase online fundraising.

Literature Review

Over the six years of its existence, the popularity of Twitter has grown quickly. What started as a project by a San Francisco based podcasting company in 2006 and was named "best blogging tool" by the influential South by Southwest festival (Hamilton, 2007), is today one of the leading social media platforms worldwide. Alexa.com (2012) lists Twitter as the eighth most popular website in the U.S. and as ninth in the world. Almost 10% of global Internet users use Twitter every day.

Public Relations, Traditional News Media, and Twitter Use

Twitter has not only gained great popularity among users and recognition throughout the world, but has also become a valuable tool for companies, organizations and the traditional news media to monitor conversations, build an online following and communicate with stakeholders and influencers. It constructs personal identities through self-presentation and dialogue, which has received extensive attention for the way it empowers the public relations function by humanizing an organization, a cause, an event or a public figure (Smith, 2010).

Twitter gained worldwide attention especially because of its role in major news events, such as the Mumbai terror attacks in 2008, the Green Revolution in Iran in 2009, the earthquake in Haiti in 2010, and the Middle East uprisings in 2011. Additionally, Twitter has become an international phenomenon as it demonstrates its potential for political and promotional impact. Its use as a campaigning tool in the 2008 U.S. presidential election underlined its potential for public relations and fundraising (Garrison-Sprenger, 2008; Shirky, 2011; Smith 2010). Researchers have documented an increase in the use of social media tools, such as Twitter, by individuals seeking political office because it allows them to reach out directly to potential voters to develop seemingly personal relationships with them (Zhang, Johnson, Seltzer & Bichard, 2010). However, and perhaps most importantly, these sites allow candidates to concentrate on how they want to be presented to the voting public, which has a significant influence on how people perceive the candidates because of increasing reliance on social media rather than on traditional news outlets (Waters & Williams, 2011; Jackson & Lilleker, 2009). A study conducted by Sungwook (2012) on the strategic use of Twitter to manage personal public relations looked at corporate leaders specifically. The study concluded that they should consider adopting and actively utilizing Twitter in order to develop effective personal public relations and to promote a positive organizational image by achieving an open two-way communication with consumers.

Rybalko and Seltzer (2010) extended the investigation of online relationship building by examining the Twitter profiles of Fortune 500 companies to understand how these companies use the popular social networking site to facilitate dialogic communication with their stakeholders. The study demonstrated that Fortune 500 companies' Twitter feeds tend to target different sections of the public compared to those targeted by websites, which implies that companies use different online tools to reach different people with different needs.

Much of the early use of Twitter was by news organizations, because "its speed and brevity make it ideal for pushing out scoops and breaking news to Twitter-savvy readers" (Farhi, 2009, p. 28). But media companies struggled to use Twitter beyond news promotion purposes and failed to use it to its full potential (Lowery, 2009). A study by Messner, Linke and Eford (2012) found that Twitter was primarily used by news organizations to promote *shovelware* from their websites by including links to their own websites in almost every tweet. The researchers found that very little content posted on Twitter was original and the engagement level with the news organizations' followers was very low. Smith, Miles and Lellis (2010) presented similar findings and also observed that news organizations' tweets included very few Twitter-specific functions that would indicate direct conversations with other users.

As a public relations tool, Twitter is being underutilized by organizations in facilitating dialogic communication with stakeholders and influencers, which is unfortunate since Twitter seems to be designed for the sole purpose of stimulating dialogue between users (Rybalko & Seltzer, 2010). Regardless, Twitter is increasingly becoming a mainstay in organizational communication and strategic communication campaigns. Although the dominant use of the service revolved around an agency's need to release information in a one-way manner, it was also used significantly to foster relationship growth with other Twitter users (Waters & Williams, 2011).

Whether using the site to augment word-of-mouth marketing campaigns or engage in conversations with stakeholders, Rybalko and Seltzer (2010) stated that Twitter has become the leading online social media outlet for marketing and public relations efforts. They stressed that Twitter should not be treated as just another means through which to disseminate the same advertisements and publicity pieces that stakeholders are already receiving through other traditional media channels.

Nonprofit Organizations and Social Media

The impact of a nonprofit organization can be limited by two primary factors: money and access to its stakeholders and constituents. With the explosion of the Internet in the 1990s and the development of social media applications over the past 10 years, both of these factors have been minimized, presenting nonprofit organizations with the opportunity to flourish. Greenberg and MacAulay (2009) stated that platforms such as Facebook, Twitter, MySpace, YouTube, and Flickr have created new opportunities for organizations to engage the public. These social media present a platform for nonprofits to engage new constituents, more quickly mobilize stakeholders, and develop a dialogue. However, like other researchers, Greenberg and MacAulay (2009) found this not to be the case. Their study focused on the use of Web 2.0 social media programs by Canadian environmental nonprofit organizations (ENPO) and found that, "they are using their online presence to disseminate messages broadly to a mass audience but are doing little in the way of using the web presence to foster a two-way flow of communication" (p. 74). The data suggest these nonprofits are failing to tap into online communities to promote collaborative work.

In a similar study, Waters, Burnett, Lamm, and Lucas (2009) looked at the use of Facebook by nonprofit organizations. Facebook provides a venue to create an interactive relationship between organizations and their constituents, whereas websites predominantly remain static vehicles of information pertaining to the structure and purpose of the organization. The authors sought to examine the use and impact of nonprofit organizational Facebook profiles through a content analysis of 275 randomly selected nonprofits. Findings indicated that, while nearly all organizations openly disclosed administration and structural information, very few actively engaged in the distribution of organizational news. The agencies relied heavily on contact e-mail addresses to encourage the community to contact them about information, while limiting disseminated information to external links to news, photographs, and discussion board posts.

Curtis, Edwards, Fraser, Gudelsky, Holmquist, Thornton, & Sweetser (2010) conducted a study to examine public relations practitioners in nonprofits and found differences between men and women. Based on the united theory of acceptance and use of technology, the researchers used online surveys to explore familiarity, level of participation, and usage behaviors. Overall, results indicated that nearly all participants used some form of social media, with a majority using e-mail, social networks, and video sharing. However, differences between usage by men and women were found. Women scored significantly higher for the factor performance expectancy and attitudes. Whereas, men scored significantly higher for the factors social influence and facilitating conditions (Curtis et al., 2010). The authors concluded that those nonprofit organizations that have a dedicated public relations department are more likely to adopt and use various social media platforms. In addition, initial results indicated that men and women differ in how they perceive the role of social media and incorporate it into their communication strategies.

Communications professionals in general viewed Twitter as an important tool in their early strategies (McCorkindale, 2009). Wright and Hinson (2010, 2012) also found that the importance attributed to Twitter by public relations practitioners has increased year-on-year. Consequently, Kanter and Fine (2010) concluded that compelling social media engagement is necessary for nonprofit organizations. Successful social media campaigns must engage people in conversations, build relationships and organize communities to drive social change (Kanter & Fine, 2010). Lovejoy, Waters, and Saxton (2012) stated that Twitter offers nonprofit organizations real-time feedback about announcements and promoted dialogue engagement with important stakeholders.

In reality, however, Muralidharan, Rasmussen, Patterson and Shin (2011), in their study of nonprofit organizations' engagement on social media, found that two-way communication on Facebook and Twitter is rare. Similar to news organizations, they merely use social media channels to disseminate information through links. Lovejoy et al.'s (2012) study supported these statements. They found minimal results to demonstrate that the use of social media, Twitter specifically, created conversations and community building. The researchers argued that these organizations were using the platform no differently than news outlets that support traditional one-way information sharing. While no study has yet analyzed the social media engagement of nonprofit health organizations, Nemovicher, Christopherson, Nagle, and Kartt (2012) pointed out that "the real opportunity for nonprofits in the social media world is deeper engagement with their audience, their community" (para. 4). But they also point out that "in the rush to 'go social,' many nonprofits are failing to think through their strategy" (para. 2). Henderson and Bowley (2010) also underlined the importance of authenticity in any social media engagement to attract and engage audiences. Researchers pointed to a disconnect between data supporting the power of social media and public relations practitioners' belief in the power of, as well as the connection between, public relations and customer service.

As the review of literature has shown, there are very few studies at this point that explore how nonprofit organizations engage their audiences on Twitter. Scholars stressed that nonprofits need to engage their audiences in two-way communication, but there are no research findings indicating that it has become common practice, yet. For this reason, the following research question was derived:

RQ1: How are nonprofit organizations engaging with their audience on the microblogging platform Twitter?

Another way of measuring engagement online is to examine linking patterns on social media platforms. Research has shown for instance that news organizations have very few external links in their tweets. Research on nonprofit engagement is again lacking on this point. Therefore, the second research question for this study attempted to explore this important area of online engagement:

RQ2: What are the linking patterns of nonprofit organizations on the microblogging platform Twitter?

In examining nonprofit organizations' Twitter engagements, it was also important to analyze the individual engagement of nonprofits and compare them to each other. This examination will allow conclusions to be drawn about macro and micro trends in nonprofit organizations' Twitter engagements. Therefore, the following two research questions were derived based on the literature review:

RQ3: Is there a difference between nonprofit organizations in their engagement with their audience on the microblogging platform Twitter?

RQ4: Is there a difference between nonprofit organizations in their linking patterns on the microblogging platform Twitter?

Method

This study was conducted to analyze the Twitter engagement of nonprofit health organizations and thereby an important part of their overall public relations strategy. A content analysis was designed and carried out in the first quarter of 2012 based on an amended measurement scale initially developed by Messner et al. (2012), who had previously studied the Twitter engagement of major news organizations.

Sample

For this study a sample of nonprofit organizations was drawn from the Forbes magazine list of the 200 Largest U.S. Charities for 2011 (Forbes, 2011). Health is one of the most important areas for nonprofit organizations on this list. Therefore, a sample of health-focused nonprofit organizations was drawn from the list through an already available category listing. Sampling the largest and most well-funded nonprofit organizations allowed this study to analyze the best practices in the health nonprofit sector. This resulted in a sample of 22 nonprofit organizations, all of which had a Twitter account. However, during the content analysis it was found that the National Cancer Coalition had never used its account and that the Leukemia & Lymphoma Society had not tweeted on any of the days sampled for this study. For this reason, both organizations were excluded from the final sample, which included the following 20 nonprofit organizations:

> Alzheimer's Association, American Cancer Society, American Diabetes Association, American Heart Association, American Kidney Fund, Arthritis Foundation, Autism Speaks, Chronic Disease Fund, Cystic Fibrosis Foundation, Easter Seals, Entertainment Industry Foundation, Foundation for the NIH, Fred Hutchinson Cancer Research Center, Juvenile Diabetes Research Foundation, March of Dimes Foundation, Michael J. Fox Foundation for Parkinson's Research, Muscular Dystrophy Association, National Multiple Sclerosis Society, Susan G. Komen for the Cure, and The Arc of the United States (see Appendix 7.1).

Content from the Twitter accounts of these 20 nonprofit organizations was sampled during a constructed two-week time period between January 1 and March 31, 2012. Each day of the week was randomly selected twice within the three-month period, leading to a sample of the following 14 non-consecutive days: January 4, 8, 19, 23, 26; February 6, 14, 17, 24; March 7, 10, 13, 24, 25. This sampling technique allowed for control of potential bias caused by certain news events involving these nonprofit organizations during the limited time period. For instance, the controversy surrounding the Susan G. Komen for the Cure organization (Robbins, 2012), which occurred in early 2012, only played a role in the tweets on two of the sampled days and did not dominate the content of tweets during the selected period.

Operationalization

The unit of analysis for this study was the individual tweet. On each of the days in the sample, each tweet by each of the 20 nonprofit organizations was included in the analysis. This led to an overall set of 948 tweets for the data analysis. The distribution of tweets for the sampled days varied greatly across nonprofit organizations, from frequently tweeting organizations (e.g., the March of Dimes Foundation $n = 155$, the Muscular Dystrophy Association $n = 144$, the American Heart Association $n = 135$, and Autism Speaks $n = 88$) to rarely tweeting ones (e.g., the Entertainment Industry Foundation $n = 6$, the Alzheimer's Association $n = 8$, the Chronic Disease Fund $n = 10$, and the American Cancer Society n = 10).

To determine the Twitter engagement level of the nonprofit organizations, each tweet was analyzed for the use of other Twitter handles as indicators for direct communications with other Twitter users. This was operationalized as a Twitter handle used at the beginning of the tweet. The analysis was also coded for use of retweets (RT) or modified tweets (MT) in the tweets. In addition, it was determined whether a hashtag was used in the tweets, which is indicated by the use of the # symbol. Finally, it was also analyzed whether a link was used in the tweet and what kind of website the link led to. It was of interest to determine whether the link led to the organization's website, to another web presence, or to external information. In addition, the number of tweets on each organization's account was recorded on March 31, 2012 as well as the number of followers and number of people each organization followed.

Two trained coders conducted the analysis. A pre-test was conducted and the coding manual was revised before the actual coding began. Overall, intercoder reliability was assessed by the two coders on 10% of the coding material at .88 for *Scott's Pi* (Scott, 1955).

Results

To determine the Twitter engagement of nonprofit organizations in the health sector, this study analyzed 948 tweets by 20 nonprofit organizations during a constructed two-week period in the first quarter of 2012. On average, each nonprofit organization tweeted 47.4 times during the two-week period and 3.4 times per day. However, as noted in the methodology, the distribution of tweets varied greatly by nonprofit organization (see Table 7.1). Based on their averages, five of the organizations did not post tweets every day.

The distribution of tweets also varied by the day of the week. The number of overall tweets on average weekdays generally ranged between 72 and 83, with a higher rate of 123 tweets on an average Thursday. However, there were fewer tweets on the weekends with averages of 22 tweets on Saturdays and 17 tweets on Sundays. The most tweets by a nonprofit organization on a single day were 83.

The four research questions posed for this study are discussed separately in the following sections.

RQ1: How are nonprofit organizations engaging with their audience on the microblogging platform Twitter?

The data analysis showed that each nonprofit organization had, on average, tweeted 2,765 times during the lifetime of its Twitter account. The average number of followers was 26,673 and the average number of people followed by each organization was 14,589. The content analysis

Table 7.1   Percentage of tweets by nonprofit organization

Nonprofit organization	Tweets (%)
Alzheimer's Association	00.8
American Cancer Society	01.1
American Diabetes Association	05.3
American Heart Association	14.2
American Kidney Fund	02.4
Arthritis Foundation	01.8
Autism Speaks	09.3
Chronic Disease Fund	01.1
Cystic Fibrosis Foundation	02.4
Easter Seals	05.4
Entertainment Industry Foundation	00.6
Foundation for the NIH	01.4
Fred Hutchinson Cancer Research Center	02.3
Juvenile Diabetes Research Foundation	05.9
M. J. Fox Foundation for Parkinson's Research	03.7
March of Dimes Foundation	16.4
Muscular Dystrophy Association	15.2
National Multiple Sclerosis Society	02.0
Susan G. Komen for the Cure	07.3
The Arc of the United States	01.5

Note: $n = 948$.

showed that almost half of the tweets by the 20 nonprofit organizations involved direct communication with the audience through the use of Twitter handles and retweets or modified tweets. It also found that more than half of all tweets were targeted toward a specific audience through the use of hashtags. On average, 28.2% of all tweets directly addressed another Twitter user through the use of a Twitter handle at the beginning of the tweet, and an additional 21.3% of all tweets were either retweets or modified tweets of users' Twitter posts. Hashtags were used in 53.8% of all tweets.

RQ2: What are the linking patterns of nonprofit organizations on the microblogging platform Twitter?

Of the overall tweets by the 20 nonprofit organizations, on average 53.5% included a link while 46.5% did not. Of the 507 links, 62.5% directed the audience to the organizations' websites or other web presences such as blogs, Facebook accounts or photo and video upload sites. While 0.6% of the links were broken and could not be identified, 36.9%

led the audience to external websites that were not affiliated with the organization posting the tweet.

RQ3: Is there a difference among nonprofit organizations in their engagement with their audience on the microblogging platform Twitter?

The Twitter activities of the 20 nonprofit organizations showed broad differences in frequency of use and audience engagement. While the average number of tweets for the different lifetimes of the Twitter accounts is 2,765 per organization, the individual number of tweets vary greatly and range from high frequencies by the Michael J. Fox Foundation for Parkinson's Research (n = 9,136) and Autism Speaks (n = 6,740) to lower frequencies by the Alzheimer's Association (n = 720) and the Entertainment Industry Foundation (n = 820). Even greater variety exists in the numbers of followers and the following of other Twitter users. While the averages are 26,673 followers and a following of 14,589 other users, the number of followers varied greatly from the American Cancer Society (n = 264,289) to the Entertainment Industry Foundation (n = 1,033), and the following of other users ranged from the American Cancer Society (n = 198,547) to the American Diabetes Association (n = 184). For three nonprofit organizations, the Alzheimer's Association, the American Diabetes Association, and the National Multiple Sclerosis Society, the number of users they followed was less than 10% the number of users that followed them, while four organizations, Chronic Disease Fund, Cystic Fibrosis Foundation, Easter Seals, and the Foundation for the NIH, were following more or almost as many users as the number of users who were following them (see Table 7.2).

While more than a fourth of the overall tweets directly communicated with another Twitter user through the use of a Twitter handle at the beginning of the tweet, and more than one fifth of the tweets were retweets or modified tweets, the Twitter audience engagement differed greatly among the 20 nonprofit organizations. While nine organizations used fewer than 10% of their tweets for direct communication with other users, eight organizations used more than 25% of their tweets for this purpose. Three organizations, the American Diabetes Association, the Cystic Fibrosis Foundation, and the Susan G. Komen for the Cure, used more than half of their tweets for direct communication on Twitter. On the other hand, the Alzheimer's Association, the American Cancer Society, and the Chronic Disease Fund never communicated directly with other users.

Table 7.2 Overall Twitter account demographics by nonprofit organization

Nonprofit organization	Number of tweets	Number of followers	Number following
Alzheimer's Association	720	14,064	647
American Cancer Society	2,346	264,289	198,547
American Diabetes Association	1,698	25,558	184
American Heart Association	5,682	24,951	3,568
American Kidney Fund	829	1,784	525
Arthritis Foundation	2,114	8,259	5,531
Autism Speaks	6,740	62,737	33,784
Chronic Disease Fund	1,746	1,461	1,205
Cystic Fibrosis Foundation	2,211	7,379	6,952
Easter Seals	2,691	4,351	4,069
Entertainment Industry Foundation	820	1,033	285
Foundation for the NIH	1,267	1,455	1,948
Fred Hutchinson Cancer Research Center	1,951	4,528	1,445
Juvenile Diabetes Research Foundation	1,939	9,259	1,715
M. J. Fox Foundation for Parkinson's Research	9,136	23,201	20,207
March of Dimes Foundation	1,046	11,325	3,758
Muscular Dystrophy Association	5,247	8,622	896
National Multiple Sclerosis Society	951	14,197	209
Susan G. Komen for the Cure	4,686	41,006	4,589
The Arc of the United States	1,470	3,997	1,711
Average	2,765	26,673	14,589

The analysis of the use of retweets and modified tweets showed similar differences among the nonprofit organizations. Six organizations used fewer than 10% of their postings for retweets or modified tweets, while five organizations used more than 25% of their tweets for the purpose of information sharing. This ranged from the American Cancer Society never using retweets or modified tweets to the Juvenile Diabetes Research Foundation using more than three-fourth of its posts for these purposes.

The use of hashtags, on the other hand, was much more frequent. The nonprofit organizations who used them did so in at least more than 10% of their posts to target them to specific audiences. Six organizations used hashtags in the majority of their tweets. The Alzheimer's Association, the American Kidney Fund, the Juvenile Diabetes Research Foundation, the March of Dimes Foundation, the Muscular Dystrophy Association, and National Multiple Sclerosis Society used hashtags in more than 70% of their tweets (see Table 7.3).

RQ4: Is there a difference among nonprofit organizations in their linking patterns on the microblogging platform Twitter?

Table 7.3 Twitter audience engagement by nonprofit organization

Nonprofit organization	Twitter handle (%)	RT/MT (%)	Hashtag (%)
Alzheimer's Association	00.0	12.5	75.0
American Cancer Society	00.0	00.0	20.0
American Diabetes Association	52.0	04.0	48.0
American Heart Association	44.4	11.1	52.6
American Kidney Fund	17.4	08.7	78.3
Arthritis Foundation	05.9	05.9	11.8
Autism Speaks	31.8	14.8	31.8
Chronic Disease Fund	00.0	20.0	10.0
Cystic Fibrosis Foundation	65.2	04.3	13.0
Easter Seals	03.9	17.6	21.6
Entertainment Industry Foundation	16.7	66.7	33.3
Foundation for the NIH	07.7	53.8	61.5
Fred Hutchinson Cancer Research Center	04.5	40.9	22.7
Juvenile Diabetes Research Foundation	05.4	76.8	92.9
M. J. Fox Foundation for Parkinson's Research	08.6	34.3	42.9
March of Dimes Foundation	21.9	23.9	78.1
Muscular Dystrophy Association	25.7	21.5	71.5
National Multiple Sclerosis Society	41.1	10.5	78.9
Susan G. Komen for the Cure	56.5	14.5	26.1
The Arc of the United States	28.6	07.1	35.7
Average	28.2 ($n = 267$)	21.3 ($n = 202$)	53.8 ($n = 510$)

The analysis showed that every nonprofit organization used a link in every third tweet at least, linking to additional information and thereby extending the maximum of 140 characters allowed in a tweet. Many organizations use links much more often than that. The Alzheimer's Association, the American Cancer Society, the Arthritis Foundation, the Chronic Disease Fund, the Easter Seals, the Entertainment Industry Foundation, and the Juvenile Diabetes Research Foundation used links in over 80% of their tweets.

While 12 organizations used most of these links to lead their audience to additional information on their websites or other web presences affiliated with the organization, six organizations used the majority of their links to connect the audience to external information provided by others. Two organizations used the same number of internal and external links.

The uses of internal and external links varied greatly between individual nonprofit organizations. While the Juvenile Diabetes Research Foundation used 90.0% of its links to guide its audience to external

Table 7.4   Twitter linking patterns by nonprofit organization

Nonprofit organization	Tweets with links (%)	Internal links (%)	External links (%)
Alzheimer's Association	087.5	042.9	057.1
American Cancer Society	100.0	050.0	050.0
American Diabetes Association	050.0	084.0	016.0
American Heart Association	039.6	049.1	050.9
American Kidney Fund	034.8	087.5	012.3
Arthritis Foundation	088.2	073.3	026.7
Autism Speaks*	052.3	060.9	037.0
Chronic Disease Fund	090.0	000.0	100.0
Cystic Fibrosis Foundation	034.8	062.5	037.5
Easter Seals	082.4	071.4	028.6
Entertainment Industry Foundation	083.3	000.0	100.0
Foundation for the NIH	076.9	090.0	010.0
Fred Hutchinson Cancer Research Center	063.6	042.9	057.1
Juvenile Diabetes Research Foundation	089.3	010.0	090.0
M. J. Fox Foundation for Parkinson's Research	071.4	084.0	016.0
March of Dimes Foundation*	016.8	057.7	038.5
Muscular Dystrophy Association*	064.6	083.9	015.1
National Multiple Sclerosis Society	068.4	100.0	000.0
Susan G. Komen for the Cure	055.1	076.3	023.7
The Arc of the United States	071.4	050.0	050.0
Average	053.5 ($n = 507$)	062.5 ($n = 317$)	36.9 ($n = 187$)

Note: *Three of the total links were broken and could not be analyzed further. Therefore, the sum of internal and external links for these organizations will not equal 100%. The total average of tweets with links includes the three broken links.

information, the Muscular Dystrophy Association used 83.9% of its links to guide followers to its own web content (see Table 7.4).

Discussion

The purpose of this study was to analyze the Twitter engagement of leading nonprofit organizations in the U.S. health sector as part of their overall public relations strategy. Data were collected from a constructed two-week period during the first quarter of 2012. The analysis showed that the use of Twitter as a platform to communicate with followers, target specific audiences, and provide links for additional information is very different in individual organizations.

The difference in frequency of tweeting by the 20 organizations shows that each one has different priorities for Twitter. Some organizations, like the March of Dimes Foundation and the Muscular Dystrophy Association, use Twitter as a regular communication tool every day. Other organizations, like the Alzheimer's Association and the Entertainment Industry Foundation, only tweet every other day. While it is expected that organizations will make fewer tweets on weekends, it is unusual for leading nonprofits not to engage on Twitter on a regular basis, as shown during the two-week sampling period of this study.

The overall results for health sector nonprofit organization Twitter engagement through direct communication with other users, retweets and modified tweets as well as their use of hashtags, show a collective that engages very well on the microblogging platform. However, a comparison of individual organizations also revealed great differences among them, which is evident in the lifetime number of tweets, followers, and followings for each Twitter account. Some have built large Twitter communities through their own followings and are regularly communicating with their followers. Others, however, show discrepancies between follower and followings with little effort to engage with the community beyond one-way communication activities.

The use of Twitter handles at the beginning of tweets, the posting of retweets and modified tweets, as well as the use of hashtags, allow an assessment of the community engagement of these nonprofit organizations. Nonprofits that use fewer than 10% of their tweets for direct communication with their followers, or for retweets or modified tweets, do not use Twitter to its full potential. Nevertheless, the overall use of hashtags by the 20 organizations shows that all of them at least target their tweets to a specific audience.

Also, the linking patterns do not reveal a collective trend. While most organizations have at least some engagement with content associated with others and do not solely use Twitter to promote their own content, there is still room for improvement. Organizations that do not use external links and do not retweet content from others, do not utilize the advantages of easy information-sharing that Twitter offers them and their audience.

Overall, the results suggest that nonprofit health organizations are still in need of best practice guidelines for Twitter to better build and engage with communities on the microblogging platform. Using Twitter without communicating directly with other users, specifying information channels, and sharing information is an ineffective and inefficient use of communication team resources at these organizations. A return on investment in a social media strategy would only be achieved through increased Twitter engagement.

Although this sample was limited to 20 nonprofit organizations in the health sector, it demonstrated Twitter engagement among nonprofit organizations. The study observed a brief constructed two-week period. The low frequency of tweets by some of the nonprofits might be attributed to the constructed sampling time period.

Studies on the social media engagement of nonprofit organizations are still rare, even though Twitter has been in existence for six years. This is surprising as the online activities of nonprofits have a great potential to advance the mission of nonprofit organizations with a health focus. The information they provide can make a difference for online audiences, impact quality of life, and strengthen connections to key stakeholders.

Appendix 7.1 Nonprofit Organizations

The Twitter accounts of the non-profit organizations were accessed through the following URLs:

Alzheimer's Association (http://twitter.com/#!/alzassociation)
American Cancer Society (http://twitter.com/#!/AmericanCancer)
American Diabetes Association (http://twitter.com/#!/amdiabetesassn)
American Heart Association (http://twitter.com/#!/american_heart)
American Kidney Fund, (http://twitter.com/#!/KidneyFund)
Arthritis Foundation (http://twitter.com/#!/arthritis_org)
Autism Speaks (http://twitter.com/#!/autismspeaks)
Chronic Disease Fund (http://twitter.com/#!/CDFund)
Cystic Fibrosis Foundation (http://twitter.com/#!/CF_Foundation)
Easter Seals (http://twitter.com/#!/Easter_Seals)
Entertainment Industry Foundation (http://twitter.com/#!/EIFoundation)
Foundation for the NIH (http://twitter.com/#!/FNIH_org)
Fred Hutchinson Cancer Research Center (http://twitter.com/#!/HutchinsonCtr)
Juvenile Diabetes Research Foundation (http://twitter.com/#!/JDRF)
March of Dimes Foundation (http://twitter.com/#!/marchofdimes)
Michael J. Fox Foundation for Parkinson's Research (http://twitter.com/#!/michaeljfoxorg)
Muscular Dystrophy Association (http://twitter.com/#!/mdanews)
National Multiple Sclerosis Society (http://twitter.com/#!/mssociety)
Susan G. Komen for the Cure (http://twitter.com/#!/komenforthecure)
The Arc of the United States (http://twitter.com/#!/thearcus).

The Twitter accounts of the National Cancer Coalition (http://twitter.com/#!/nationalcancer) and the Leukemia & Lymphoma Society (http://twitter.com/#!/llsusa) were excluded from the sample due to an absence of tweets.

References

Alexa.com. (2012). Twitter. Retrieved from http://www.alexa.com/siteinfo/twitter.com

Curtis, L., Edwards, C., Fraser, K. L., Gudelsky, S., Holmquist, J., Thornton, K. & Sweetser, K. D. (2010). Adoption of social media for public relations by nonprofit organizations. *Public Relations Review, 36*(1), 90–92.

Farhi, P. (2009). The Twitter explosion. *American Journalism Review*. Retrieved from http://www.ajr.org/Article.asp?id=4756

Forbes. (2011). The 200 largest U.S. charities for 2011. Retrieved from http://www.forbes.com/lists/2011/14/200-largest-us-charities-11_rank.html

Fox, S. (2010). Mobile health 2010. *Pew Research Center's Internet & American Life Project*. Retrieved from http://pewinternet.org/Reports/2010/Mobile-Health-2010.aspx

Fox, S. (2011). The social life of health information, 2011. *Pew Research Center's Internet & American Life Project*. Retrieved from http://www.pewinternet.org/Reports/2011/Social-Life-of-Health-Info.aspx

Garrison-Sprenger, N. (2008). Twittery-do-dah, twittering pays. *Quill, 96*(8), 12–15.

Greenberg, J. & MacAulay, M. (2009). NPO 2.0? Exploring the web presence of environmental nonprofit organizations in Canada. *Global Media Journal, 2*(1), 63–88.

Hamilton, A. (2007). Why everyone's talking about Twitter. *Time*. Retrieved from http://www.time.com/time/business/article/0,8599,1603637,00.html

Henderson, A., & Bowley, R. (2010). Authentic dialogue? The role of "friendship" in a social media recruitment campaign. *Journal of Communication Management, 14*(3), 237–257.

Jackson, N. A., & Lilleker, D. G. (2009). MPs and e-representation: Me, Myspace, and I. *British Politics, 4*(2), 236–264.

Kanter, B., & Fine, A. (2010). *The networked nonprofit: Connecting with social media to drive change*. Hoboken, NJ: Wiley.

Lenhart, A., Purcell, K., Smith, A., & Zickuhr, K. (2010). Social media and mobile Internet use among teens and young adults. *Pew Research Center's Internet & American Life Project*. Retrieved from http://pewinternet.org/Reports/2010/Social-Media-and-Young-Adults.aspx

Lovejoy, K., Waters, R. D., & Saxton, G. D. (2012). Engaging stakeholders through Twitter: How nonprofit organizations are getting more out of 140 characters or less. *Public Relations Review, 38*(2), 313–318.

Lowery, C. (2009). An explosion prompts rethinking of Twitter and Facebook. *Nieman Reports*. Retrieved from http://www.nieman.harvard.edu/reportsitem.aspx?id=101894

McCorkindale, T. C. (2009). *Can you see the writing on my wall? A content analysis of the Fortune 50's Facebook social networking sites.* Paper presented at the annual meeting of the International Public Relations Research Conference, Coral Gables, FL.

Messner, M., Linke, M., & Eford, A. (2012). Shoveling tweets: An analysis of the microblogging engagement of traditional news organizations. *#ISOJ Journal, 2*(1), 76–90.

Muralidharan, S., Rasmussen, L., Patterson, D., & Shin, J.-H. (2011). Hope for Haiti: An analysis of Facebook and Twitter usage during the earthquake relief efforts. *Public Relations Review, 37*(2), 175–177.

Nemovicher, S., Christopherson, E. G., Nagle, J., & Kartt, J. (2012). Tweeting for a better world. *Bridgespan Group.* Retrieved from http://www.bridgespan.org/tweeting-for-a-better-world.aspx

Robbins, T. (2012). Komen struggles to regain footing, and funding. *National Public Radio.* Retrieved from http://www.npr.org/2012/03/26/149396029/komen-struggles-to-regain-footing-and-funding

Rybalko, S. & Seltzer, T. (2010). Dialogic communication in 140 characters or less: How Fortune 500 companies engage stakeholders using Twitter. *Public Relations Review, 36*(4), 336–341.

Scott, W. A. (1955). Reliability of content analysis: The case of nominal scale coding. *Public Opinion Quarterly, 19*(3), 321–325.

Shirky, C. (2011). The political power of social media. *Foreign Affairs, 90*(1), 28–41.

Smith, B. (2010). Socially distributing public relations: Twitter, Haiti, and interactivity in social media. *Public Relations Review, 36*(4), 329–335.

Smith, J., Miles, S., & Lellis, L. (2010). *Tweeting the news: Broadcast stations' use of Twitter.* Paper presented at the annual meeting of the Association for Education in Journalism and Mass Communication, Denver, CO.

Sungwook, H. (2012). The strategic use of Twitter to manage personal public relations. *Public Relations Review, 38*(1), 159–161

Waters, R. D., Burnett, E., Lamm, A., & Lucas, J. (2009). Engaging stakeholders through social networking: How nonprofit organizations are using Facebook. *Public Relations Review, 35*(2), 102–106.

Waters, R. D., & Williams, J. (2011). Squawking, tweeting, cooing, and hooting: Analyzing the communication patterns of government agencies on Twitter. *Journal of Public Affairs, 11*(4), 253–363.

Wright, D. K., & Hinson, M. (2010). How new communications media are being used in public relations: A longitudinal analysis. *Public Relations Journal, 4*(3). Retrieved from http://www.prsa.org/Intelligence/PRJournal/Documents/2010tWrightHinson.pdf

Wright, D. K., & Hinson, M. (2012). *A four-year longitudinal analysis measuring social and emerging media use in public relations practice.* Paper presented at the annual meeting of the International Public Relations Research Conference, Coral Gables, FL.

Zhang, W., Johnson, T. J., Seltzer, T., & Bichard, S. L. (2010). The revolution will be networked: The influence of social networking sites on political attitudes and behavior. *Social Science Computer Review, 28*(1), 75–92.

Zickuhr, K. (2010). Generations 2010. *Pew Research Center's Internet & American Life Project.* Retrieved from http://pewinternet.org/Reports/2010/Generations-2010.aspx

8

Public Relations in a Virtual World: A Second Life Case Study

John C. Sherblom and Sara Green-Hamann

Second Life is one of the largest and most well-known, three-dimensional virtual worlds that exists today (Koles & Nagy, 2012). Since its launch by Linden Labs in 2003, Second Life has grown rapidly and currently boasts millions of participants worldwide (Jin & Bolebruch, 2009). In 2005 Second Life was recognized as having become a major public relations opportunity (Cere, 2007; Martin, 2008; Nikolaou, Bettany, & Larsen 2010); and in 2006 the global public relations firm Text 100 International opened a Second Life office (Text 100, 2006). However, by 2007 public relations professionals began voicing skepticism over the possibility of developing any truly useful and important public relations campaigns in Second Life. In 2010, following results published by the University of Southern California (USC) Annenberg School to a survey of 400 executives' responses to their public relations practices, Second Life was declared officially dead as a public relations tool.

Those survey results showed a lack of enthusiasm among public relations professionals for using virtual worlds in their work. On a scale of 1 to 7, where 1 is low and 7 is high, public relations professionals ranked their current use of virtual worlds as a 1.4 and their planned use as a 1.6 (Ciarallo, 2010). They ranked future use well below use of online videos (5.2), Twitter (4.2), weblogs (3.9), podcasts (3.8), wikis (2.6), and even below "other" digital social media (1.8). The USC report makes a special comment about those virtual world results, saying that: "The poor showing of once-hot Virtual Worlds is noteworthy" (USC Annenberg School, 2010, p. 19). However, the same report notes that "nonprofits [in particular] are very aggressive users of digital/online tools ... [and anticipate using] social networking sites to a greater degree than any other type of surveyed organization" (p. 24).

A series of Pew reports show that the percentage of donations made to nonprofit charitable organizations through an online medium has increased in recent years. Thirteen million Americans made donations online for Hurricanes Katrina and Rita relief (Morris & Horrigan, 2005). Mobile phone users texted millions of dollars to aid Haiti earthquake relief (Smith, 2012). In fact, Americans under the age of 40 were more likely to donate to the Japanese tsunami disaster relief fund through Internet websites and texting from their cell phones than through more traditional telephone, in person, or postal mail methods (Purcell & Dimock, 2011).

This trend toward making charitable contributions through an online medium has grown among Second Life participants as well. The American Cancer Society reports that their annual Relay for Life event held in Second Life in 2004 had 99 participants who raised $2,000. That same event had 315 participants who raised $5,000 in 2005, 1570 participants who raised $41,000 in 2006, and 1831 participants who raised $118,500 in 2007. In 2008, 2009, and 2010 that annual event had more than 1500 participants and raised more than $200,000 each year (Relay for Life of Second Life, 2012). Clearly, Second Life holds some potential for public relations fund raising. The challenge for real-world organizations is to develop strategies and ways of doing business that facilitate their real-world goals (Smith & Zook, 2011).

Virtual worlds like Second Life represent a relatively new phenomenon and there is much about doing business in a virtual world that is only recently being discovered (Jin, 2009). The purpose of this chapter is to identify a set of strategic public relations principles and practices that facilitate awareness and fund-raising efforts in a virtual world like Second Life. These principles and practices were applied to a World AIDS Day awareness and fund-raising event held in Second Life.

The Virtual World of Second Life

Second Life is a three-dimensional virtual world with the visual dimensions of physical space and the social characteristics of a virtual community (Green-Hamann, Eichhorn, & Sherblom, 2011). This type of virtual world is sometimes referred to as a *meta-universe*, or more commonly *metaverse*, and is distinguished from online games in that participants do not have a single, pre-set goal or objective the way players of a game do (Kumar, Chhugani, Kim, Kim, Nguyen, Dubey, Bienia &Kim, 2008). Participants use avatars to represent themselves and can explore, play, work, join groups, engage in social activities, interact with others, and build their own residences and social communities within this virtual space (Bloomfield, 2009; Koles & Nagy, 2012; Martin, 2008; Nikolaou et al., 2010; Wood, 2011). The virtual physicality provides a sense of personal immediacy and interactivity within a social community (Nikolaou et al., 2010). Participants create and modify virtual objects, negotiate meanings, and construct social knowledge in ways that influence individual participant identity and build a social presence (Jin & Bolebruch, 2010; Kumar et al., 2008; Sherblom, 2010; Yildiz, 2009).

Participants communicate with each other in real-time, but can remain personally anonymous, identified only by their avatar name and image. Over time, however, participants develop online reputations and identities within the virtual community. They get to know each other as they interact, negotiate meanings, and construct social knowledge in ways that are symbolically similar to face-to-face conversations. This type of communication facilitates the development of social presence, trust, and personal relationships (Green-Hamann et al., 2011; Koles & Nagy, 2012; Sherblom, 2010; Sherblom, Withers, & Leonard, 2009).

Participant Identity

An individual develops an identity and online reputation over time through participation in the ongoing communication and social practices of the virtual community (Monberg, 2005). Second Life, however, provides opportunities for individuals to construct their identities in unique and varied ways that emphasize how individuals wish to express themselves (Boras, 2009; Koles & Nagy, 2012; Williams, 2007). "The embodied self shifts from skin-bound into the highly extendible and socially-constructed world within and with which users *dwell*" (Jarmon, 2009, p. 4). Avatars, as agents of participant identity, make a virtual world presence attainable that may not be possible in the physical world (Bente, Ruggenberg, Kramer, & Eschenburg, 2008; Biocca, 1997; Taylor, 2009). These individual identities become part of the larger social network of the virtual community (Pizarro, 2007). The individual, as an active participant, helps construct the community identity and, reciprocally, the individual identity is shaped by the values of the virtual community (Sherblom et al., 2009). By becoming a member of the virtual community an individual validates the community's shared values, relationships, symbolic use of space, and meaningful experiences (Gouveia, de Albuquerque, Clemente, & Espinosa, 2002; Waisbord,

1998). Collectively, participants create interconnected identities and lifestyles within that community, and embody the community norms and values (Nikolaou et al., 2010).

The boundary between the virtual and the physical world is becoming increasingly fluid (Nikolaou et al., 2010). Hence, developing an identity in Second Life can provide public relations opportunities in the physical world as well (Jin & Bolebruch, 2010; Nikolaou et al., 2010). Numerous cities, corporations, national embassies, nonprofit organizations, and universities have created a virtual presence in Second Life (Kumar et al., 2008); and there are over 200 real-world brands present in Second Life, including Coca-Cola, Pepsi, Kraft, and Pizza Hut (Wood, 2011). IBM uses Second Life to conduct virtual meetings. Little Wonder Studio uses it to design new toys. Crescendo Design creates detailed, three-dimensional models of environmentally friendly buildings, and Starwood Hotels tests new hotel lobby designs (Wood, 2011). Many groups and organizations have seen positive real-world results from their Second Life ventures. Successfully performing public relations in Second Life, however, requires an understanding of the relationships among participant-avatar social identity needs and community practices (Nikolaou et al., 2010).

Four Attributes of a Public Relations
Event in Second Life

The researchers identified four attributes important to promoting public relations in Second Life. These attributes were: (a) online reputation, (b) presence, (c) interactivity, and (d) virtual community. Table 8.1 shows the application of each of these attributes in the preparation and participation phases of staging a public relations event in Second Life. Each of these four attributes has a preparatory and a participatory phase. An online reputation can be built upon the real-world reputation of an organization, but that reputation must be extended into the virtual world. The participatory phase consists in having a spokesperson avatar who is not only knowledgeable, but attractive and sophisticated in appearance. Presence involves the creation of a virtual space that is visually attractive in which, during the participation phase, avatars can engage in immersive activities. Interactivity necessitates the preparation of full-avatar-body events that proactively encourage participation. Virtual community requires building a word-of-mouth network that creates a social identity.

Table 8.1 Four attributes of holding a public relations event in Second Life

Attribute	Preparation	Participation
Online reputation	Co-create an online reputation	Credible spokesperson avatars
Presence	Create visually attractive spaces	Active, immersive experiences
Interactivity	Plan full-avatar-body events	Proactively encourage, involve avatars
Virtual community	Build a word-of-mouth network	Symbolic, visual social identity

Online Reputation

Co-create an online reputation

Developing a solid online reputation is particularly important to a virtual-world organization due to the fluidity of self-representation that is possible in virtual environments. Building trust in one's reputation among the participants of a virtual community is important (Orange, 2011). Perceptions of informational usefulness, decisions about potential involvement with a company or event, and levels of participant enjoyment are built upon this trust (Chen, Shih, Chiang, & Lin, 2010; Hassanein & Head, 2006). Community participants who are consulted and treated as collaborators in the co-creation of an organization's reputation develop a perception that the organization cares about their thoughts and concerns. These perceptions can help establish the organization's long-term reputation (Smith & Zook, 2011). When evaluating a product or event newer community members consider the experiences of these trusted older participants to be more accurate predictors of a company's true identity than the pre-packaged company materials, and they pay more attention to the recommendations made by these older, more experienced, expert community members (Smith & Zook, 2011). Spokesperson avatars can provide trustworthy advice to community members. Hence, a credible public relations spokesperson avatar can have a strong influence on a virtual community (Jin & Bolebruch, 2010; Orange, 2011; Smith & Zook, 2011).

Credible spokesperson avatars

Credible spokesperson avatars who represent the expertise, knowledge, and online reputation of an organization are important sources of organizational messages in a virtual world (Jin, 2009). These avatars, as dynamic agents of participant identity, offer a direct sense of immediacy, interactive trustworthiness, and personal expertise that help build a company's online reputation (Jin & Bolebruch, 2010). Sophisticated, attractive-looking avatars, representing real people, can make recommendations, reduce uncertainty, and enhance a participant's interaction experience (Jin & Bolebruch, 2009). Interacting with a physically attractive spokesperson avatar increases participant enjoyment, perceptions of the value of information, positive attitudes toward a product, and engaged behavior toward a service or event (Jin, 2009; Jin & Bolebruch, 2009). The technical sophistication of the avatar spokesperson, visual as well as informational, and the realistic setting in which the interaction takes place, including sophisticated whole-body movements and the use of space, can contribute to a participant's overall positive communication experience and sense of presence (Aymerich-Franch, 2010).

Presence

Presence is defined in the literature as a combination of: telepresence – sense of immediacy within a medium (Nowak & Biocca, 2003); social presence – extent to which a medium conveys the perception of being involved with other participants (Biocca, Harms, & Burgoon, 2003; Walther, Slovacek, & Tidwell, 2001); copresence – sense of mutual awareness, connection, and satisfaction among participants (Nowak, 2001); and social copresence – sense of mutual connectedness, emotional accessibility, and communication satisfaction in the medium (Fägersten, 2010). Thus, presence describes the feelings of connection, immediacy, and involvement that participants have in a virtual environment (Jin & Bolebruch, 2009; Lee, 2004; Nowak, 2001).

Create visually attractive spaces

The visual attractiveness and realism of Second Life spaces enhance this sense of presence and foster positive interactions and evaluations of events held there (Blascovich, Loomis, Beall, Swinth, Hoyt &Bailenson, 2002). Presence can be facilitated further by the strategic decisions made within the medium in ways that affect the cognitive dispositions of participants (Daugherty, Gangadharbatla, & Bright, 2010). The virtual spaces of Second Life have the look and feel of real-life places. Participants have pre-existing emotional associations with symbols present in these real-life places, and creating visual similarities in the virtual space increases the sense of presence (Westerman & Skalski, 2010).

Active, immersive experiences

Active, immersive social experiences, such as interacting with other avatars within the Second Life medium, further facilitate this sense of presence (Daugherty et al., 2010; Freeman, Lessiter, & Ijsselsteijn, 2001; Lombard & Ditton, 1997; Li, Daugherty, & Biocca, 2002). Building virtual spaces that are visually similar to real ones, and that develop the sense of presence through the construction of active, immersive experiences, can facilitate the success of a public relations event. This feeling of presence increases interpersonal trust, participation, and intent to contribute to an event (Gefen, Karahanna, & Straub, 2003).

Interactivity

Plan full-avatar-body events

Social media activity has moved beyond passive attention, through attraction, to participation (Smith & Zook, 2011). Pushing information out to recipients in an email, or creating an attractive website as a location for searchers to find that information, are less effective means of engaging and persuading people than finding ways to actively involve them in an event. Interactivity is an important relationship-development strategy for public relations (Waters, Burnett, Lamm, & Lucas, 2009). Interactivity may include conversations with experienced customers, contact with opinion leaders, or communication with brand owners (Smith & Zook, 2011). Second Life provides opportunities for all three of these types of interaction. In addition, Second Life permits the development of full-avatar-body participation events such as dances, races, and sporting events as further opportunities for positive interaction. Designing an event that enhances the interactivity of avatars in Second Life is an important aspect of virtual public relations. Virtual conversations and testimonials are useful, but dances, races, and sporting events not only engage the avatar, but involve the person behind that avatar more fully as well.

Proactively engage and involve avatars

Second Life provides a medium in which participants can communicate easily, interact reciprocally with others, and mingle with whomever, whenever and wherever they want (Smith & Zook, 2011). Credible spokesperson avatars who proactively engage and involve participants increase both the sense of presence and the strategic interactivity of a virtual community (Jin, 2009). By proactively engaging participants in full-body-avatar events, spokesperson avatars can facilitate participant involvement, create more positive interaction among the participants themselves, and enhance their intentions to act (Jin & Bolebruch, 2009; Skalski & Tamborini, 2007). Interactivity in a planned event, coordinated by spokesperson avatars, can strategically involve participants in the shared goals and experiences of the virtual community (Chen et al., 2010).

Virtual Community

Virtual communities engage members in shared experiences of common interest (Willson, 2006). However, communities vary in the degree of participant involvement and interaction (Chen et al., 2010). The virtual communities in which participants are the most heavily engaged and most fully identified are the ones in which they are the most active. These communities are the ones that have the strongest influence on participants.

Build a word-of-mouth network

The social influence of a virtual community can be as persuasive as that of a physical one. The virtual communities with which participants are engaged communicate with them through word-of-mouth networks that provide information about events and activities of interest (Dumrongsiri, 2010). The information that is conveyed through this word-of-mouth network is considered trustworthy and is a source of vicarious learning and perspective taking. Participants are influenced by the real and imagined social pressure of other community members in ways that affect their attitudes and behaviors (Dumrongsiri, 2010). The more individuals perceive themselves to be members of that virtual community and the more deeply the community holds a conviction, value, or belief, the greater the community's social influence on the individual's behavior and the greater the likelihood of individual conformity (Blascovich et al., 2002; Swinth & Blascovich, 2001).

Symbolic, visual social identity

The virtual goods of Second Life are not used to meet material needs; there are no material needs in Second Life. However, the use of virtual goods is not irrational, meaningless, or valueless. In Second Life virtual goods take on socially assigned symbolic values expressing: belonging, identity, individuality, power, social status, sophistication, and style. Second Life affirms the value of originality and uniqueness by explicitly restricting, although not eliminating, the ability to steal, copy, or replicate certain virtual goods (Martin, 2008). Virtual goods are imbued with normatively charged values of status and reputation within the community, and express the social needs and desires of the virtual participant. The value of virtual goods is in their use to create a coherent avatar social identity. Participants are able to customize their avatars by purchasing, modifying, and displaying virtual goods, and by performing a self-presentation that shows how much money, time, and effort they have invested in their avatar (Martin, 2008). The constructed social identity is seen and appreciated by other participants for its coherence and expressive aesthetic as displayed in the virtual shape, skin, hair, clothing, jewelry, and other items that are chosen and worn by a participant (Martin, 2008).

Through the use of virtual goods an individual constructs an identity that expresses a self-image through which to interact with others in the virtual community. Hence, virtual goods are used to create a symbolic balance between the individual and community in ways that assist participants in forming coherent social identities, and linking those identities to the values of the community. A participant's identity affects their ability to achieve self-motivated goals and the quality of their experience within the community. Therefore, the identity associations created through the use of virtual goods create opportunities for persuasive interactions within the virtual community (Martin, 2008).

Online reputation, presence, interactivity, and virtual community are four of the key attributes that influence the development of public relations in Second Life. Each of these attributes interacts with, and builds upon, the others, and each has a preparation and a participation phase. The following public relations event held in Second Life on World AIDS Day, December 1, 2009, illustrates the preparation and participation phases of these four attributes.

Case Study

A case study provides a method of observation and reflection on the context and underlying influences of a specific event. Through direct observation a researcher examines the pattern of influences on an event and attempts to describe a holistic model of the context surrounding that event. Although the particulars of a case study cannot be generalized, the holistic analysis that explores issues, describes processes and practices, depicts the complex interactions among influences, and develops the implications of consequence, can be applied to a broader set of cases (Yin, 1994). This case study analysis examines the interacting influences of online reputation, presence, interactivity, and virtual community in ways that positively affect awareness and fund raising in a public relations event held in Second Life.

World AIDS Day Recognition in Second Life

The World AIDS Day public relations event was designed primarily to provide a virtual world event-planning experience for a group of 30 public relations trainees. The 30 trainees met twice a week for six weeks, first to learn how to participate in Second life, and then to plan and organize the World AIDS Day event. To build an online reputation this group of trainees coordinated the event with several pre-existing AIDS awareness and prevention groups who already operated in both Second Life and in real life. The design and success of this project owes much to the ongoing interaction with these groups, and to the efforts of Lynnette Leonard, throughout the preparation and participation phases.

Online Reputation

Co-create an online reputation

The three-dimensional model of an HIV virus created by Madcow Cosmos on Karuna Island in Second Life that appeared on the cover of the August 2009 special issue of the *Journal of Virtual Worlds Research* inspired the development of this World AIDS Day public relations event in Second Life. The creation of this detailed, interactive model demonstrated expertise, sophistication, and trustworthiness and the trainee group established a link to the model's location. In addition, the group built links to the Second Life home of the Bronx AIDS Services, which houses a large amount of information about HIV and AIDS prevention, and to the activist group Stop Aids Now.

Establishing these links to informational resources was important to the development of the group's online reputation within the Second Life virtual community. The group also contacted Second Life newspapers and media services, such as the *The Alphaville Herald*, and learned about popular places and types of activities present in Second Life. One of the most popular activities in Second Life is dancing, especially dancing to the music that is streamed by disc jockeys. Members of the group investigated the popularity of various Second Life disc jockeys and asked three popular disc jockeys to participate in the event. Each of these disc jockeys had a personal reason for participating in the World AIDS Day event.

Second Life disc jockeys function as opinion leaders. They maintain a list of followers who frequent the events at which they play. Each disc jockey who participated sent notices to their followers. This connected the event to a network of people unlikely to be reached by other means. In addition, group members explored social gathering places in Second Life – pubs, dance halls, jazz clubs, other popular recreational spots – and developed individual networks of friends. These efforts created lists of friends to whom announcements could be sent prior to, and on the day of, the event.

The trainee group prepared multiple visual symbols for the event. Red ribbons, tee-shirts, and tank tops were made for event attendees. Logos and signs were created that connected the Second Life event to real-life organizations. Large World AIDS Day ribbons and a word cloud were produced for display at the event site. The word cloud showed a visual representation of the words that HIV and AIDS brought to mind. The importance of each word was shown by its font size and color. Prominent in the word cloud were: awareness, cure, education, hope, pain, prevention, protection, research, stigma, suffering, and understanding.

Credible spokesperson avatars

This group of event planners first had to become familiar with Second Life and with their avatars. They had to learn how to walk, fly, communicate with others, purchase items, and modify their self-images so that they did not look or act like participants who are new to Second Life, often called *newbies*, who are frequently discounted or ignored by other Second Life participants. Once group members had developed sophisticated looking avatars and the ability to engage in activities, they began exploring Second Life. The purpose of this exploration was two-fold: to develop an understanding of the activities that attract participants to events, and to create a network of friends who might be interested in participating in the World AIDS Day event. The idea behind developing these lists of participants to invite was not to build an event participation list, but to build a potential cascading snowball effect for event participation. Second Life allows participants to view the locations where large numbers of avatars are gathered. Built on the principle that people go where people are, in the expectation that a large group means something worth visiting, the idea was to build an exciting place to visit, attract a core group of participants who might then invite friends to join them, and through this initial concentration in avatar numbers create an event that would attract the attention of larger numbers of curious strangers (Bloomfield, 2009).

Presence

Create visually attractive spaces

The group built two visually attractive virtual locations. Each location had participant activities and clearly identified teleport stations to provide links for participants to travel easily between them. Each location also provided teleport links to the HIV model and to the two-story building housing the Bronx AIDS Services with its plethora of HIV and AIDS prevention information.

The first location contained two installations, The first housed a tunnel constructed with several branches of HIV/AIDS information. One branch of the tunnel included information on the history of AIDS in the United States. Another branch held AIDS awareness tips for prevention. A third branch contained facts specific to the AIDS epidemic in Africa and more general information on AIDS around the world. Participants could walk inside the interestingly lit tunnel and proceed through one or all three of the branches. The second installation at this location was a two-story, open-air dance hall with a flashing color-tile floor, a disco dance ball, a small bar upstairs, and lots of room to dance to live-streamed disc-jockey music. Teleport stations were located at the ends of each tunnel branch, and on both floors of the dance hall, to facilitate participant navigation between the tunnel, the dance hall, and to the other locations of interest.

The second location contained a large quilt, designed after the AIDS quilt, containing personal stories of people in Second Life with AIDS mounted on its panels. Participants could walk along the panels to view the stories. This location also included an art gallery with paintings, jewelry, and sculptures created by Second Life artists. These were on display and listed for sale, with the artists pledging a portion of their sale profits to the event.

Active, immersive experiences

The information tunnel, AIDS quilt, art gallery, and links to the HIV virus model and AIDS prevention information all provided participant experiences designed to engage attention and activity. The dance hall created an active experience and was designed as part of the overall strategy to get participants involved. The use of pictures and other graphics in the tunnel, site signage, red-ribbon symbolism, and teleport stations that eased travel around the sites, created a sense of presence for the site as a whole and facilitated participant thinking about HIV and AIDS. Donation boxes textured with the word cloud were prominently displayed at strategic locations around the site and became a part of the larger immersive experience.

Interactivity

Full-avatar-body events are important

In addition to the activities, special items of clothing – tee-shirts, tank tops, and wearable red ribbons – were designed to give to each visitor. These pieces of clothing included tucked and un-tucked versions of men's T-shirts saying "Celebrate Life: World AIDS Day," and women's tank tops saying "Lead the Fight", and T-shirts and tank tops displaying red ribbons on the front. Each of these items was available in multiple colors and was offered to participants upon arrival, on the dance floor, and after a donation was made. In addition to walking through the tunnel, interacting with the quilt, viewing the art, and dancing, these pieces of clothing created the potential for a participant to have a full-avatar-body experience.

Proactively encourage and involve participants

On arrival participants were proactively engaged by a greeter who offered them a T-shirt or tank top to wear and who described the different events. Avatar-greeters on the dance floor encouraged participants to dance and offered another piece of clothing. The donation boxes posted the name of the most recent donor and the name of the current largest donor over the top of the box. For each new donation, a greeter publicly thanked the donor by avatar name and offered the donor another clothing item. The clothing cost little to produce and was relatively easy to modify. The idea behind creating the large selection of clothes was to encourage participants to strive toward collecting as many items as possible, thus involving participants in visiting, dancing, and donating. Participants not only wore the shirts, T-shirts, and tank tops during the event, but also wore them when they left, advertising the event across Second Life.

Virtual Community

Build a "word-of-mouth" network

Prior to the event, planners built word-of-mouth networks. On the day of the event, the planners sent notices of the event to their lists of friends, provided notices for the disc jockeys to send to their followers, and sent notices to other Second Life nonprofit organizations to send to their members. Using these multiple word-of-mouth networks helped stimulate interest and participation in the events on the day.

Symbolic, visual social identity

The symbolic identity created by prominently displaying red ribbons and the links to existing AIDS groups connected this Second Life event to real-life organizations, symbols, and themes and that helped develop its online reputation. The design of the sites, planned activities, and symbolic clothing worn at the event created a sense of group presence and immediacy. The avatar-greeters who invited participants to dance, offered gifts of clothing, recognized donations, and encouraged interactivity and involvement. Together, as participants gathered and danced wearing themed T-shirts the sense of a virtual community of avatars dressed alike, moving in rhythm, and having a singular purpose emerged.

The attractiveness of the activities, outgoing friendliness of the spokesperson avatars, and emergent energy of the group created a desire to participate and be part of this virtual community and cause. More than 500 participants attended and the event raised approximately $900. Although this group of 30 trainees did not create a major fund-raising event in Second Life, they did raise awareness and the event offered a good opportunity for trainees to consider the preparation processes, participation procedures, event challenges, and organizational opportunities of using virtual world events as part of their overall public relations strategies. To stage a truly successful event a longer-term organizational presence would need to be created in Second Life and, as shown by the American Cancer Society example at the beginning of this chapter, promoted over time. Hosting the same event annually over several years helps create an online presence and reputation.

Discussion

Second Life provides a visual, textual, and audio communication medium that holds public relations awareness and fund-raising potential. However, developing an online reputation, presence, interactivity, and virtual community are necessary prerequisites to establishing a truly successful public relations event in Second Life. These characteristics interact to build identity and participation among members of a self-defined virtual community. Preparation is important: creating an online reputation, constructing visually attractive and easily navigated spaces, planning full-avatar-body events, and creating word-of-mouth networks make successful events possible. Participation builds upon that preparation with credible (knowledgeable, trustworthy, attractive, friendly) avatars acting as spokespeople who involve participants in an active, immersive experience, proactively involve them in interaction, and offer them symbolic personal identities within a desirable, and now desired, virtual community.

An online reputation is built by carefully selecting pre-existing Second Life and real-world images, symbols, and organizations with which to be associated, and by developing credible spokesperson avatars. Yet, in a world where everyone can look exactly as they wish, a credible spokesperson avatar must provide an authentic portrayal of the person and organization represented. The time and effort spent embodying oneself in an avatar becomes important, not to look like a newbie, be too plain or too outrageous, but be crafted with a professional demeanor within the cultural expectations of Second Life.

Presence is created in visually attractive spaces in Second Life. Building an attractive space takes time and talent and Second Life is full of beautiful places to visit. To attract visitors a new space must be aesthetically pleasing, unique in some way, and linked to a network of existing, appropriately-themed sites. The new site must facilitate engagement in active, immersive experiences. This requires an overall site design that includes the buildings, appearance of spokesperson avatars, teleport stations, signage, choice of participant clothing gifts, and appropriate interactive events.

Interactivity is best developed by offering a spectrum of events, from the common to the unique. Dancing is a common event in Second Life. Most Second Life participants have learned the technical aspects of how to animate their avatars by touching the dance ball, and understand the social courtesies of dancing, such as when it is appropriate to join others in a line dance or in couples dancing, and when to stand and chat. More unique animated events may require clear, straightforward directions for participation. A spokesperson avatar can proactively encourage and involve participants in activities and events, but discussions of the purpose of the event are more meaningful than repeated instructions on how to engage in activities.

A virtual community develops through a word-of-mouth network and by doing things together over time. It takes longer than the six weeks allotted to this training project to develop an authentic community. Linking into pre-existing social networks, such as the disc jockeys or the already established groups, can help, but at least six months to a year spent in Second Life should be allowed to develop a social network and reputation.

Public relations in Second Life is a full-bodied avatar sport of active engagement and participation in a virtual community with its visual symbols, social meanings, and identities. Once established, the four aspects of online reputation, social presence, interactivity, and virtual community can create opportunities for public relations awareness and fund raising in both the virtual and real worlds of an organization. However, each of these aspects takes careful preparation and engaged participation to develop.

References

Aymerich-Franch, L. (2010). Presence and emotions in playing a group game in a virtual environment: The influence of body participation. *Cyberpsychology, Behavior, and Social Networking, 13*(6), 649–654.

Bente, G., Ruggenberg, S., Kramer, N. C., & Eschenburg, F. (2008). Avatar-mediated networking: Increasing social presence and interpersonal trust in net-based collaborations. *Human Communication Research, 34*, 287–318.

Biocca, F. (1997). The cyborg's dilemma: Progressive embodiment in virtual environments. *Journal of Computer-Mediated Communication, 3*(2). Retrieved from http://www.ascusc.org/jcmc/vol3/issue2/biocca2.html

Biocca, F., Harms, C., & Burgoon, J. K. (2003). Toward a more robust theory and measure of social presence: Review and suggested criteria. *Presence, 12*(5), 456–480.

Blascovich, J., Loomis, J., Beall, A., Swinth, K., Hoyt, C., & Bailenson, J. (2002). Immersive virtual environment technology as a methodological tool for social psychology. *Psychology Inquiry, 13*, 103–124.

Bloomfield, R. (2009). World of Bizcraft. *Journal of Virtual Worlds Research, 2*(3).

Boras, S. D. (2009, February). *Lost in translation: Regulation of the situated self in an age of digital discourse.* Paper presented at the annual meeting of the Western States Communication Association Convention, Phoenix, AZ.

Cere, J. (June 5, 2007). A second look at Second Life. *Marketing Profs.* Retrieved from   http://www.marketingprofs.com/articles/2007/2378/a-second-look-at-second-life

Chen, C. C., Shih, D. H., Chiang, H. S., & Lin, C. H. (2010). An empirical study of blog marketing based on trust and purchase intention. *International Review on Computers and Software, 5*(1), 97–105.

Ciarallo, J. (2010). It's official: Second Life is dead, for PR at least. *PRNewser.* Retrieved from http://www.mediabistro.com/prnewser/its-official-second-life-is-dead-for-pr-at-least_b3782

Daugherty, T., Gangadharbatla, H., & Bright, L. (2010). Telepresence and persuasion. In C. C. Bracken & P. Skalski (Eds.), *Immersed in media: Telepresence in everyday life* (pp. 113–136). New York, NY: Routledge.

Dumrongsiri, A. (2010). Impact of electronic word-of-mouth to consumer adoption process in the online discussion forum: A simulation study. *World Academy of Science, Engineering and Technology, 65*, 180–189.

Fägersten, K. (2010). Using discourse analysis to assess social copresence in the video conference environment. In L. Shedletsky & J. E. Aitken (Eds.),

Cases in online discussion and interaction: Experiences and outcomes (pp. 175–193). Hershey, PA: IGI Global.

Freeman, J., Lessiter, J., & Ijsselsteijn, W. (2001). An introduction to presence: A sense of being there in a mediated environment. *The Psychologist, 14,* 190–194.

Gefen, D., Karahanna, E., & Straub, D. (2003). Trust and TAM in online shopping: An integrated model. *MIS Quarterly, 27*(1), 51–90.

Gouveia, V. V., de Albuquerque, J. B., Clemente, M., & Espinosa, P. (2002). Human values and social identities: A study in two collectivist cultures. *International Journal of Psychology, 37*(6), 333–342.

Green-Hamann, S., Eichhorn K. C., & Sherblom J. C. (2011). An exploration of why people participate in Second Life social support groups. *Journal of Computer-Mediated Communication, 16,* 465–491.

Hassanein, K., & Head, M. (2006). The impact of infusing social presence in the web interface: An investigation across different products. *International Journal of Electronic Commerce, 10*(2), 31–55.

Jarmon, L. (2009). An ecology of embodied interaction: Pedagogy and homo virtualis. *Journal of Virtual Worlds Research, 2*(1). Retrieved from http://jvwresearch.org

Jin, S. A. (2009). Modality effects in Second Life: The mediating role of social presence and the moderating role of product involvement. *Cyberpsychology & Behavior, 12*(6), 717–721.

Jin, S. A., & Bolebruch, J. (2009). Avatar-based advertising in Second Life: The role of presence and attractiveness of virtual spokespersons. *Journal of Interactive Advertising, 10*(1), 51–60.

Jin, S. A., & Bolebruch, J. (2010). Virtual commerce (v-commerce) in Second Life: The roles of physical presence and brand-self connection. *Journal of Virtual Worlds Research, 2*(4). Retrieved from http://journals.tdl.org/jvwr/article/view/867

Koles, B., & Nagy, P. (2012). Who is portrayed in Second Life: Dr. Jekyll or Mr. Hyde? The extent of congruence between real life and virtual identity. *Journal of Virtual Worlds Research, 5*(1). Retrieved from http://journals.tdl.org/jvwr/issue/view/254

Kumar, S., Chhugani, J., Kim, C., Kim, D., Nguyen, A., Dubey, P., Bienia, C., & Kim, Y. (2008). Second Life and the new generation of virtual worlds. *Computer, 41*(9), 48–55.

Lee, K. M. (2004). Presence, explicated. *Communication Theory, 14*(1), 27–50.

Li, H., Daugherty, T., & Biocca, F. (2002). Impact of 3-D advertising on product knowledge, brand attitude, and purchase intention: The mediating role of presence. *Journal of Advertising, 31*(3), 43–58.

Lombard, M., & Ditton, T. (1997). At the heart of it all: The concept of presence. *Journal of Computer-Mediated Communication, 3*(2). Retrieved from http://jcmc.indiana.edu/vol3/issue2/lombard.html

Martin, J. (2008). Consuming Code: Use-value, exchange-value, and the role of virtual goods in Second Life. *Journal of Virtual Worlds Research, 1*(2). Retrieved from http://journals.tdl.org/jvwr/article/view/300

Monberg, J. (2005). Trajectories of computer-mediated communication research. *Southern Communication Journal, 70*(3), 181–186.

Morris, S., & Horrigan, J. B. (2005). Relief donations after Hurricanes Katrina and Rita and use of the internet to get disaster news. Retrieved from http//:pewinternet.org/Reports/2005/13-million-Americans-made-donations-online-after-Hurricanes-Katrina-and-Rita.aspx

Nikolaou, I., Bettany, S., & Larsen, G. (2010). Brands and consumption in virtual worlds. *Journal of Virtual Worlds Research, 2*(5). Retrieved from http://journals.tdl.org/jvwr/article/view/845/711

Nowak, K. (2001). *Defining and differentiating co-presence, social presence and presence as transportation.* Paper presented at the annual meeting of Presence, Philadelphia, PA. Retrieved from http://citeseerx.ist.psu.edu/viewdoc/summary?doi=10.1.1.19.5482

Nowak, K., & Biocca, F. (2003). The effect of the agency and anthropomorphism on users' sense of telepresence, copresence, and social presence in virtual environments. *Presence, 12*(5), 481–494.

Orange, E. (2011, July–August). Augmented, anonymous, accountable: The emerging digital lifestyle. *The Futurist, 45*(4), 37–41.

Pizarro, N. (2007). Structural identity and equivalence of individuals in social networks. *International Sociology, 22*(6), 767–792.

Purcell, K., & Dimock, M. (2011, March 23). *Americans under age 40 are as likely to donate to Japan disaster relief through electronic means as traditional means.* Retrieved from http://pewinternet.org/Reports/2011/Japan-Donations.aspx

Relay for Life of Second Life. (2012). Retrieved from http://wiki.secondlife.com/wiki/ relay_for_life_of_second_life#history_of_relay_for_life

Sherblom, J. C. (2010). The computer-mediated communication (CMC) classroom: A challenge of medium, presence, interaction, identity, and relationship. *Communication Education, 59*(4), 497–523.

Sherblom, J. C., Withers, L. A., & Leonard, L. G. (2009). Communication challenges and opportunities for educators using Second Life. In C. Wankel & J. Kingsley (Eds.), *Higher education in virtual worlds: Teaching and learning in Second Life* (pp. 29–46). Bingley, UK: Emerald.

Skalski, P., & Tamborini, R. (2007). The role of social presence in interactive agent-based persuasion. *Media Psychology, 10*(3), 385–413.

Smith, A. (2012). *Why mobile phone users texted millions of dollars in aid to Haiti earthquake relief and how they got their friends to do the same.* Retrieved from http://pewinternet.org/Reports/2012/mobilegiving.aspx

Smith, P. R., & Zook, Z. (2011). *Marketing Communications.* Philadelphia, PA: Kogan Page.

Swinth, K., & Blascovich, J. (2001). *Conformity to group norms in an immersive virtual environment.* Paper presented at the annual meeting of the American Psychological Society, Toronto, Ontario.

Taylor, P. G. (2009). Can we move beyond visual metaphors? Virtual world provocations and Second Life. *Journal of Virtual Worlds Research, 2*(1). Retrieved from http://jvwresearch.org

Text 100. (2006). *Global public relations.* Retrieved from http://www.text100.com/media/ press-releases/text-100-opens-first-public-relations-office-second-life-aedhmar-hynes

USC Annenberg School for Communication and Journalism. (2010). *Communications and public relations general accepted practices report 3: Areas of responsibility, digital/social media, evaluation.* Retrieved from http://ascjweb.org/gapstudy/

Waisbord, S. (1998). When the cart of media is before the horse of identity: A critique of technology-centered views on globalization. *Communication Research, 25*(4), 377–398.

Walther, J. B., Slovacek, C. L., & Tidwell, L. C. (2001). Is a picture worth a thousand words? *Communication Research, 28*(1), 105–134.

Waters, R., Burnett, E., Lamm, A., & Lucas, J. (2009). Engaging stakeholders through social networking: How nonprofit organizations are using Facebook. *Public Relations Review, 35*(2), 102–106.

Westerman, D., & Skalski, P. (2010). Computers and telepresence. In C. C. Bracken & P. Skalski (Eds.), *Immersed in media: Telepresence in everyday life* (pp. 63–86). New York, NY: Routledge.

Williams, M. (2007). Avatar watching: Participant observation in graphical online environments. *Qualitative Research, 7*(1), 5–24.

Willson, M. A. (2006). *Technically together: Rethinking community within techno-society.* New York, NY: Peter Lang.

Wood, N. T. (2011). *Marketing in virtual worlds.* Boston, MA: Prentice Hall.

Yildiz, S. (2009). Social presence in the web-based classroom: Implications for intercultural communication. *Journal of Studies in International Education, 13*(1), 46–65.

Yin, R. K. (1994). *Case study research: Design and methods* (2nd ed.). Thousand Oaks, CA: Sage.

Part III

Social Media Policies/Practices and Legal/Ethical Considerations

9
Organizational Social Media Policies and Best Practice Recommendations

Melissa D. Dodd and Don W. Stacks

Ellen Simonetti, or the Queen of the Sky, began blogging as a method of therapy following her mother's death in 2003. As a Delta flight attendant, Simonetti typically blogged about her travels, offering practical travel advice; however, one day, Simonetti posted seductive photos of herself posing in her uniform on a grounded plane. Although she never provided her last name or that of the airline, was off-duty when the photos were taken, and Delta had no policy regarding such matters, Simonetti was terminated (Simonetti, 2004). She subsequently made appearances on *The Today Show* and filed suit against Delta in 2005. This very public case is considered one of the first controversial instances of employee social media use. Nearly a decade later, it would be expected that most organizations have implemented clear social media policies; however, this does not seem to be the case as evidenced by a 2011 YouTube video by Starbucks barista Christopher Cristwell. In the video, Cristwell sings about the finicky Starbucks customers wearing only his apron and underwear (Cristwell, 2011). Further, a 2010 study by Manpower found that 75% of employers (of the 34,400 responses worldwide) say their organizations do not have formal policies regarding social media.

Organizations today are faced with widespread social media (SM) use among both the external public as well as employees internal to the organization. For example, research found that 8% of Internet users, approximately 12 million American adults, maintain a blog, and approximately 57 million American adults read blogs (Lenhart & Fox, 2006), and a report from Weber Shandwick (2009) notes that there are more than 20 million people on Twitter in the U.S., and 50 million worldwide. Moreover, according to TechCrunch (2009), Twitter acquires 18 million new users each year, and more than 4 million tweets are posted daily. Social media such as Facebook and LinkedIn have become some of the fastest growing forms of SM. Facebook recently celebrated reaching 400 million members internationally (Dybwad, 2010), and it is estimated that one new member joins LinkedIn every second (Marketing Charts, 2010). Similarly, video-hosting sites such as YouTube have experienced increased popularity in recent years. Approximately 63 million people, 16 million of whom are from the U.S., view videos in a single month on YouTube (comScore, 2006).

Strategic communication professionals were quickly identified as those most capable of managing SM due to their existing expertise in communication, public and media relations. Public relations professionals in particular are using and managing SM on behalf of their organizations, as evidenced by the overwhelming amount of practical and scholarly publications that are easily found across these disciplines. For example, a simple search of books on Amazon with the keywords public relations and social media returned more than 2,300 results, 1,100 of which were categorized as "professional & technical" by Amazon. Wright & Hinson (2009b) note the importance that public relations professionals place on SM for their organizations. The authors found significant gaps between the importance professionals indicated organizations were placing on the various SM and the importance professionals believed *should* be placed on SM. Relatedly, Dodd & Campbell (2011a, 2011b) sought to longitudinally compare the results of Wright & Hinson's (2009a) research to the expectations of the Millennial Generation, that is those born between the years 1982 and 2001 (Wellner, 2000; Almash, 2000), who not only represent 27% of the U.S. population (81.1 million), but are also those most likely to use SM (Tapscott, 2009). In both studies Dodd & Campbell concluded that in comparison to the expectations of Millennials regarding organizational communication via SM, what public relations professionals believed *should* be occurring with their organization's (or clients') SM use did not show significant differences for the majority of expectations by Millennials. On the other hand, and similar to the conclusions of Wright & Hinson (2009a), significant gaps existed between Millennials' expectations and what practitioners indicated was happening in actuality for organizational SM use.

Clearly, then, strategic communicators have sought to embrace SM on behalf of their organizations both out of necessity for bottom-line objectives, and also due to the voice and subsequent power SM has provided for constituencies. This is not surprising in that communication via

SM has the potential to impact a number of public relations outcomes important to organizations (e.g., relationship, reputation, trust, goodwill, credibility, confidence, and so on) (Stacks, 2011). Wright & Hinson (2009a) found that across one year, agreement as to whether or not SM had impacted internal communications grew from 38% in 2008 to 45% in 2009. Elving (2005) suggested that, "applications emerging from this new technology offer a wide range of opportunities for reaching two of the main goals of internal communication: (a) communication to inform and (b) communication aimed at creating a community" (Friedl & Vercic, 2011, p. 84). Recent research by Supa & Kelly (2012) reviewed the SM policies of 26 higher education institutions, concluding that half ($n = 13$) of the policies were administered by marketing, communications, public affairs, or university relations departments, and 12% by an interdepartmental task force ($n = 3$). Additional research by Wright & Hinson (2009a) revealed that public relations professionals are steadily implementing research and measurement surrounding employees communications via blogs, with the following data indicative of such initiatives across four years: 3% in 2006, 11% in 2007, 15% in 2008, and 25% in 2009.

Additionally, there are potential legal ramifications for SM use. As Terilli, Driscoll, & Stacks (2008) note, "the role and scope of commercially driven Internet activity continues to grow as businesses and their public relations firms enter the Internet Age and advocate their positions through the Internet and specifically blogs" (p. 1). In particular, they focused on the classification of corporate reflective blogs and the likelihood that SM use by employees (either official or personal) facilitates the likelihood of legal action from lower to higher. They point in particular to the travails of Edelman Public Relations Worldwide in their use of blogging for two clients: Wal-Mart and Microsoft (as in Terilli et al., 2008; Are Freebies, 2007; O'Brien, 2007; Nolan, 2006; Sullivan, 2006). Adding to this controversy, Gordon & Franklin (2006) noted that "[no] laws specifically regulate "blogging," and there is virtually no case law to provide guidance". In the analysis by Terilli et al. (2008), it is recommended that the use of Twitter and YouTube meet the same legal standards as blogs. In all instances, where an employee is blogging, tweeting, or uploading to YouTube, the organization must have a policy set forth that clearly delineates intended use of SM, on and off the job.

So, what is the state of Internet law? Recent legislation attempts have been made, but have not met with much success. For example, the United States House of Representatives recently rejected an amendment to give the Federal Communications Commission the power to stop employers from requesting passwords for personal SM from job applicants (Purewal, 2012). In the absence of such laws, then, the importance of organizational policies becomes even greater, and it would appear that various organizational (namely, corporate) policies currently stand in as legal recourse to SM mistakes. However, such policies, as noted earlier, are neither widely employed nor are they well-discussed.

It is important to note here that strategic communication among the internal public has long been the domain of public relations professionals, and as such, the public relations professional appears to be the most qualified to address SM policy among employees. That is not to say that other departments should not play a significant role in the process, but rather to note the expertise of the public relations professional in this capacity; that is, in regards to communication, SM, and employee relations. Perhaps, then, it can be posited that the lack of existing organizational SM policies (Manpower, 2010) or the ineffectiveness of some policies, stems from a lack of knowledge or guidance on behalf of organizational leadership in deciding who should be involved in the creation and administration of such policies, and/or a lack of overall importance prescribed to such policies. Many practical articles exist on this subject (Black, 2010; Dishman, 2010; Lauby, 2009; Pick, 2010); however, most are superficially brief discussions (blog posts) at best. Similarly, several online directories of existing SM policies exist for reference by professionals; however, these directories offer little in terms of guidance for organizational creation or implementation. Turning to scholarship in the area, there is little academic research, aside from the aforementioned, that seeks to address internal SM use, let alone policy. Thus, the current research seeks to fill this gap through an in-depth examination of existing organizational SM policies and an offering of best practice for the construction and implementation of organizational SM policies, encouraging future research in the area. The following research questions were used to guide this examination of existing organizational social media policies:

RQ1: What themes are prevalent among the organizational social media policies examined in this research?

RQ2: How do the social media policies examined demonstrate the inclusion or exclusion of public relations concepts related to internal communication?

Method

To answer these questions, an in-depth reading and content analysis of existing organizational SM policies aimed at internal audiences was conducted to identify themes and facilitate a discussion of best practice. A broad list of existing and freely available SM policies was downloaded from ComplianceBuilding.com, a blog managed by lawyer Doug Cornelius on compliance and business ethics. The site has been honored by LexisNexis as one of the Top 25 Blogs, 2010 in the category of business law. At the time of this research, ComplianceBuilding.com contained web links to 236 SM policies that met the criteria of being freely available online via the site. The researchers crosschecked with other online directories of SM policies, and found this list to be the most comprehensive. Therefore, the Compliance Building list was used because not only was it freely available, but it was also found to be the most comprehensive of those identified by the researchers. The directory included corporate, nonprofit, and government listings as well as media, education, health, and religious organizations (as categorized by the site's author). It is important to note here that it is possible that: (a) the directory could have omitted many policies, so the researchers conducted primary research and made five additions to the list; and, (b) many organizations do have private SM policies, not available to the public, and thus, these organizations were not included in the final sample ($n = 241$). However, the Manpower (2010) study indicates that a majority of organizations do not have formal policies in place. From the directory, the researchers determined that 15 policies from each category (corporate, nonprofit, and government) would comprise the sample for this study. Thus, the directory was randomized, and the researchers selected the first 15 for each category from the list. Policies that were aimed at external audiences (e.g., Bank of America has Community Guidelines for external customers) were skipped as this study is concerned primarily with employees, members, or volunteers. Further, universities comprised a large portion of the overall list 12% ($n = 28$), so the researchers categorized publicly funded universities as government organizations, and privately funded universities as corporate organizations.

Of the 45 organizations, 19% of the total directory used in this study, the following demographic variables resulted: 16 organizations (36%) had international operations, and the remaining 29 organizations (64%) had operations at a national or local level. Organizations were subcategorized within industries as follows: education 17%; professional services 9%; religious 9%; healthcare 9%; retail 9%; charity 7%; technology

7%; youth organizations 7%; federal government 7%; state government 4%; city government 4%; county government 4%; activist 2%; advisory committee 2%; manufacturing 2%; and media 2%. One organization was subcategorized as both professional services and retail as there was no primary emphasis on either. Organizations were further categorized within the respective corporate, nonprofit, and government categories used in this study.

Corporate. Organizations were subcategorized by industry as follows, with the percentage reflecting the category only ($n = 15$): professional services 27%; retail 27%; technology 20%; education 13%; healthcare 7%; media 7%; and manufacturing 7%. One organization was subcategorized as both professional services and retail as there was no primary emphasis on either.

Nonprofit. Organizations were subcategorized by industry as follows, with the percentage reflecting category only ($n = 15$): religious 27%; healthcare 20%; charity 20%; youth organization 20%; activist 7%; and advisory committee 7%.

Government. Organizations were subcategorized by industry as follows, with the percentage reflecting category only ($n = 15$): education 40%; federal 20%; state 13%; city 13%; and county 13%.

The researchers further performed primary research to determine approximately how many internal audience members (employees/volunteers/members, as applicable, and hereafter referred to as employees) the SM policies were likely to reach. In calculating these data, estimates made were conservative. For example, in calculating the internal audience of organizations reporting membership, only the number of locals was included (as opposed to the number of total members, for example). Further, an outlier of one million volunteers was removed. As a result, the average number of internal audience members of the 45 organizations used in this research was 50,031 (minimum = 7, maximum = 426,751). It should be noted here that although estimates were conservative, the researchers did not (could not) determine to whom SM policies were actually distributed, and it is possible that organizations only distributed policies to upper-level employees, which would greatly reduce the average. However, this average is important in understanding the size of organization used in this study. Most of them have thousands of employees, and as a result, would be classified as large organizations. The researchers also performed primary research to understand the revenues/endowments/budgets of the organizations used in this research. All were in the millions, and most were in the billions.

Results

Across this qualitative examination of SM policies, 12 policy themes emerged that were used to analyze how the SM were defined, implemented, and managed. Further, six public relations concepts emerged from the themes. Data were analyzed in order to determine whether the theme or concept was included in the SM policy and, if so, it was then examined as to whether it was implicitly or explicitly stated.

Table 9.1 presents the findings as collapsed across classifications (corporate, governmental, and nonprofit, *n* = 45). In terms of the policy

Table 9.1 Social media policy themes and public relations concepts: across classifications

Theme	Included in policy statement		Not included in policy statement
Policy themes	Explicit	Implicit	
Social media defined	36	0	9
Specific personnel identified	15	4	26
Personal vs. organization use	37	1	7
Mission/vision/values/objectives	15	6	24
Branding (copy-right/trademark)	32	1	12
Ownership of content	27	3	15
Prohibited content	41	0	4
Privacy	40	0	5
Personal use	30	4	11
Management	25	0	20
How-to information	10	5	30
Monitoring	18	4	23
Evaluation	8	3	34
Legal	21	0	24
On-the-job use	17	2	26
Disciplinary actions	17	2	26
Public relations concepts			
Reputation	21	16	8
Trust	11	10	24
Ethics	34	1	10
Transparency	29	10	6
Honesty/accuracy	24	5	16
Dialogue	22	8	15
Relationship	16	11	18
Empowerment	7	12	26

Note: n = 45.

themes, all themes were found in the sample of SM policies. Of those found in the policy statements, most were explicitly stated. Interestingly, the themes that were *not* found in the majority of policy statements dealt with on-the-job usage policy, disciplinary actions policy, and SM management components to include how to create and implement, monitor, and evaluate SM as well as the legalities related to such efforts. In terms of the public relations concepts found in the SM policies, reputation, ethics (transparency and honesty/accuracy), dialogue, and relationships with stake/stockholders were included in the majority. Only trust and employee empowerment were not included in the majority of policy statements. For trust, the number included was almost evenly split between explicit statements and those that were determined to be implicit in the policy. For employee empowerment, the content was more inclined to be specified implicitly.

There were some differences in themes that are worthy of note among the three classifications of corporate, governmental, and nonprofit institutions (n = 15 each). As demonstrated in Tables 9.2 through 9.4, the major difference in policy themes that arose between classifications was found between the nonprofit and corporate/governmental institutions. For nonprofits, seven themes were not included in their SM policies, as compared to two in the other classifications. The majority of nonprofit themes not included dealt more with ownership, management, operational, and personal use themes. For nonprofits, almost all themes were explicitly stated. This held true for the other two classifications as well.

The analysis of policy statements for public relations concepts yielded similar findings. Once again, the nonprofits included fewer public relations concepts in their SM policies, with three – trust, honesty/accuracy, and empowerment – found less often (see Table 9.4). Where found, however, most public relations concepts were explicitly stated. With the exception of employee empowerment, the corporate institutions' inclusions were more explicitly than implicitly stated (see Table 9.2). Interestingly, for governmental institutions all public relations concepts were included, with a mix stated explicitly and implicitly (see Table 9.3).

Specifically, the majority of government organizations identified the personnel responsible for organizational SM, whereas the majority of corporate and nonprofit organizations did not. Likewise, government organizations explicated the management of SM policies to include how-to, monitoring, and evaluation information whereas corporate

Table 9.2 Social media policy themes and public relations concepts: corporate

Theme	Included in policy statement		Not included in policy statement
Policy themes	Explicit	Implicit	
Social media defined	13	0	2
Specific personnel identified	7	0	8
Personal vs. organization use	11	0	4
Mission/vision/values/objectives	8	0	7
Branding (copy-right/trademark)	9	0	6
Ownership of content	14	0	1
Prohibited content	14	0	1
Privacy	14	0	1
Personal use	14	0	1
Management	6	0	9
How-to information	3	0	12
Monitoring	6	0	9
Evaluation	2	0	13
Legal	11	0	4
On-the-job use	7	0	8
Disciplinary actions	7	1	7
Public relations concepts			
Reputation	7	6	2
Trust	8	0	7
Ethics	11	1	3
Transparency	11	3	1
Honesty/accuracy	10	0	5
Dialogue	9	1	5
Relationship	5	2	8
Empowerment	4	1	10

Note: $n = 15$.

and nonprofit policies did not. In regards to public relations concepts, government organizations identified the theme of relationship in the majority of policies whereas this concept was not present in the majority of policies for corporate and nonprofit organizations.

For the identification of mission/vision/values/objectives, the majority of corporate policies identified how such things were relevant to SM, whereas nonprofit and government organizations did not. Likewise, the majority of corporate policies identified legalities associated with SM and its management as well as disciplinary actions to be taken for

Table 9.3 Social media policy themes and public relations concepts: government

Theme	Included in policy statement		Not included in policy statement
Policy themes	Explicit	Implicit	
Social media defined	11	1	3
Specific personnel identified	5	4	6
Personal vs. organization use	13	1	1
Mission/vision/ values/objectives	1	5	9
Branding (copy- right/trademark)	12	1	2
Ownership of content	12	3	0
Prohibited content	15	0	0
Privacy	14	1	0
Personal use	11	4	0
Management	13	0	2
How-to information	5	5	5
Monitoring	7	4	4
Evaluation	5	3	7
Legal	6	0	9
On-the-job use	3	2	10
Disciplinary actions	3	1	11
Public relations concepts			
Reputation	4	9	2
Trust	2	9	4
Ethics	15	0	0
Transparency	8	7	0
Honesty/accuracy	10	5	0
Dialogue	7	7	1
Relationship	7	7	1
Empowerment	2	10	3

Note: $n = 15$.

misuse, whereas the majority of nonprofit and government organizations did not.

For the identification of ownership associated with SM content produced as well as personal use themes, the majority of government and corporate policies included this, whereas the majority of nonprofit policies did not. In regards to public relations concepts apparent in the SM policies, trust, honesty/accuracy, and dialogue were apparent in the majority of government and corporate policies, whereas the majority of nonprofit policies did not include such themes.

Table 9.4 Social media policy themes and public relations concepts: nonprofit

Theme	Included in policy statement		Not included in policy statement
Policy themes	Explicit	Implicit	
Social media defined	12	0	3
Specific personnel identified	3	0	12
Personal vs. organization use	13	0	2
Mission/vision/ values/objectives	6	1	8
Branding (copy- right/trademark)	11	0	4
Ownership of content	1	0	14
Prohibited content	12	0	3
Privacy	12	0	3
Personal use	5	0	10
Management	6	0	9
How-to information	2	0	13
Monitoring	5	0	10
Evaluation	1	0	14
Legal	4	0	11
On-the-job use	7	0	8
Disciplinary actions	7	0	8
Public relations concepts			
Reputation	10	1	4
Trust	1	1	13
Ethics	8	0	7
Transparency	10	0	5
Honesty/accuracy	4	0	11
Dialogue	6	0	9
Relationship	4	2	9
Empowerment	1	1	13

Note: *n* = 15.

Discussion

The differences that emerged among the overall themes for the three categories (corporate, government, and nonprofit) were particularly interesting when used comparatively. For example, understanding what was included in the government policies helped to understand what, perhaps, should be included in the nonprofit policies, and so on. Thus, this study proceeds to recommend the best practices that stem from the policies as a whole and may be useful despite the organizational categorization.

In order to effectively facilitate recommendations for best practice, this research developed a template for organizational SM policies (see Appendix 9.1). To begin with, however, it is important that the creation of the policy be a collaborative effort on behalf of the public relations, legal, and IT representatives. A bi-annual schedule should be created for updates/revisions to the policy among this team, and it is further recommended that employee sign-off be obtained following the dissemination of the policy, perhaps in the form of a brief survey that indicates understanding. A detailed description, inclusive of quotes used in policies in this study, is discussed as follows.

Section One: Summary, purpose, and scope. The policy should begin with an endorsement from the organization's leadership both formally as well as through the writing of a summary letter that can be used as the executive summary or introduction to the policy. So, for example, a one-page summary of the policy in the form of a letter from the CEO adds credibility and salience to the policy as a whole (Kodak, 2009). Next, the purpose of the policy should be outlined such that the intention of the policy is not to stifle personal expression or limit the rights of employees. Rather, the purpose of the policy is in explicitly empowering and encouraging employee SM use while simultaneously setting forth guidelines to protect the organization's reputation. For example, "These Online Social Media Principles have been developed to help empower our associates to participate in this new frontier of communications, represent our Company, and share the optimistic and positive spirits of our brands" (Coca-Cola Company, 2009, p. 1). Additionally, inclusion of the scope of the policy is appropriate here; that is, to whom the policy specifically applies. For example, "B&D Personnel means all partners, principals, attorneys, professionals, paralegals, staff members, interns and temporary employees of B&D" (Baker & Daniels Consulting, 2011, p. 1). An important component of the scope should also be in detailing whether the policy applies only to official organizational or also to personal SM accounts (or both). So, for example:

> In general, what you do on your own time is your affair. However, activities in or outside of work that affect your IBM job performance, the performance of others, or IBM's business interests are a proper focus for company policy.... When the company wishes to communicate publicly as a company – whether to the marketplace or to the general public – it has well established means to do so. Only those officially designated by IBM have authorization to speak on behalf of the company. (IBM, 2010, Detailed Discussion section, para. 2)

Section Two: Introduction to social media, its use and the organization's expectations. This section should first seek to define SM and describe major types and/or platforms. The researchers recommend blogs, Facebook, Twitter, and YouTube; however, the policy should further note that it covers other SM not described at length, and as SM is an ever-changing tool, the policy will be updated regularly but also extends to cover new and emerging SM (e.g., YMCA, 2010).

Of utmost importance for this section is differentiating personal versus organizational SM accounts (as noted in the scope of the policy). The University of Michigan (2010), for example, provides general, personal, and official use guidelines. Personal SM accounts are those private accounts of individuals associated with the organization, whereas organizational accounts are those SM accounts maintained by personnel authorized to speak on behalf of the organization. If there are particular personnel or departments assigned to organizational SM accounts, they should be noted in this section with contact information. If an employee receives a request from the media, list to whom they should forward such requests. Employees who are using personal accounts, but have publicly affiliated themselves or may be perceived as a spokesperson for the organization should include a disclaimer statement: "The views and opinions expressed here are my own." Additionally, technical distinctions among major platforms can be made in this section (e.g., a Facebook Fan Page and verified Twitter handle are used for organizational accounts, and a Facebook Group or Profile is intended for small groups of friends or colleagues and individuals, respectively). Best practice across platforms should be referenced here, such that they are included in *Section Three: Management of official social media accounts and you.* These best practices are applicable to both personal use of SM as well as organizational use. (e.g., Xerox, 2011).

Further, connecting SM to the overarching mission, vision, values, goals, and/or objectives of the organization is important in order that an understanding of organizational expectations of SM is achieved among employees. The organization should understand that the purpose of SM is in fostering relationships and creating community and dialogue, not in marketing to them. So, for example, "Goal: To recruit potential Girl Scouts, volunteers, and donors, and retain current Girl Scout membership...To continue to strengthen the message that we are building girls of courage, confidence, and character, who make the world a better place" (Girl Scouts, 2009, p. 1). Similarly, Coca-Cola (2009) connects the policy to organizational values that include: leadership, collaboration, integrity, accountability, passion, diversity, and quality.

Relatedly, it should be explicitly stated that personal employee use of SM can impact trust in the organization and the reputation of the organization to the public. For example,

> If you choose to identify yourself as a part of United Way (UW) or discuss matters related to UW on a personal website, social site, or blog, many readers will assume you are speaking on behalf of UW. In order to protect the reputation of UW Worldwide and the UW network, your communication must be transparent, ethical and accurate. (United Way, 2011, p. 1)

Each expectation should be further detailed for personal and official use such that the policy describes transparency, honesty/accuracy, and acting ethically via SM. In addition, it is recommended that a link to the organization's Code of Ethics/Conduct be included in the policy for further explication of what it means to act ethically as a representative of the organization both on-the-job and off. For example:

> You need to determine your own comfort level in discussing work in your personal communications. If you choose to talk about your Red Cross work via your personal online accounts, please disclose your relationship with the Red Cross and be responsible. Remember that National Headquarters Social Media Team will see all mentions of the Red Cross and may contact you to praise your discussion, invite you to contribute to our corporate online spaces, or to give you guidance about how to talk about your work responsibly. Always follow our Fundamental Principles [link included here]. (American Red Cross, 2009, Frequently Asked Questions section, para. 1)

Next, although the policy is meant to empower employees to use SM as ambassadors for the organization, it is important for organizations to explicitly mention those kinds of content that are strictly prohibited by the organization. Prohibited content can include any or all of the following: (a) official representation of the organization, (b) copyright/trademark, (c) private information, and (d) content that is disparaging toward the organization, and so on (e.g., Sears Holdings, 2009). Oftentimes, employees may use SM to vent about workplace frustrations. This section should further detail to whom, and the process by which, anonymous (or free from retribution) complaints/criticisms can be submitted.

Moreover, organizations are often concerned with security risks associated with the use of SM. For example,

> 'Loose tweets sink fleets' is a modern-day take on a classic saying that loose communication can affect [Operations Security]...When posting information online, everyone should be cognizant that your audience is likely larger than just those to whom you think you're talkin. (United States Navy Command, 2010, p. 7)

A discussion of the privacy risks and settings for SM sites is appropriate here. Additionally, the use of SM poses risks in regards to phishing, spam, malware, and so on that can compromise the security of the organization's data and operations. Collaborate with IT departments to fully explicate this section.

Finally, legal terms are an important component for any policy. Such terms may include: (a) legal responsibility for SM (personal or official); (b) organizational monitoring of SM; (c) ownership of content produced when it is branded alongside the organization (e.g., local chapters of national nonprofits); (d) rights to distribution; (e) friending/following (appropriate for conflicts of interest such as doctor-patient relationships and manager-subordinate relationships or for relationships with minors, as may be present in youth group organizations); (f) use of SM during work hours; and (g) disciplinary actions to be taken if misuse is apparent. Collaborate with legal departments to fully explicate this section based on your organization's legal policies regarding such matters.

Section 3: Management of official social media accounts and you. While this section serves primarily as a guide to those authorized employees who will be using SM in an official capacity, it offers further suggestions that can be applied to personal best practices for SM use. Thus, it is important to again note who will administer official SM accounts on behalf of the organization and provide the information for those accounts (e.g., @Organization; organization.facebook.com, etc.). It has previously been noted that public relations/communications personnel are those most qualified to perform such functions. In the case that an employee would like to create/host an account on behalf of the organization, as in the case of a local chapter of a national nonprofit, for example, procedures should be detailed as to how and from whom authorization should be obtained. These procedures should remind the employee of the time commitment and expectations of the organization in regards to managing an official account (frequency, content). It is generally recommended that the following SM be updated with each respective frequency: blogs, at least bi-monthly; Facebook, at least twice per week; Twitter, at least once each day; and, YouTube, at least monthly. Also, official SM accounts should be checked daily for comments and feedback. SM administrators should respond to content in a substantive way. For example, responses should not simply refer a user to another source but should seek to provide primary assistance.

Next, it is important for policies to describe the expectations of content posted on behalf of the organization in an official capacity, as well as when speaking about the organization via personal accounts. This is the opposite of prohibited content; rather, it is content that *should* be used. It should be explicitly noted by the policy that content should add value and initiate dialogue as well as be transparent, honest/accurate, and ethical. Specific examples of content that demonstrates these concepts can be included as well. Further, content should not only link to internal sources, but also to external sources to add credibility, but only when external sources have been investigated for transparency and accuracy that match the values of the organization.

A particularly large concern for organizational SM is in the moderation of content. If an organization makes a *mistake*, it should be immediately remedied. The original content should generally not be deleted but amended to include a statement regarding the *unfortunate error*. A discussion to this extent should be included in the policy. Some SM sites allow for settings that enable users to approve/deny comments before they appear publicly. While it is recommended that these settings not be used for official accounts, they may be recommended for personal accounts among employees or necessitated by organizational circumstances (*not* to exclude comments that are negative toward the organization; everyone is entitled to their opinions). An explanation of how to respond to negative comments should be detailed in the policy. For example, Xerox recommends the following, which is further detailed in the company's policy: "avoid public disputes," "avoid sarcasm," and "think before responding" (2011, pp. 4–5). Similarly, the organization should have clear guidelines for what content necessitates deletion from an official account. For example:

> We will moderate all comments and responses to Bread's social media. We will ensure that no spam, profanity, defamatory, inappropriate or libelous language will be posted to our sites. Neither will we use such

language when we post comments to other people's sites. (Bread for the World, 2009, Our Principles section, para. 11)

Likewise, a policy for blocking a user from an organizational SM site should be detailed.

Next, a largely neglected concept regarding organizational SM use is how the effectiveness of use should be evaluated as it pertains to organizational goals and objectives. SM evaluation metrics have become more commonplace for organizations and in many cases are provided free. For example, Facebook Fan Pages provide free "insights" to include "likes," "reach," "talking about this," and "check-ins"; free Google Analytics can easily be added to blogs to include "visits," "unique visitors," "page views," "average visit duration," and so on; and there are many existing Twitter applications that can be used to track comments, feedback, and mentions. Moreover, more advanced SM evaluation and measurement tools are available from the scholarly and professional literature (e.g., KDPaine's PR Measurement Blog, 2012). Policies should not only detail the evaluation metrics to be used, but also detail how often evaluation should be performed. It is generally recommended that evaluation be performed quarterly; however, if an organization is launching an online campaign, it is also important that benchmarks are set in advance and assessed as indicators of the overall effectiveness of the campaign.

Finally, this research recommends a concluding section that details best practices across major SM platforms (blogs, Facebook, Twitter, and YouTube). Because platforms differ in regard to the expectations of users or the culture surrounding them, there are recommendations that can be made for each. For example, it is not appropriate to post multiple times per day on Facebook; however, on Twitter, it is an expectation. There are several existing best practices available online that can be included here, but the researchers recommend the Xerox policy as a good starting point. Discussion here will only make best practice recommendations across platforms, such as "Don't blog when you're unhappy. Negative tone will come through in your writing," and also reinforce many of the aforementioned concepts (trust, reputation, relationships, ethics, transparency, honesty/accuracy, and dialogue), such as "Be yourself [on Twitter]. Losing the trust of your followers can damage a reputation" (Xerox, 2011, p. 6). As previously stated, these best practices are focused on organizational SM use; however, they also have real implications for and serve to further the organization's SM policy regarding personal use.

Appendix 9.1   Organizational Template for Social Media Policies

Section 1: Summary and introduction

I. Executive summary
II. Purpose and scope

Section 2: Social media, its use, and the organization's expectations

III. Social media defined
IV. Personal versus organizational use
V. The importance of social media use, both personal and organizational:
   a. For the organization's mission, vision, values, goals and/or objectives
   b. For its impact on trust and the reputation of the organization to the public
   c. Ethics: Code of ethics/conduct is appropriate here.
VI. Prohibited content
VII. Security concerns
VIII. Legal terms

Section 3: Management of official social media accounts and you

IX. Personnel and procedures
   a. Social media administrators
   b. Expectations of content and moderation
   c. Evaluation and measurement
X. Best practices for each major platform (blogs, Facebook, Twitter, and YouTube)

References

Almash, J. (2000). Key to marketing successfully to Gen X and Gen Y? Break all your rules. *Card News, 15*(3), 1.

American Red Cross. (2009). *Social media handbook for local Red Cross units*. Retrieved from https://docs.google.com/View?docid=df4n5v7k_216g5jdd7c8&hgd=1&pli=1

Are freebies a blogosphere taboo? (2007, January 12). *PR Week*, 18.

Baker & Daniels Consulting. (2011). *Social media policy*. Retrieved from http://www.bakerdstreamingvid.com/publications/Baker_Daniels_Social-Media-Policy.pdf

Black, T. (2010). How to write a social media policy. *Inc.* Retrieved from http://www.inc.com/guides/2010/05/writing-a-social-media-policy.html

Bread for the World. (2009). *Social media policy*. Retrieved from http://www. socialmedia.biz/social-media-policies/bread-for-the-worlds-social-media-policy/

Coca-Cola Company. (2009). *Online social media principles*. Retrieved from http://www.thecoca-colacompany.com/socialmedia/

comScore.com (2006, October 11). *comScore data confirms reports of 100 million worldwide video streams from YouTube.com in July 2006*. Retrieved from http://comscore.com/Press_Events/Press_Releases/2006/10/YouTube_Worldwide_Video_Streams/(language)/eng-US

Cristwell, C. (2011, July 20). *The Starbucks rant song* [Video file]. Retrieved from http://youtu.be/MUTrJW-0xtc

Dishman, L. (2010). Corporate social media policies: The good, the mediocre, and the ugly. *Fast Company*. Retrieved from http://www.fastcompany.com/1668368/social-media-policies-the-good-the-bad-and-the-ugly

Dodd, M. D., & Campbell, S. B. (2011a). *The strategic use of social media in managing relationships with the Net Generation*. Paper presented at the annual meeting of the International Communication Association Conference, Boston, MA.

Dodd, M. D., & Campbell, S. B. (2011b). *The strategic use of social media in managing relationships with the Net Generation: A longitudinal examination*. Paper presented at the annual meeting of the National Communication Association, New Orleans, LA.

Dybwad, B. (2010). Facebook passes 400 million user mark. *Mashable*. Retrieved from http://mashable.com/2010/02/04/facebook-400-million/

Elving, W. J. L. (2005). The role of communication in organisational change. *Corporate Communications: An International Journal, 10*(2), 129–138.

Friedl, J., & Vercic, A. T. (2011). Media preferences of digital natives' internal communication: A pilot study. *Public Relations Review, 37*(1), 84–86.

Girl Scouts of the Missouri Heartland. (2009). *Social Media Policy*. Retrieved from http://www.docstoc.com/docs/20086803/Social-Media-Guidelines

Gordon, P., & Franklin, K. (2006, November 6). *Can law firms keep the blogosphere at bay?* Retrieved from http://www.law.com/jsp/article.jsp?id=900005466205&slreturn=20130215123200

IBM. (2010). *IBM social computing guidelines*. Retrieved from http://www.ibm.com/blogs/zz/en/guidelines.html

KDPaine's PR Measurement Blog. (2012). Retrieved from http://kdpaine.blogs.com/

Kodak, Eastman. (2009). *Social media tips*. Retrieved from http://www.kodak.com/US/images/en/corp/aboutKodak/onlineToday/Kodak_SocialMediaTips_Aug14.pdf

Lauby, S. (2009). 10 must-haves for your social media policy. *Mashable*. Retrieved from http://mashable.com/2009/06/02/social-media-policy-musts/

Lenhart, A., & Fox, S. (2006). Bloggers: A portrait of the internet's new storytellers. *Pew Internet & American Life Project*. Retrieved from http://www.pewinternet.org/~/media/Files/Reports/2006/PIP%20Bloggers%20Report%20July%2019%202006.pdf.pdf

Manpower, Inc. (2010). Social networks vs. management? Harness the power of social media. *Fresh Perspectives*. Retrieved from http://files.shareholder.com/downloads/MAN/1269766382x0x346214/1a3ff810–1a69–453e-8b59–47abdd11016f/MANP_285779_WHITE_1up.pdf

Marketing Charts. (2010). 'Mass mingling' brings consumers closer together. *Marketing Charts.* Retrieved from http://www.marketingcharts.com/direct/mass-mingling-brings-consumers-closer-together-13150/

Nolan, H. (2006, October 23). Edelman acknowledges mistakes in blog matter. *PR Week*, 3.

O'Brien, I. K. (2007, January 8). Edelman defends ethics of Vista PC gifting tactic. *PR Week*, 6.

Pick, T. (2010). How to write a social media policy. *Socialmediatoday.* Retrieved from http://socialmediatoday.com/tompick/191412/how-write-social-media-policy

Purewal, S. J. (2012, March 29). Facebook password amendment rejected by congress. *PCWorld.* Retrieved from http://www.pcworld.com/article/252837/facebook_ password_amendment_rejected_by_congress.html

Sears Holdings. (2009). *Social media policy.* Retrieved from http://www.docstoc.com/docs/20088030/Sears-Holdings-Social-Media-Policy

Simonetti, E. (2004, December 16). Perspective: I was fired for blogging. *CNET.* Retrieved from http://news.cnet.com/I-was-fired-for-blogging/2010-1030_3-5490836.html

Stacks, D. W. (2011). *Primer of public relations research,* 2nd ed. New York: Guilford Publications, Inc.

Sullivan, L. (2006, October 30). Hard-lessons-always: Wal-Mart's cybereducation. *Information Week*, 17.

Supa, D. W., & Kelly, M. (2012). *Normative versus communicative: Understanding the impact of social media on public relations objectives.* Paper presented at the annual meeting of the International Public Relations Research Conference, Miami, FL.

Tapscott, D. (2009). *Grown up digital: How the Net Generation is changing your world.* New York: McGraw-Hill.

TechCrunch. (2009, April 9). *Twitter eats world: Global visitors shoot up to 19 million.* Retrieved from http://techcrunch.com/2009/04/24/twitter-eats-world-global-visitors-shoot-up-to-19-million/

Terilli, S. A., Driscoll, P. D., & Stacks, D. W. (2008). Business blogging in the fog of law: Traditional agency liability principles and the less-than-traditional Section 230 immunity in the context of blogs about businesses. *Public Relations Journal*, *2*(2), 1–22.

United States Navy Command. (2010). *Social media handbook.* Retrieved from http://www.slideshare.net/USNavySocialMedia/navy-command-social-media-handbook-web

United Way. (2011). *Social media policy and guidelines.* Retrieved from http://www.nationalassembly.org/Publications/documents/socialmediaguidelines2011_uw_sm_v10.pdf

University of Michigan. (2010). *Voices of the staff: Guidelines for the use of social media.* Retrieved from http://voices.umich.edu/docs/Social-Media-Guidelines.pdf

Weber Shandwick. (2009). *Fortune 100 companies on Twitter.* Retrieved from http://www.webershandwick.com/resources/ws/flash/twittervention_study.pdf

Wellner, A. (2000). Generational divide. *American Demographics*, *22*(10), 52.

Wright, D. K., & Hinson, M. D. (2009a). An updated look at the impact of social media on public relations practice. *Public Relations Journal*, *3*(2), 1–33.

Wright, D. K., & Hinson, M. D. (2009b). Examining how public relations practitioners actually are using social media. *Public Relations Journal, 3*(3), 1–33.

Xerox. (2011). *Social media guidelines.* Retrieved from http://www.xerox.com /downloads/usa/en/s/Social_Media_Guidelines.pdf

YMCA, Metropolitan Dallas. (2010). *Social networking policy.* Retrieved from http://www.campgradyspruce.org/images/upload/Social%20Media%20 Policy.pdf

10
Legal and Ethical Use of Social Media for Strategic Communicators

Daxton R. Stewart and Catherine A. Coleman

Social media tools present great opportunities for strategic communicators to engage with their audience in ways that were impossible just a decade ago. However, the benefits social media allow communicators are tempered by the risks inherent in tools that allow messages to be sent immediately and that can spread rapidly. Further, laws and professional ethics policies drafted with a 20th century understanding of mass media may not be in tune with communication tools that constantly emerge, develop, spread and change. What steps can strategic communication organizations take to prevent embarrassing, unprofessional, or even illegal behavior when its employees use social media tools?

For example, Chrysler ran a highly successful ad campaign during the Super Bowl in 2011, highlighting the rebirth of the American auto industry and the resiliency of the city of Detroit in an advertisement featuring the music of rapper Eminem. Just over a month later, the Chrysler Twitter account, @ChryslerAutos, posted this message: "I find it ironic that Detroit is known as the #motorcity and yet no one here knows how to f****** drive" (Kiley, 2011, para. 2). Chrysler deleted the tweet, but not before it was retweeted numerous times. The company apologized for the incident and chose not to renew its contract with New Media Strategies, the company staffing the Twitter account (Kiley, 2011).

Potential social media dangers are not limited to Twitter. In 2010, Novartis Pharmaceutical Corporation received a cease-and-desist letter from the Federal Food and Drug Administration (FDA) regarding the way it allowed visitors to its website to share information about a leukemia drug on Facebook (Hobson, 2010). For its drug Tasigna, Novartis created a 'Facebook share social media widget' on its website that allowed users to repost information on Facebook about the drug, where friends could then comment about it. The FDA found that this allowed access to information about the 'efficacy' of Tasigna but "fail(ed) to communicate **any** risk information associated with the use of this drug" in violation of FDA regulations (Rulli, 2010, p. 1). Further, the FDA found that Novartis' Facebook share widget had not been submitted to the FDA for preview before disseminating it to the public, also in violation of FDA regulations (Rulli, 2010).

Beyond rogue tweets and incomplete Facebook pages, strategic communicators face other dangers from social media use. After the oil spill in 2010 became both an environmental disaster for the Gulf of Mexico and a public relations disaster for BP, a parody Twitter account made things more difficult. The humorous @BPGlobalPR had more than 10 times as many followers as BP's official Twitter feed, with comments purporting to be from the company's embattled CEO, such as, "Safety is our primary concern. Well, profits, then safety. Oh, no – profits, image, then safety, but still – it's right up there" (Cohen, 2010, para. 6). This Web 2.0 twist on public relations – feedback in kind from disaffected members of the public – drew a request from BP that the parody site refrain from trying to confuse the public about its origin and intentions. Further, the Public Relations Society of America (PRSA) offered an article that advised members on handling fake Twitter accounts, including the suggestion that companies develop social media policies and incorporate them into their crisis plans (Schock, 2010).

As social media tools such as Facebook, Twitter, Flickr, Pinterest and YouTube have become prevalent ways for people to share and connect, professional communicators have increasingly incorporated these tools into their daily practice. The purpose of this chapter is to provide an ethical and legal framework for strategic communication professionals when using social media. First, the authors examine codes of ethics and social media guidelines and policies from leading strategic communication companies, identifying common areas of concern to professional practitioners and how they are being addressed. Then they focus on the legal dangers strategic communicators face to help them evaluate risks while maximizing effective use of social tools. Informed by the review of professional codes and legal issues, this chapter concludes with an analysis of the ethical challenges embedded in social media communications that the law and professional codes have yet to address, focusing on the roles of dialogue and power in the relationship between strategic communicators and the public.

Guidance from Professional Codes of Ethics

Formal guidance about using social media in professional codes and guidelines created by strategic communication organizations is still in its developmental stage. Professional codes of ethics such as those by the Public Relations Society of America, the American Advertising Federation (AAF) and the Word of Mouth Marketing Association (WOMMA) have only recently been updated, and a 2010 study found that just 29% of U.S. companies had social media guidelines in place (Axon, 2010). The prevalent adoption of social media as a strategic tool suggested that such policies would be implemented at a much greater rate in 2012, but it is still imperative that strategic communicators adopt and implement social media policies that address the legal and ethical challenges practitioners face.

In general, these policies embrace the positive aspects of social media use, such as building new avenues for engaging the public and new ways to maximize clients' positive images. In a blog post announcing its social media guidelines, Ogilvy Public Relations Worldwide (2010) called for its employees to display "insatiable curiosity" regarding development of "new angles, new methods and new platforms" for communication (para. 13). Mediasmith Inc., an advertising company in San Francisco, reminds its employees to "be yourself and have fun," reflecting the company's "spirit, creativity, savvy and awesome talent" in all their online communications (S. Engle, personal communication, November 11, 2010). The PRSA guidelines call for public relations professionals to "create a sense of excitement when communicating through social media outlets" (Public Relations Society of America, 2011, p. 7).

A review of social media guidelines and policies for professional communicators has shown a number of common themes: (a) transparency by users, (b) friending/following rules, (c) clearances before use, (d) personal vs. professional use, (e) ensuring confidentiality and privacy, and (f) tone of discussion. Each of these themes is discussed below, with examples from a variety of social media policies and guidelines.

Transparency

For this most common theme, strategic communication organizations emphasize the need for professionals to be transparent, focusing mostly on blogging and posting comments online. These transparency guidelines parallel those in the PRSA Member Code of Ethics (2000), which say that members should "(b)e honest and accurate in all communications" and "(r)eveal the sponsors for causes and interests represented" (pp. 3–4).

Social media policies generally identify three areas of concern. The first is avoiding anonymity; as Mason, Inc. (2010) notes:

> Identify yourself – State your name and (when relevant) position at Mason, Inc. When discussing Mason or Mason related matters you must write in the first person, and make it clear that you are speaking for yourself and not on behalf of Mason, Inc. (para. 2)

Most policies require people to identify themselves by name and title.

A second area of concern is pretending to be someone else. As Ogilvy Public Relations Worldwide (2010) notes in its policy, "Be Yourself: Never assume a 'fake' identity in social media and always be transparent about who you are and who you represent" (para. 21). Ogilvy Public Relations Worldwide requires employees to be transparent about their relationship with clients, for example, while using Twitter, "this is generally done by adding a (disc: client) or (cl) when space is limited" (para. 34).

Third, most policies encourage use of social media but require employees to post disclaimers about the extent of their personal comments. The Public Relations Society of America (2011) recommends that, when writing about the organization, it should be made clear that "comments or postings are strictly your opinions" (p. 8).

Friending/Following Rules

Strategic communication organizations offer few guidelines regarding who should become friends with whom through social media. Ogilvy Public Relations Worldwide (2010) urges its employees to use social media tools to "build a following" by "promot(ing) yourself and finding and sharing information that will be interesting to your friends and followers and useful for them to share" (para. 22). The Greteman Group (2009) also offers guidance regarding using social networking sites (SNS) to build a network of friends, suggesting that employees use Facebook and MySpace as their "personal network," and not to feel pressured to friend "coworkers, vendors or clients" (para. 16). For professional networking, Greteman suggests using LinkedIn instead.

Clearance and Review

Because strategic communication professionals are representing both their organization and the clients they represent, social media guidelines are much more specific regarding who is authorized to speak through certain social media channels. Speaking on behalf of the organization via social media requires clearance from a manager at Mediasmith, "to be sure that their online activities are part of their expected job duties" (S. Engle, personal communication, November 11, 2010). Ogilvy Public Relations Worldwide (2010) reminds its employees they are "not an official 'spokesperson' for Ogilvy PR and there are many cases when we must leave speaking for Ogilvy up to them" (para. 29). Razorfish (2009) has a similar policy, noting that employees "are personally responsible for what we write on blogs including Twitter. Irresponsible blogging can risk legal action against Razorfish" (p. 1).

Personal vs. Professional

Similar to news organizations, strategic communication organizations noted the blurring line between one's personal and professional life. These policies were similar, including phrases such as "do not believe anything is private" (S. Engle, personal communication, November 11, 2010) and "know you're always 'on'" (Ogilvy Public Relations Worldwide, 2010, para. 23).

The Greteman Group (2009) offered Microsoft's "bone-simple" blogging policy as an example for its employees: "Be smart" (para. 5). Greteman goes on to note that the "ability to publish things that may never go away and can be forwarded endlessly, well, it gives us pause and we hope it does you, too" (para. 5).

Ogilvy Public Relations Worldwide (2010) suggests that its employees "assume that your social media usage is visible to clients, managers and prospects...be sure to manage what and with whom you are sharing" (para. 23). Further, Ogilvy Public Relations Worldwide (2010) notes that Facebook and Twitter are not the best place to air the "occasional work frustration" (para. 23).

Confidentiality and Privacy

Preserving confidentiality is another great concern for strategic communication organizations, and every social media policy reviewed in this context provided some guidelines regarding confidentiality. This follows the PRSA's requirement that members "(s)afeguard the confidences and privacy rights" of clients and "(p)rotect privileged, confidential, or insider information" divulged by a client (Public Relations Society of America, 2000, p. 5).

Confidentiality concerns were manifested in several ways in social media policies. First, strategic communication professionals should keep matters regarding clients as confidential, particularly when these matters are part of representation agreements. As Mason (2010) notes, matters such as business strategies and product development are rightly the property of the clients and should not be divulged without their approval. Permission from the client is very important. Ogilvy Public Relations Worldwide (2010) requires "explicit permission from your client and manager" when discussing clients or potential clients online (para. 20). Razorfish (2009) provides additional detail, noting that "(e)ven acknowledging a client relationship on Twitter can violate a client privacy agreement" (p. 1).

Greteman Group (2009) extends this to location-based social media, recommending that employees not check in on "Foursquare, Gowalla and the like" at client locations because "we don't want to clue in our competition on which potential (and current) clients we're visiting and when" (para. 33).

Second, several policies require approval from clients to quote them or use their information on social media. Mediasmith, for example, recommends "(w)hen quoting clients, partners or suppliers, always get their approval on quotes before publishing something. It's a common courtesy that goes a long way" (S. Engle, personal communication, November 11, 2010).

Finally, as the Institute of Advertising Ethics (2011) notes, it is imperative for strategic communicators to preserve the public's reasonable expectation of privacy: "Advertisers should never compromise consumers' personal privacy in marketing communications, and their choices whether to participate in providing their information should be transparent and easily made" (p. 8). This suggestion is made in light of the development of behavioral advertising on the web, which has been made very easy through online tracking strategies.

Tone

Remaining calm in the face of the possibility of instantaneous publication through social media can be difficult, and most strategic communication organizations emphasize the importance of maintaining a civil tone when using social media. The Public Relations Society of America (2011) guidelines recommend that communicators adopt a conversational tone, writing "in a manner that invites a response and encourages comment" (p. 7). Key to this approach, though, is doing so without "starting fires," as the Public Relations Society of America (2011, p. 7) notes.

Guidelines also included obvious advice against using insults, obscene language or ethnic slurs in online communications as part of a general call not to offend the audience, in the case of Mediasmith (S. Engle, personal communication, November 11, 2010), and to "(b)e civil and human" (Ogilvy Public Relations Worldwide, 2010, para. 24). When professional communicators are dealing with members of the public who are arguing with them or are not engaging with a civil tone online, they are encouraged to take the high ground and "(b)e diplomatic," as Mediasmith notes (S. Engle, personal communication, November 11, 2010). Mason (2010) suggests that employees "respect the audience," and when disagreements arise, employees should not "pick fights" (p. 1). When you do get into an argument, Razorfish (2009) suggests, "it's not cool to attack others with unprofessional remarks;" rather, one should "exercise grace" (p. 2).

Correcting mistakes was another common theme in these policies. As the PRSA guidelines note, "Take Ownership. If You Make a Mistake, Admit It" (Public Relations Society of America, 2011, p. 7). This advice could be seen in the handling of the Chrysler rogue tweet disaster mentioned in the introduction to this chapter.

Legal Pitfalls in Social Media

Principle 7 of the Institute of Advertising Ethics code, for example, says advertisers "should follow federal, state and local advertising laws" (2011, p. 9) and the PRSA social media guidelines make specific recommendations about being careful about legal issues. Two particular concerns are prominent for strategic communicators using social media: federal commercial speech regulations and intellectual property laws such as copyright, trademark, and online impersonation.

It is well established that commercial speech activities have some protection under the First Amendment, even if that protection is not as robust as it is for political speech or other individual, artistic expression. In spite of these protections of free speech, strategic communicators must operate within a framework of laws and regulations that have passed constitutional muster. It is unquestioned, for example, that false or deceptive advertising falls outside of First Amendment protections, justifying federal and state Deceptive Trade Practices Acts. But other commercial speech that may be deceptive or incomplete can trigger scrutiny by the FDA and the Federal Trade Commission (2009), who place numerous limits and burdens on communicators regarding the promotion and labeling of products and services. Statements made on social networks are certainly subject to these regulations, some of which have been revised in recent years to adapt to the new challenges consumers and communicators face.

Federal Commercial Speech Regulations

Ogilvy Public Relations Worldwide (2010) mentions the Federal Trade Commission guidelines that require companies to disclose payments or free products given to reviewers or other bloggers, requiring its employees to "fully disclose" these relationships, and to "(n)ever talk about a product or organization in social media in exchange for cash. If you receive a product or service to review for free, you must disclose it in your post or review" (para. 25). The revised FTC guidelines are clear on the duties of both marketers and bloggers who endorse their products/services. In essence, any "material connections" between the company making the product/service and the endorser must be disclosed. Under the Code of Federal Regulations section 255.5, these "connections" include any benefits the endorser receives from the company that "might materially affect the weight or credibility of the endorsement," particularly when the audience would not reasonably expect there to be such a connection (Federal Trade Commission, 2009, p. 10).

This usually entails receiving free products or services from the company in exchange for a positive review. Strategic communicators must disclose any relationship that confers a benefit on the reviewer or endorser, even if they are merely discounts, coupons for products, or chances to win a gift card in a blog or Twitter contest. The point of the guidelines is to make it clear to the audience if something is motivating the blogger to slant his or her review of a product/service.

Such disclosures must be "clear and conspicuous." For example, requiring readers to click through to a separate disclaimers and disclosures page probably would not suffice. The disclosure – "I received XYZ from the company in connection with the publication of this review" – should be on the same page in a place that would be easy for the reader to see. Similarly, sponsored tweets should be noted, such as with the hashtag #ad or other mention that it is a commercial message. Because of the 140-character limit on tweets, the communicator may use back-to-back messages issued seconds apart to include the disclosure, with "(1 of 2)" or "MORE" at the end of the first message to make it clear to the audience that additional information is following shortly. Similarly, posts on the social review site Yelp would require disclosure of such financial relationships between reviewers and service providers. Companies that do not follow these disclosure guidelines face being fined and investigated by the FTC (Vilaga, 2009).

Unfortunately, at the time of the writing of this chapter, such formal regulatory guidance for social media communications about prescription drugs was not in place. The FDA conducted hearings in 2009 on social media marketing, but by early 2012, the agency had released just one set of draft guidelines, which covered how pharmaceutical companies should respond to public requests for information about off-label use of prescription drugs (Food and Drug Administration, 2012). The guidelines suggest that unsolicited requests should be responded to by scientific or medical, rather than marketing or communications, personnel. Further, responses should be made privately (one-to-one) rather than through public channels, such as social media. One example the Food and Drug Administration (2012) provides in these draft guidelines is, if a pharmaceutical company announces results of a study via Twitter suggesting that an off-label use is safe, "any comments and requests received as a result of the original message about the off-label use would be considered solicited requests" (p. 6) and thus subject to other FDA rules limiting how companies may intentionally communicate or promote off-label uses. While these guidelines are only in draft form, and are only limited to one topic of pharmaceutical communications, they are indicative of a very conservative approach. Strategic communicators should be very cautious when making statements on social media, even when asked questions in a public forum by citizens.

Intellectual Property

The PRSA Member Code of Ethics notes that members should "(p) reserve intellectual property rights in the marketplace" (Public Relations Society of America, 2000, p. 3), and this is sometimes mentioned in the social media policies of strategic communications organizations. As Mediasmith notes, "be aware that images, photos, music, and art work make up a good portion of copyright material and cannot be used unless specified otherwise" (S. Engle, personal communication, November 11, 2010). Ogilvy Public Relations Worldwide (2010) also notes that words and ideas are mostly fine to share – "It's OK to quote or Re-Tweet others" – as long as proper credit is given, but that employees should avoid using "language, photography, or other information" that belong to someone else (para. 25).

Section 102 of the United States Copyright Act grants copyright protection to people who create works of authorship such as photographs, music, lyrics, books, articles, architecture, dance choreography, sculptures and more. If the work is original – that is, shows some creative spark beyond mere compilation like a list of addresses in a phone book – and is "fixed in a tangible medium of expression," meaning it is more than just an idea, it may be copyrighted (Copyright Act, 1976, §102(a)).

This presents a danger for strategic communicators who may want to share images using social media such as Twitpic, Pinterest or Facebook or share videos on YouTube. If a strategic communicator did not create the work or pay for a license to use, somebody else probably holds that right. Further, the fair use exception in section 107 of the Copyright Act (1976) – which protects secondary uses for news, education, research or criticism/commentary purposes – is unlikely to apply to a strictly commercial use that would be typical for advertising or public relations professionals.

Thus, strategic communicators should actively seek permission to use items that they have neither (a) created themselves, nor (b) been granted a license for commercial use. This includes music and video shared by the public through social tools. Just because users post their creative works on the web does not mean that the works are in the public domain. Rather, copyright still automatically attaches to that work at the moment of creation, and the content creator would have a valid action in a federal court for damages if their copyright is infringed without permission or other licensed use of the work.

These concerns appear in some social media policies. Razorfish (2009) suggests that employees be aware of the terms of service of social media sites before using or sharing content from them. For example, according to the terms of service of YouTube (2010), videos posted on YouTube do not belong to YouTube but to the creator of the video, and permission must be received from the creator before reusing. Similarly, photographs posted on the photosharing site Flickr do not become public domain, but the service has partnered with the Library of Congress and Creative Commons to create a searchable database of photos that are either public domain or can otherwise be used with a mere attribution rather than requiring permission and licensing in advance (Flickr, 2012).

For strategic communicators, trademark law presents another challenge. Federal and state trademark laws protect logos, slogans, names and other items that businesses use to identify themselves to the public for commercial purposes and to distinguish their products and services from their competitors. Strategic communicators should be cautious about using the trademarks of other companies in their social media communications if the use is likely to cause confusion to the public, or if it tarnishes or otherwise dilutes the value and goodwill of the trademark. Similarly, communicators should be on the lookout for uses on social media that cause confusion, tarnishment or dilution, such as the aforementioned @BPGlobalPR account.

Several states, including New York, Texas, and California, have enacted laws to protect against online impersonation through fake social media accounts, but they are generally aimed at protecting individuals rather than companies or brands. Nevertheless, strategic communication professionals with clients who may be parodied through social networking sites should be aware of such *e-personation* laws and what rights they give to people who may be hurt or tarnished through online mockery. For example, California's e-personation law, which went into effect in 2011, makes it a misdemeanor punishable by up to a year in jail and up to a $1,000 fine if any person "knowingly and without consent credibly impersonates another actual person through or on an Internet Web site or by other electronic means for purposes of harming, intimidating, threatening, or defrauding another person" (California Penal Code, 2011, §528.5).

As is the case for professional social media guidelines and policies, the law is aimed at regulating the conduct of individuals and companies. Strategic communication as a field, from an institutional perspective, also has an important role to play in the ethics of communicating using social media tools. This role is explored in the next section.

Advancing Ethical Use of Social Media By Strategic Communicators

In the proceedings of the 2007 U.S. Media Summit, Cooper and Christians (2008) concluded that media fields are on both a downward trajectory of lapses in practice and judgment and an upward trajectory inspired by increased interest in ethical reasoning as guides to action. The codes of professional organizations such as the Public Relations Society of America (2000), the American Advertising Federation (2012), and the International Association of Business Communicators (2012) state, among their core values, the obligation of ethical practice; yet changes in communication technology and their use have outpaced practitioners' and scholars' attention to and evaluation of ethical frameworks to address the myriad challenges posed. New media platforms, including social media, offer uncharted territory that the codes may not address sufficiently (Ward & Wasserman, 2010). Drumwright and Murphy (2009), for example, found that advertising industry leaders were greatly concerned about "the Wild West" of new media in general and, "moreover, no consensus has emerged regarding what is ethical behavior, and there is no sense that industry participants are collaborating to build consensus on these topics" (p. 87). The lack of an underlying ethical framework to support and guide imperatives such as truthfulness is highly problematic, especially in fields like public relations and advertising where manifestations of truth may differ, are bound to other prescriptives such as advocacy and confidentiality in the client relationship, and are expected to be biased (Bivins, 2008).

For strategic communicators, organizations, and the public, both the promise and the problems of social media have become paramount. Stevenson and Peck (2011) suggest, "social media use may require a fresh ethical framework for decision making and/or evaluating of actions made online" (p. 56). As a model for evaluating social media the authors propose double effect reasoning, the legacy of Aquinas, in differentiating intention and choice when determining the good or evil of an act. But this approach neither addresses, nor proposes to address, the complexities of moral knowledge and mediated social dialogue in organizational settings and for persuasion communication.

But while double effects reasoning does not achieve this, the nature of social media may offer an opportunity to develop an ethical framework that encompasses organizations and the public as communicators and undergirds strategic communication practices. In other words, not only have developments and problems in social media precipitated a need to consider an ethical framework to deal with this context, but also this context of social media could provide an opportunity to reconceptualize and build an ethical framework for stakeholder relationships and practice in strategic communication. To begin working through this possibility, the authors of this chapter focus on three key aspects of the contemporary market environment that are highlighted through social media: (a) globalism/multiculturalism, (b) relationship/collaboration and (c) power.

Words such as collaboration, community, engagement, connection, dialogue, information, relationships, conversation, personalization, and empowering have been proposed to help professional strategic communicators and the public understand the values of social media through different lenses (Lester, 2007; Lavrusik, 2010; Maul, 2009). Social media have become a powerful global tool, connecting people and organizations around the world. They are not bound by time and space in the manner of more traditional forms of communication.

Further, scholars and practitioners have discussed social media as a space of unprecedented opportunity to connect with the public. Increasingly, companies are turning their branding efforts to Facebook and Twitter, where they can amass followers and where, many believe, consumers engage more with their messages and build more "honest and human" relationships with the brand (Newman, 2011). The concept of the organization–public relationship takes on new meaning with options such as friending a company making the connection more human (Sweetser, 2010). Discussions on the future of social media for public relations and advertising point to the fact that while conversations about social platforms and earnings are important, the most important factor is the human one that emphasizes the relationship between organizations, professional communicators, and the public (Swallow, 2010).

Many of the professional standards of practice incorporate various guides for addressing the public or consumer (such as, with truthfulness, fairness, and transparency or information), but they do not adequately address how they should behave in dialogue with the public – that is, dialogue in which organization, professional communicator, and the public have a voice, as in social media settings. For advertising and public relations, social media offers a space for collaboration and co-creation, should potential stakeholders choose to accept it as such. The concept of co-creation is not new to social media. Generally, widespread modern theories of consumer society, for example, recognize that consumer practices do more than fulfill physical needs, they also fulfill cultural needs – the need to have meaning and to be empowered in the process of shared meaning, much of which is created by and passed through our cultural imagery and discourse, including advertising and public relations messages. But, the concept of collaborative meaning may have greater levity in the context of social media.

At the same time, the concept of power is important in understanding these relationships. Practitioners have come to understand that engaging in dialogue with consumers through social media requires a willingness to relinquish some control over the message. While this can build stronger relationships with the public, it also can have a detrimental effect when not understood and handled properly (Sweetser, 2010). Also, brand messages preferred by the public may not always be the ones preferred by those managing the brand and public relationships. While it is important to recognize this ceding of control to the public, there is another aspect of power that is, in some ways, more difficult to reconcile. While relationship building and co-creation are exciting concepts, organizations and professional communicators tend to have resources not available to the general public. There remains in many cases an imbalance of power that should not be neglected in a proper ethical framework.

Dialogic Ethics for Social Media

Dialogic ethics – asserting humanness as a fundamental value, developed and achieved in the social realm through communication – offers an appropriate framework for social media ethics in strategic communication. Dialogic deontology is based on a responsibility to humanness that presides in relation to others (Christians, 2007). It is a trinitarian worldview that incorporates mind, body and spirit (the symbolic, interpretive domain). In human interpretive capacity resides the ability to see ourselves subjectively, to represent ourselves and our world symbolically, and to do so through mediated systems that, as such, are "inescapably human creations as well" (Christians, 1997, p. 10). Dialogic ethics has an expectation that communicative partners are viewed as the end, rather than as a means to the end. Humanity is created and expressed through communication, in the dialogic, through interdependent reflection and action. This is important in strategic communication contexts because it may help to overcome imbalances of power, by ensuring that the public are not viewed as subjects to be persuaded to meet organizational ends but as inter-subjective, co-constitutive partners in the process of meaning-making. To this end, it may help to consider Cunningham's (1999) use of Hannah Arendt's communicative conceptualization of power and social contract theory to propose a contractualist approach to advertising ethics. Advertisers' power is granted by the public and thereby requires being responsible to the public.

One frequently proposed version of dialogic ethics is Habermas' discourse ethics, which places ethics in public communication practices as dialogic rather than monologic, derived from "communicative action – the process of giving reasons for holding or rejecting particular claims" (Christians, 2007, p. 126). Previous scholarship has proposed discourse ethics as an alternative to the situational ethics instituted in professional codes. Leeper (1996) connected the discourse ethics of Habermas to the Grunig-Hunt symmetrical model of two-way communication and applied it to ethics in public relations, suggesting that code development from this perspective is "continuous real dialogue" (p. 141). While Leeper (1996) does stress a means of assuaging criticisms of Habermas, the Habermasian discourse theory has sustained significant challenges for failing to be "deeply holistic, gender inclusive, or culturally constituted" and for being ethnocentric in insisting "public discourse conform to generalizable interests" (Christians, 2007, p. 126), thereby failing to demonstrate how subcultural interests may be met. In marketing terms, these subcultures may constitute specific target audiences, so a view that fails to consider such interests is both strategically and ethically problematic.

But as Christians (2007) points out, dialogic ethics still provides "a distinctive model for both ethical theory and professional practice" (p. 125). He is speaking of news and reporting, but consider its adequacy for strategic communication:

> A more sophisticated concept of news, consistent with dialogical ethics, is authentic disclosure. In this perspective, reporting must be grounded historically and biographically, so that complex cultures are represented adequately...Moral duty is nurtured by the demands of social linkage and not produced by abstract theory. (Christians, 2007, p. 126)

Authentic disclosure requires the capacity for authentic exchange, which can only occur when all parties have the capacity that comes through knowledge and critical thought. Transparency, information and truthful representation are bound into our humanness because they are a necessary component of dialogue. Further, social institutions are implicit in the expression of humanness, such that humans as acting, transforming and creative beings "produce not only material goods – tangible objects – but also social institutions, ideas, and concepts. Through their continuing praxis, men and women simultaneously create history and become historical-social beings" (Freire, 2006, p. 101). It is reasonable to expect social institutions to have the capacity to act responsibly and to be made responsible (Christians, 1988), as well as, through dialogic exchange, making the public responsible as collaborators in meaning. Our inter-subjectivity in dialogic ethics expects this of all parties as part of the fabric of social being.

Discussion

Social media tools are transformational methods of communication. As Boyd and Ellison (2008, p. 211) noted, social networking sites are marked by the public nature of their interconnectivity – people create public profiles, share lists of friends, and make new connections. Businesses that use social tools enter a culture of interaction and sharing, a culture quite different to traditional advertising and public relations models. But this culture has codes of ethics drafted decades ago and laws drafted to address communication issues before or during the early days of the Internet.

This chapter has aimed to clarify legal and ethical challenges at two levels. First, at the individual and corporate level, all strategic communication organizations should develop codes of conduct – either through a social media guideline or a policy – that makes employees aware of company expectations and their obligations in this field. Codes of conduct should be regularly updated to reflect the changing nature of social media communications; guidelines drafted in 2010 may very well address Facebook and Twitter but may not be aimed at the particular challenges presented by Pinterest, which became one of the most heavily trafficked social media tools less than a year after its launch in 2011.

Second, at the institutional level, strategic communication as a field should consider the role it plays in persuasion and public dialogue through social media. Any codes of conduct should be developed with forethought for ethical implications and should be grounded in guiding ethical theory. As strategic communicators navigate the spaces of social media relationships and collaborations, as they communicate with and in globalized and multicultural contexts, and as they act on and are acted on by consumers and the public, dialogic ethics offers a substantial ethical basis for code- and decision-making. In this context, humanness is situated in the interpretive domain, the domain of dialogue, which requires active listening to uncover the truth of the other in any exchange (Christians, 1997); thereby, cultural differences do not supersede humanness. Some organizations' social media guidelines reflect this sentiment, to "be civil and human" (Ogilvy Public Relations Worldwide, 2010, para. 24).

Further, dialogic ethics by definition require relationship and collaboration. In practice, dialogic ethics not only highlight, but also require principles such as transparency, so that all parties are entering an authentic exchange. One cannot truly listen to and interpret the other without context. To disengage context is to disengage from authentic exchange.

Finally, dialogic ethics further requires that symbol systems and organizational systems, both of which are activated in social media contexts, are recognized as fundamentally human creations. Social media technologies have been hailed as tools of public/audience/consumer empowerment, but they are embedded in complex systems of organizational power. In recognizing organizations and social institutions as human creations, and in situating humanness in the interpretive domain, organizations and audiences must both be given voice and be made responsible in dialogic encounters. As with the adherence to tone implemented in some of the current codes, the tone must be made to encourage conversation.

Social media has the potential to allow more people to engage and interact in open exchange. If all exchanges involving strategic communicators were transparent and informed, they would certainly satisfy the legal and ethical requirements of the field. When they are not, the public is at a power disadvantage in relation to the persuasive communicator, particularly when public users are depersonalized, on the other side of a computer screen or network from the message sender. This potentially dehumanizes both the receiver and the sender of the message by failing to acknowledge that communication is at the core of humanness.

The actions of strategic communicators shape conversation and interaction among members of the public using social media. As an institution, the strategic communication field should recognize its power and influence to preserve social media as a transparent, free, and open public space.

References

American Advertising Federation. (2012). *Advertising ethics and principles.* Retrieved from http://www.aaf.org/default.asp?id=37

Axon, S. (2010, February 3). Most companies don't have a social media policy. *Mashable.com.* Retrieved from http://mashable.com/2010/02/03/social-networking-policy/.

Bivins, T. (2008). The future of public relations and advertising ethics. In T. W. Cooper, C. G. Christians, A. S. Babbili, & J. M. Kittross (Eds.), *An ethics trajectory: Visions of media past, present and yet to come* (pp. 233–238). Urbana, IL: University of Illinois, Institute of Communications Research.

Boyd, D. M., & Ellison, N. B. (2008). Social network sites: Definition, history, and scholarship. *Journal of Computer-Mediated Communication, 13*(1), Retrieved from http://jcmc.indiana.edu/vol13/issue1/boyd.ellison.html

California Penal Code §528.5. (2011). Retrieved from http://leginfo.ca.gov/pub/09–10/bill/sen/sb_1401–1450/sb_1411_bill_20100927_chaptered.html

Christians, C. G. (1988). Can the public be held accountable? *Journal of Mass Media Ethics, 3*(1), 50–58.

Christians, C. G. (1997). The ethics of being in a communication context. In C. Christians & M. Traber (Eds.), *Communication ethics and universal values* (pp. 3–23). Thousand Oaks, CA: Sage.

Christians, C. G. (2007). Utilitarianism in media ethics and its discontents. *Journal of Mass Media Ethics, 22*(2/3), 113–130.

Cohen, N. (2010, June 7). For dueling BP feeds on Twitter, biting trumps earnest. *The New York Times.* Retrieved from http://www.nytimes.com/2010/06/07/business/media/07link.html?_r=1

Cooper, T. W., & Christians, C. G. (2008). The state of the field: Summits yet to come. In T. W. Cooper, C. G. Christians, A. S. Babbili, & J. M. Kittross (Eds.),

An ethics trajectory: Visions of media past, present and yet to come (pp. 265–268). Urbana, IL: University of Illinois, Institute of Communications Research.

Copyright Act, 17 U.S.C. § 101 et seq. (1976). Retrieved from http://www.copyright.gov/title17/92chap1.html

Cunningham, A. (1999). Responsible advertisers: A contractualist approach to ethical power. *Journal of Mass Media Ethics, 14*(2), 82–94.

Drumwright, M. E., & Murphy, P. E. (2009). The current state of advertising ethics: Industry and academic perspectives. *Journal of Advertising, 38*(1), 83–107.

Federal Trade Commission. (2009). *Guides concerning the use of endorsements and testimonials in advertising.* Retrieved from http://www.ftc.gov/os/2009/10/091005revisedendorsementguides.pdf

Flickr. (2012). *Explore/Creative Commons.* Retrieved from http://www.flickr.com/creativecommons/

Food and Drug Administration. (2012). *Guidance for industry: Responding to unsolicited requests for off-label information about prescription drugs and medical devices* (Draft Guidance). Retrieved from http://www.fda.gov/downloads/drugs/guidancecomplianceregulatoryinformation/guidances/ucm285145.pdf

Freire, P. (2006). *Pedagogy of the oppressed.* 30th anniversary edition. New York, NY: Continuum.

Greteman Group. (2009, January 14). *Social media policy.* Retrieved from http://www.gretemangroup.com/social-media-policy/

Hobson, K. (2010). FDA dings Novartis for Facebook widget. *Wall Street Journal.* Retrieved from http://blogs.wsj.com/health/2010/08/06/fda-dings-novartis-for-facebook-widget/tab/print/

Institute of Advertising Ethics. (2011). *Principles and practices for advertising ethics.* Retrieved from http://www.aaf.org/images/public/aaf_content/images/ad%20ethics/IAE_Principles_Practices.pdf

International Association of Business Communicators. (2012). *IABC Code of Ethics for Professional Communicators.* Retrieved from http://www.iabc.com/about/code.htm

Kiley, D. (2011, March 10). Chrysler splits with new media strategies over f-bomb tweet. *AdAge Digital.* Retrieved from http://adage.com/article/digital/chrysler-splits-media-strategies-f-bomb-tweet/149335/

Lavrusik, V. (2010). Top 20 mashable reader responses to "what is social media?". *Mashable.com.* Retrieved from http://mashable.com/2010/06/11/top-20-mashable-reader-responses-to-what-is-social-media/

Leeper, R. V. (1996). Moral objectivity, Jurgen Habermas's discourse ethics, and public relations. *Public Relations Review, 22*(2), 133–150.

Lester, R. (2007). Social media: Marketing mix. *Marketingweek.* Retrieved from http://www.marketingweek.co.uk/home/social-media-marketing-mix/2058820.article

Mason. (2010). *Mason, Inc., social media guidelines.* Retrieved from http://socialmediagovernance.com/Mason_Inc_SM_Policy.pdf

Maul, K. (2009, October). Reality check. *PRWeek,* 34–42.

Newman, A. A. (2011). Brands now direct their followers to social media. *The New York Times.* Retrieved from http://www.nytimes.com/2011/08/04/business/media/promoting-products-using-social-media-advertising.html

Ogilvy Public Relations Worldwide. (2010, February 14). Empowering communications via a social media policy. *Ogilvy PR 360 Digital Influence Blog.* Retrieved from http://blog.ogilvypr.com/2010/02/empowering-communicators-via-a-social-media-policy/

Public Relations Society of America. (2000). *PRSA Member Code of Ethics*. Retrieved from http://www.prsa.org/AboutPRSA/Ethics/documents/Code%20of%20 Ethics.pdf

Public Relations Society of America. (2011). *Social media policy*. Retrieved from http://www.prsa.org/AboutPRSA/GuidelinesLogos/SocialMediaPolicy/secured /PRSASocialMediaPolicy.pdf

Razorfish. (2009). *Razorfish employee social influence marketing guidelines*. Retrieved from http://www.razorfish.com/img/content/RazorfishSIMguideWebJuly2009. pdf

Rulli, K. (2010). *Letter Re: NDA #022068, Tasigna capsules. Food and Drug Administration*. Retrieved from http://www.fda.gov/downloads/Drugs /GuidanceComplianceRegulatoryInformation/EnforcementActivitiesbyFDA /WarningLettersandNoticeofViolationLetterstoPharmaceuticalCompanies /UCM221325.pdf

Schock, N. (2010). Handling a fake Twitter account. *Public Relations Strategist*, 16(3), 9–10.

Stevenson, S. E., & Peck, L. A. (2011). "I am eating a sandwich now": Intent and foresight in the Twitter age. *Journal of Mass Media Ethics*, 26, 56–65.

Swallow, E. (2010). The future of public relations and social media. *Mashable.com*. Retrieved from http://mashable.com/2010/08/16/pr-social-media-future/

Sweetser, K. D. (2010). A losing strategy: The impact of nondisclosure in social media on relationships. *Journal of Public Relations Research*, 22(3), 288–312.

Vilaga, J. (2009). FTC responds to blogger fears: That $11,000 fine is not true. *Fast Company.com*. Retrieved from http://www.fastcompany.com/blog/jennifer-vilaga/slipstream/ftc-bloggers-its-not-medium-its-message-0

Ward, S. J. A., & Wasserman, H. (2010). Towards an open ethics: Implications of new media platforms for global ethics discourse. *Journal of Mass Media Ethics*, 25(4), 275–292.

YouTube. (2010). *Terms of service*. Retrieved from http://www.youtube.com /static?gl=US&template=terms

11
#knowwhatyoutweet: The FTC is Watching

Holly Kathleen Hall, Myleea D. Hill and Mary Jackson Pitts

In a cluttered media market, strategic communications professionals are constantly looking for new ways to cut through consumer overload, connect with target audiences and enhance a brand. The growth of social media has generated a host of new tools and tactics for accomplishing those ends such as blogger outreach programs and consumers' increased ability to post and access reviews of products and services.

Every year, public relations firm Edelman publishes a Trust Barometer that measures attitudes about the state of trust in business, government, non-governmental organizations, and media across 25 countries. In 2012, Edelman's barometer revealed that public distrust of corporations, government and other established institutions is waning, that "a person like me" is seen as highly credible, ranking only behind academics and technical experts. Social media sites also saw a remarkable increase in their trusted source status (Edelman, 2012). A 2009 Nielsen Global Online Consumer Survey revealed "recommendations from personal acquaintances or opinions posted by consumers online are the most trusted forms of advertising" (Nielsen Wire, 2009, para. 1).

With the realization of the importance of trusted sources, many firms and agencies now see social media outreach programs and sponsored conversations as a necessity for connecting with consumers, not a perk. Some of the early attempts at these programs highlighted serious ethical issues, such as the blogger outreach campaign for Microsoft Windows Vista. Bloggers received laptops pre-loaded with Vista. The program was criticized for the lack of disclosure on the part of the bloggers. It was not clear to many readers that Microsoft was the one who sent the computers to the bloggers for purposes of review (Hobson, 2006). Paying bloggers to mention and promote products is tantamount to an advertorial or product placement. As one public relations executive at Edelman stated about some mommy bloggers (women who write about home-life, family issues and products relevant to those subjects), "They aren't really writing about juggling work and home and kids. These blogs are created to get products or to make money" (Ramirez, 2009, para. 7). One momosphere participant even wrote, "I no longer believe that mommy blogging is a radical act. It is a commercial act" (Ramirez, 2009, para. 9). One school of thought was that the practice was simply a new marketing model and, if it one day went too far in customers' minds, the system would self-regulate and there would be no need for the Federal Trade Commission (FTC) to step in and create new guidelines (Lasica, 2005). The FTC thought otherwise.

The Federal Trade Commission's Updated Guides on Testimonials and Endorsements

In 2006 the FTC did not taken the task of producing guidelines for sponsored conversations when they issued a formal staff opinion in response to a petition from Commercial Alert, a consumer watchdog group (Hespos, 2006). The FTC concluded that while it was likely that deceptive practices were occurring in the context of sponsored conversations, they did not feel specific guidelines were needed.

Then the Commission seemed to reverse their reasoning. By 2008 the FTC began talking about the need for new guidelines and regulations. They noted that, "with changes taking place at a dizzying pace, effective consumer protection is more important – and more relevant – than ever" (Federal Trade Commission, 2008a, p. 4). Acknowledging the now robust and empowered consumer movement, the explosion of media channels, and the increasingly obscure division between consumers and advertisers, the FTC stepped forward to suggest a need for new strategies to police sponsored conversations. This signaled the first revision of their guidelines for editorials and testimonials since 1980 (MacMillan, 2009).

The FTC published recommendations for updating the guidelines and allowed the public to review them and provide feedback through March 2009 (Federal Trade Commission, 2008b). The FTC then announced the new guidelines on October 5, 2009, and set December 1, 2009, as the effective date (Federal Trade Commission, 2009). Even though the guidelines are only advisory, existing rules already forbade deceptive business practices. Actions to enforce the Guides can be brought under the current FTC Act (Solis, 2009).

The Guides define testimonials and endorsements as "any advertising message that consumers are likely to believe reflects the opinions, beliefs, findings, or experience of a party other than the sponsoring advertiser" and further explain that "endorsements may not contain any representations that would be deceptive, or could not be substantiated, if made directly by the advertiser" (Federal Trade Commission, 2009, p. 75). In addition, the FTC affirms that advertisements claiming they are using actual consumers should use actual consumers or else disclose that they are not; and, most importantly, that any connection between the seller of the product that might "materially affect the weight or credibility of the endorsement" should be fully disclosed (Federal Trade Commission, 2009, p. 75).

The Internet has seemingly operated under a Wild West mentality, free of extensive oversight and regulations, which has opened the door to unethical practices. Richard Cleland, assistant director in the FTC's advertising practices division, stated, "If you walk into a department store, you know the (sales) clerk is a clerk... Online, if you think somebody is providing you with independent advice and... they have an economic motive for what they're saying, that's information a consumer should know" (Yao, 2009, para. 4).

In a set of examples, the Federal Trade Commission highlighted some of the different scenarios that might commonly arise. The first is a consumer who regularly buys a certain dog food who chooses to buy a different type of food made by the same company and then blogs about the new food in a very positive way. The FTC deems this is not an endorsement necessitating disclosure. In the second example, the consumer gets the dog food as a gift from the manufacturer who has been tracking her purchases and offers a coupon for a free trial bag. The FTC maintains that any subsequent posting would also not be an endorsement necessitating disclosure. Finally, they offer this change in the scenario which takes it to the level of an endorsement: the consumer has become a member of "a network marketing program under which she periodically receives various products about which she can write reviews if she wants to do so. If she receives a free bag of the new dog food through this program, her positive review would be considered an endorsement under the Guides" (Federal Trade Commission, 2009, p. 51).

In addition to trying to define "an endorsement," more narrowly, the FTC also made an effort to illustrate what might be considered "a relationship" necessitating disclosure. Again, they emphasized the need for some kind of ongoing association between a consumer and a marketing program; not just a one-time coupon use or a free trial (Federal Trade Commission, 2009, p. 12).

To the extent that the new Guides inhibit free speech, the FTC very clearly asserts the new regulations will not "interfere with the vibrancy" of social media (Federal Trade Commission, 2009, p. 10). Several comments submitted in response to the initial revisions argued that many advertisers might refrain from using testimonials so as not to face an FTC challenge (Federal Trade Commission, 2009, p. 26). Another commenter maintained that there are constitutional issues with the new Guides, contending that there are less restrictive methods for preventing deception, such as mandating that "typicality" disclaimers be displayed in a more obvious fashion (Federal Trade Commission, 2009, p. 27). The FTC's response to such arguments is that deception is not determined by whether or not testimonials are involved, but in looking at the impression of the advertisement taken as a whole. And that, "the Guides call for a disclosure only if the ad is misleading (and thus not protected by the First Amendment) without a disclosure" (Federal Trade Commission, 2009, p. 28).

Furthermore, it was formerly the case that only advertisers were liable for non-disclosure of endorsement connections. Now, under the new Guides, both the advertiser and the endorser can be liable. Even though the advertiser may not control the content of an endorsement, in the FTC's view, the advertiser should make every effort to "advise these endorsers of their responsibilities and to monitor their online behavior in determining what action, if any, should be warranted" (Federal Trade Commission, 2009, p. 15).

What about, as Tom Hespoe of iMedia Connection asserts, the fact that it is always possible for a reader to miss a disclosure statement? For example, a search engine result might display part of a product review without the disclosure statement. Or an RSS feeder only sends a subscriber an excerpt, again leaving off the disclosure. The reality is that a disclosure statement will not be foolproof. The FTC will even be looking at Twitter posts. Even though Twitter posts are limited to 140 characters, Cleland declared that clear disclosure is still necessary and possible (McCarthy, 2009).

When the new Guides were first released, rumors circulated that penalties for non-disclosure could range from a warning letter to $11,000 in fines per violation. Cleland protested that the $11,000 figure was inaccurate, saying:

> Worst-case scenario, someone receives a warning, refuses to comply, followed by a serious product defect; we would institute a proceeding

with a cease-and-desist order and mandate compliance with the law. To the extent that I have seen and heard, people are not objecting to the disclosure requirements but to the fear of penalty if they inadvertently make a mistake. That's the thing I don't think people need to be concerned about. There's no monetary penalty, in terms of the first violation, even in the worst case. Our approach is going to be educational, particularly with bloggers. We're focusing on the advertisers: What kind of education are you providing them, are you monitoring the bloggers and whether what they're saying is true? (Vilaga, 2009, para. 5)

Since the Guides went into effect, the FTC has acted at least three times to deal with what it views as non-compliance. The first company to run foul of the Guides was retailer Ann Taylor. Ann Taylor LOFT invited bloggers to attend an exclusive preview of their 2010 summer collection. The retailer expected bloggers to blog about the event in exchange for gift cards ranging in value from $50 to $500. Some bloggers disclosed that there were gifts and others did not. A sign was posted at the event that did instruct bloggers to make the proper disclosure. However, the FTC deemed the sign not effective or visible enough (Indvik, 2010). Ann Taylor quickly adopted a policy for blogger outreach and did what they could to cooperate with the FTC. The FTC ultimately decided not to recommend enforcement action (Hawkins, 2011).

The second FTC investigation concerned employees of public relations firm Reverb Communications, whose client list includes ATARI and Metro-Goldwyn-Mayer Studios (Reverb Communications, n.d.). Reverb provides public relations, sales and marketing services for video game applications. The FTC found they engaged in deceptive activity by posing as consumers and posting reviews from November 2008 through May 2009 in the iTunes store on behalf of game and application developers. Reverb employees posted positive comments such as "Really Cool Game" and "One of the best apps just got better" (Clark, 2010, p. 2). Reverb was held liable. They had to remove the endorsements and could not make any representations about a product or service without clear notice of any material connection (Begley, Lanpher, & Heavner, 2011). This appears to be the first real enforcement action on the part of the FTC, meant to serve as an example and deterrent to others who contemplate being less than open in their disclosures.

In the Legacy Learning Systems case, affiliates wrote reviews, again posing as ordinary consumers. Legacy sold the Learn and Master Guitar program that used DVDs for learning how to play the guitar at home.

Endorsements appeared in content on numerous online sites close to hyperlinks leading to Legacy's website. Affiliates earned large commissions on the sales of the products that resulted from a referral, usually between 20–45% of the cost of each instrumental course sold. A sampling of some of the endorsements read: "The undisputed No. 1 training product for someone wanting to learn how to play the guitar" and "The best home study DVD course for guitar I have ever seen" (Clark, 2011, p. 2). The endorsements reportedly led to over $5 million in sales (Federal Trade Commission, 2011). The FTC faulted Legacy for not adequately monitoring the affiliates. They fined Legacy $250,000 and the company agreed to monitor their affiliates more closely (Begley et al., 2011). In each of these three cases, the FTC placed much of the burden and responsibility on the marketers/advertisers to ensure that proper disclosures are made. The entities (Ann Taylor LOFT, Reverb Communication, and Legacy Learning Systems) were faulted by the FTC for failing to provide adequate instruction and oversight of affiliates. Many small businesses that do not have the resources of larger organizations such as Ann Taylor LOFT face a monumental task. Many are choosing to use social media like Twitter to promote their products and services. Twitter is an inexpensive medium. The use of Twitter requires that small businesses are proactive in learning the Federal Trade Commission rules and regulations on their own, in essence serving as their own advertising and marketing agencies. Ultimately, many small business owners operate with no awareness of the FTC rules and regulations.

Twitter as an Advertising Medium

Twitter's use as a regulated advertising medium is complicated by its technical structure and business model. Although the service has grown in scope from its original purpose, the message character length remains at 140. Twitter has added paid promoted tweets but does not allow for third-party advertising networks, which leaves endorsements as a valued way for brands to spread the word. To help companies maximize their efforts, Twitter even includes a section called Twitter 101 for Businesses.

Just a few years ago, the thought of using tweets to promote products would have been wishful thinking. Twitter was originally called Twttr when it was developed by a startup company in 2006 as a way to broadcast instant messaging status updates to multiple friends (Carlson, 2011). With the proliferation of smartphones, Twitter now claims to have more than 100,000,000 users. Twitter describes itself as "a real-time information network that connects you to the latest stories, ideas, opinions and news about what you find interesting. Simply find the accounts you find most compelling and follow the conversations" (Twitter, 2012a, para. 1). Some of the items of interest could be services or products, and the 100,000,000 users are obviously of interest to advertisers. Recognizing its potential as an advertising medium, Twitter specifically includes an explanation of why it does not allow third-party platforms. The explanation first came in a May 24, 2010, blog post stating that Twitter would ban services that used the Twitter applications programming interface (API) from placing paid tweets into the timeline:

> As our primary concern is the long-term health and value of the network, we have and will continue to forgo near-term revenue opportunities in the service of carefully metering the impact of Promoted Tweets on the user experience. It is critical that the core experience of real-time introductions and information is protected for the user and with an eye toward long-term success for all advertisers, users and the Twitter ecosystem. For this reason, aside from Promoted Tweets, we will not allow any third party to inject paid tweets into a timeline on any service that leverages the Twitter API. (Twitter, 2010, para. 8)

In their blog, Twitter provided two main reasons for disallowing third-party advertising networks in its stream. The first was Twitter's assumption that third parties might be looking to maximize market share or profit, which would not necessarily be beneficial to the user experience. Twitter mentioned a third-party desire for click-through rates as a potential detraction. The second reason Twitter gave for banning third parties was the concern that outside interference could impede necessary innovations in the social media site's advertising network. Due to the nature of its platform, Twitter claims "a necessary focus of promoted tweets is to explore ways to create value for our users. Third party ad networks may be optimized for near-term monetization at the expense of innovating or creating the best user experience" (Twitter, 2010, para. 10).

Twitter added in the blog that third parties did not have to front the cost of supporting Twitter but had been able to profit. Industry analysts saw the banning of third-party advertising networks as a way for Twitter itself to become more profitable by drawing advertising dollars in-house. Mashable noted that the decision meant "Twitter's own advertising offering – promoted tweets – will no longer have ad competition within the stream from third-party ad networks" (Van Grove, 2010, para. 4).

CNET said simply, "The straight story is that these third-party networks – including Adly and the just launched TweetUp – now compete with Twitter itself for advertising dollars" (McCarthy, 2010, para. 4).

Somewhat ironically, Twitter told CNET that the policy against third-party advertising networks would not affect so called Tweet brokers, individuals who receive payment to promote a product. For example, CNET reported that the reality star Kim Kardashian was paid $10,000 per tweet to sponsor a product (McCarthy, 2010). Therefore, while Twitter's ban on third-party advertising networks took steps to prevent small start-ups from collecting advertising revenue, it did not address the issue of celebrities profiting from posting endorsement tweets, which would be subject to the FTC disclosure guidelines.

While Twitter use has grown exponentially in six years, it has been slower to show a profit. Twitter has walked a fine line with third-party developers, needing the developers to contribute applications to grow the business but not wanting to lose potential revenue to third-party entities. As one business site noted after Twitter posted another blog cautioning third party developers not to mimic the Twitter interface in 2012, "Twitter, which had been criticized until now on how it is going to make money, had to be strong with the party-developers" (Naidu, 2012, para. 1). Naidu (2012) added, "It is interesting to see Twitter coming down hard on a community that helped it grow all these years" (para. 4).

The reason for the crackdown on third-party developers was to develop new revenue for Twitter while blocking competing applications because "Twitter has struggled to make advertising revenues" (Naidu, 2012, para. 6). The slow growth in advertising dollars is rooted in Twitter's initial uses and outlook. In a 2009 blog post entitled *Does Twitter Hate Advertising,* Twitter said that it was not "philosophically opposed" (para. 1) to advertising and acknowledged that commercial usage could be a key to becoming a profitable business. Still, Twitter said it was not interested in banner advertising, a traditional means of advertising revenue for websites.

Instead, Twitter provides information to encourage use of the site by businesses. The section Twitter 101 for Business includes a headline "What does Twitter do for businesses?" The answer is, "[a]s a business, you can use Twitter to quickly share information, gather market intelligence and insights, and build relationships with people who care about your company. Often, there is already a conversation about your business happening on Twitter" (Twitter, 2012b, p. 1). Trying to tap into the existing buzz, or word of mouth, is a long-held practice in advertising and promotion, and Twitter's interactive nature makes it an attractive forum for such conversations. In fact, while stating that it would be avoiding traditional advertising such as banner advertisements, Twitter (2009) said that "facilitating connections between businesses and individuals in meaningful ways is compelling" (para. 3). Twitter's interface allows individuals to follow businesses as well as friends in the same stream. According to the definition of the American Marketing Association, word-of-mouth communication "occurs when people share information about products or promotions with friends" (Dictionary, 2012, para. 70). Technically, a promoted tweet by a company might not at first be seen as word of mouth, but if it is then retweeted from friend to friend, it has gone viral and meets the word-of-mouth criteria. Public relations measurement expert Katie Payne encouraged companies to take advantage of Twitter's influence as a form of online word of mouth.

> We all know that Word of Mouth is important – influencing between 20–50% of all decision, depending on whose research you're reading. Probably the easiest way to measure your "Word of Mouth" campaign is a coupon. A coupon can easily go viral on Twitter and be spread out to thousands of people in less than a week. (Payne, 2010, para. 1)

In the example given by Payne, the viral coupon would not run foul of the FTC disclosure guidelines because the coupon would be available to everyone on Twitter with no special arrangement. An *AdAge* columnist added that viral campaigns do not necessarily have to be short-lived coupon bursts but instead could leverage positive sentiment on Twitter, along with other social media, as part of a long-term strategy of engaging consumers with frequent interaction (Daitch, 2010).

However, the FTC disclosure regulations can complicate such interactions if any sort of compensation is received in exchange for the endorsement. While Twitter has several sections on how businesses can use the service, an explanation of Federal Trade Commission regulations is not prominently displayed. In fact, a search for FTC in March 2012 of the Twitter self-contained blog resulted in only one hit, which was unrelated to the disclosure regulations.

Twitter's business section includes an overview of the basics of Twitter, tips to optimize business activity including case studies, and steps to start advertising on Twitter, including promoted tweets, trends, and accounts as well as analytics. As an advertising-supported company valued at more than $5 billion, Twitter has a vested and understandable interest in encouraging business to use its own promoted tweets rather than third-party platforms or even individual endorsements. Still, with

Twitter's acknowledgement of the application to business and awareness of FTC policy as cited elsewhere on its site, the lack of specific and
prominent recommendations is a missed opportunity to clarify potential disclosure situations.

Twitter poses a unique situation because of the 140-character limit
per post. In addition, when you retweet, you lose characters. While
suggestions have been made to use certain hashtags for sponsored posts
such as #sp, #spon, or #ad, there has been no one standard established
(Hawkins, 2011). During a March 2011 speech, FTC Commissioner Julie
Brill cautioned the audience of attorneys about a Twitter incident with
rapper 50 Cent:

> 50 Cent mentioned a penny stock in a series of tweets and the
> stock price skyrocketed 240 percent. It turns out that the company
> mentioned by 50 Cent has an interest in a line of high-end head-
> phones called "Sleek by 50 Cent." While 50 Cent later tweeted in two
> follow-up messages that he actually owned stock in the company, no
> one knew that 50 Cent stood to benefit when it was first mentioned.
> (Prochnow, 2011, para. 12)

The FTC has warned that an endorser has to note those connections
regardless of character restrictions. Are hashtags the way to go? One tech
expert feels they are a good idea, but that they are only a temporary
stop-gap (Smillie, 2010). In June 2010, the FTC issued some clarification
on the Guides as they relate to Twitter:

> The FTC isn't mandating the specific wording of disclosures. However,
> the same general principle – that people have the information they
> need to evaluate sponsored statements – applies across the board,
> regardless of the advertising medium. A hashtag like "#paidad" uses
> only 8 characters. Shorter hashtags – like "#paid" and "#ad" – also
> might be effective. (Bureau of Consumer Protection, 2010, para. 26)

It appears the lack of clarity and understanding of the FTC regulations
in this area is pervasive. And the usage of Twitter among young adults
is relatively high (one in five Internet users aged 18–24 use Twitter on a
typical day) (Smith & Brenner, 2012). Children's television advertising
regulations serve as an analogue to the attempts of the FTC to regulate
testimonials and endorsements. When Congress enacted the Children's
Television Act in 1990, part of the act was aimed at assisting children
so they could distinguish between program content and commercial

content. Now the FTC is grappling with the same related issue on social media: assisting people in distinguishing between content and advertisements.

The purpose of this study was twofold. First, the researchers sought, through a qualitative content analysis, to examine the use of Twitter hashtags as recommended by the FTC to disclose compensation.

RQ1: What is Twitter's use of hashtags as related to disclosure?

Second, the researchers chose to survey college students to gauge their use of Twitter and their understanding of FTC policies.

Research questions addressed by the survey:

RQ2: What are college students' habits in using Twitter?

RQ3: For what purposes do college students use Twitter?

RQ4: What are college students' perceptions of FTC policies and recommendations regarding Twitter?

Method

To address RQ1, researchers analyzed the use of hashtags, by conducting a pilot study in early 2012. Using a researcher's established Twitter account, a researcher typed each of the FTC recommended tags into the search bar. What appeared on the screen served as a snapshot of a given point in time. The search for #paid_ad resulted in no tweets that included the specific phrase #paid_ad, although there were some tweets that included both #paid and ad in the message. For example, one message said in part, "Getting #paid daily for posting one ad for #zeckler penny auction site." The search for #paid resulted in multiple posts for the day (around 90) including an additional 20 new tweets while capturing a screenshot for analysis. Researchers also administered a pilot survey to 43 communications students in a Mid-South university to answer the remaining research questions.

To answer RQ2 (i.e., what are college students' habits in using Twitter?), researchers examined if students had a Twitter account, how many people they followed and how many followed them, and their frequency of sending tweets. Researchers used ten variables to ask students how they use Twitter, what they tweet, and what they follow on Twitter to answer (RQ3) (i.e., for what purposes do students use Twitter?). Five Likert statements were used to address RQ4: What are college students' perceptions of FTC policies and recommendations regarding Twitter? Variables addressed students' awareness of the FTC's role in regulating Twitter and awareness of FTC policy toward advertising. Forty-three students (n = 43) participated in the survey. A standard statistical package (SPSS) was used to tabulate frequencies. Because of the small sample size and pilot nature of the survey, researchers did not analyze statistical significance or correlations.

Results

The pilot qualitative content analysis of Twitter hashtags indicated that the use of #paid did not exclusively indicate disclosure of an endorsement. For example, the first two tweets that appeared were "This guy just told me to #makeitplatinum and get #paid" and "remix done, time to get #paid." A probable example of the use of #paid as recommended by the FTC can be seen in the tweet, "What exactly are paid online surveys?...exciting and fun way to earn a little extra cash. Ht.ly/8Rol3 #cash #paid." Another example considered by the researchers to be a use of #paid to note disclosure was "(A company) is hiring a C/C++ Game Developer in Palo Alto, CA. Details: (website link) #paid."

The search for #ad resulted in multiple posts, but some of them were specifically promoted tweets or directly from a company and not necessarily for disclosure. The first tweet was a promoted tweet for Fidelity Investments that did not even include the hashtag #ad, and the next three were for electronics and sporting gear. For example, a tweet for an electronics company said, "SAVE $35.77 – Phillips BDP3406/F7 1080p Blu-Ray Disc Player – Black $94.22 (website) #ad #deal #bluray_player." A tweet for a sporting goods site said, "Youth Team On The Go Vintage Hooded Sweatshirt $39.99 (website) #starstruck #ad #tweetshop."

From the qualitative portion of the pilot study, the researchers concluded that the FTC's recommended hashtags of #paid_ad, paid, and ad are imprecise and non-exclusive, which could lead to confusion or lack of awareness in the marketplace. In fact, while there is evidence the hashtags are occasionally used to indicate an endorsement, such utilization is far from uniform or even the primary use of the hashtags. This leads to issues and difficulties especially for small businesses, as they are burdened with serving as their own advertising/marketing agency consultant. Among the pilot survey's 43 respondents, the mean age was 22. Females made up the largest number of respondents (83.3%). The majority of the respondents were juniors (35.7%) and seniors (35.7%).

To answer RQ2, the majority, 98% of the sample (n = 43), had a Twitter account. The mean number of accounts followed was 294, and the mean number of followers of the students' accounts was 233; 58% reported tweeting daily, while 23% tweeted weekly and 16% tweeted monthly; 79% checked Twitter daily, while 14% checked Twitter weekly and 5% did so monthly. Students reported retweeting at the rate of 42% daily, 33% weekly, and 23% monthly.

Data to address RQ3 showed the highest number of students (91%) reported using Twitter to keep up with news. The next most common use was to communicate with friends (86%) and the third most common use was to share relevant information (81%). Table 11.1 is a window on what students are doing with Twitter. This small sample of students is less likely to follow products, political issues and sports but is still willing to tweet about subjects they do not follow on Twitter. One would assume they follow these areas through other media platforms and then tweet their opinions and thoughts. The percentage of students tweeting about brands is much less than those who follow brands (see Table 11.1).

Students were asked to list their level of agreement with statements about the FTC and Twitter to answer RQ4 (i.e., what are college students' perceptions of FTC policies and recommendations regarding Twitter?) (see Table 11.2). In response to the statement "Federal Trade Commission monitors Twitter," 61% either agreed or strongly agreed, while 42% agreed that the FTC policies affect Twitter and 0% strongly agreed. In contrast, 65% agreed that FTC policies affect advertising, and an additional 16% strongly agreed; 56% agreed or strongly agreed that #paid_ad, #paid, and #ad are recommended when someone endorses a product in a tweet.

Table 11.1 Frequencies and percentages for how students use Twitter

Tweeted about	Yes (%)	No (%)	What students follow?	Yes (%)	No (%)
Products	63	37	Products	14	86
Political issues	54	46	Political issues	45	55
Sports	74	26	Sports	52	48
Brands	38	62	Brands	50	50
Celebrities	74	26	Celebrities	84	14
Class work	43	57	Teachers	64	36
Friends	88	12	Friends	98	2
Services	29	71	Companies	62	38

Note: n = 43. One student without Twitter = 2%.

Table 11.2   Student understanding of Federal Trade Commission and Twitter regulations

Statement	Strongly disagree (%)	Disagree (%)	Agree (%)	Strongly agree (%)
FTC monitors Twitter	7	33	49	12
FTC policies affect Twitter	9	49	42	
FTC policies affect advertising	7	12	65	16
#paid ad, #paid, and #ad are recommended when someone endorses a product in a tweet	12	33	30	26

Note: n = 43. One student without Twitter = 2%; FTC = Federal Trade Commission.

The pilot study indicated that even students who are relatively heavy users of Twitter do not have a strong understanding of the FTC's general role in developing policies that affect Twitter. Perhaps most surprisingly was the large gap in the number of students who agreed/strongly agreed that FTC policies affect advertising compared with the number that agreed FTC policies affect Twitter. Additionally, there was also a disconnect, though not as large, in that more students agreed that the FTC monitors Twitter than agreed that FTC policies affect Twitter. With such a noted lack of understanding among a supposedly heavy Twitter-using population (albeit statistically small), concerns arise for the ability of many everyday consumers and potential product reviewers/affiliate marketing members to ferret out the specific situations when a disclosure is necessary. Much of the burden is shifted to the advertisers/affiliate marketers to instruct and educate their citizen-tweeters about disclosure requirements.

Discussion

With the confusion about disclosing endorsements on Twitter to comply with FTC guidelines, some advertising and public relations agencies have developed their own codes and instructions for their clients. Ogilvy, for example, updated their Social Media Engagement Code with statements such as: "If we ask an influencer to review a product and, therefore, provide the influencer with the product to enable him/her to 'experience' it, we will ask that he/she be transparent and reveal that he/she has been given the product temporarily, or permanently" (Bell, 2012, para. 25). They and other agencies frequently direct users to the Word of Mouth Marketing Association's (WOMMA) Social Media Disclosure Guide which includes a section on Clear and Prominent Disclosure stating:

> No matter which platform is used, adequate disclosures must be clear and prominent. Language should be easily understood and unambiguous. Placement of the disclosure must be easily viewed and not hidden deep in the text or deep on the page. All disclosures should appear in a reasonable font size and color that is both readable and noticeable to consumers. (Word of Mouth Marketing Association, n.d., para. 8)

The Porter Novelli agency recommends the following:

> Work with your own legal department to educate them on blogger relations, disclosure and advertising claims issues that may arise. Provide them with sources of industry information so they can keep you informed about best practices and better understand the sites with which you are working. Remember that the spirit of the FTC guidelines is protection of consumers. That intent aligns perfectly with foundations of Web 2.0 and blogging – authenticity and transparency. (Agresta, 2009, p. 6)

One organization called BlueHost.com attempted to provide instructions with as much specificity as possible, lacking the exact instructions the FTC could potentially provide agencies. The BlueHost.com directions are for disclosures to be frequent, clear, conspicuous, and require no action. Under the require no action heading, BlueHost.com explains:

> Your disclosure must be immediately evident to a typical visitor to your site who views a review, ranking or endorsement on a PC or Mac monitor. A visitor should not need to scroll, click or hover to learn that you receive compensation. If you do include a clickable link or additional information when a visitor hovers over text, the language of the link itself should reveal the fact that you receive compensation. Example of a link that requires no action: Disclosure: We are compensated for our reviews. Click here for details. Keep this in mind: Simply telling the visitor that they can "Click/hover here to read our FTC disclosure" is not adequate. You need to use the word "disclosure" and present the nature of the disclosure. (Affiliate Disclosure Requirements and Examples, n.d., para. 4)

While admirable in its coaching and direction, this example again illustrates the lack of clarity and consistency in disclosure requirements. If #disclosure is required, for example, in a tweet, the Twitter-user has already lost 11 characters out of the 140 allowed. And it begs the question, are reviewers supposed to use #ad, #paid, #paid_ad, #disclosure or some other term each agency may deem appropriate?

Though the FTC has attempted to place some parameters around sponsored conversations and provide some suggested structure and guidance, vagueness and a lack of awareness remains for the consumer. During the FTC's public comment period for the new Guides on testimonials and endorsements, the Public Relations Society of America (PRSA) noted the Guides were "lacking in the degree of clarity that enables members to meet their obligations" under the PRSA Code of Ethics which includes provisions such as ensuring the free flow of accurate information (Cherenson, 2009, p. 2). As author and social media guru Brian Solis noted, journalists have specific requirements and ethics code provisions regarding any gift-for-coverage issues. But when it comes to the ordinary citizen, the web is:

> Driven only by loosely defined and sporadically practiced methodologies that promote at-will disclosure and transparency, many brands, intentionally or deliberately, are blurring a consumer's ability to discern the distinction between partisan and genuine experiences. (Solis, 2009, para. 7)

It was hoped that the new FTC Guides would address these issues. Although the pilot study was not large enough to be statistically significant, it does appear to shed some light on the need for clarity and education in the area of FTC policy on endorsements and testimonials. If the consumers the FTC is trying to protect do not recognize or understand the purpose of the disclosure hashtags, then new strategies need to be explored for effective consumer protection.

The FTC needs to establish clear and definitive disclosure requirements for endorsements on Twitter, as well as engage in an intentional educational effort aimed at consumers and small businesses. Although there are enforcement and clarity issues, the Guides seem to be a step toward protecting the consumer in this new age of social media by making sure they have all the information they need to make an informed decision. Consumers value truthful reviews and opinions from their peers. In the end, whether FTC-mandated or self-regulated, it is all about being authentic and transparent. Advertisers and marketers involved in affiliate marketing or blogger outreach programs need to practice due diligence by informing affiliates/participants of disclosure requirements and in monitoring those affiliates/participants on a regular and disciplined basis.

The pilot study indicates that additional research is needed to investigate the disparity in students' understanding of the role the FTC plays in affecting advertising in contrast to Twitter. Additional studies could also examine the efficacy of Twitter as an advertising medium and the effects of disclosure hashtags on the credibility of tweets about brands, products, and services. After experimenting with the pitfalls and successes of endorsements on Twitter, brands may decide that long-term credibility is more important than short-term, less than transparent, and questionable consumer reviews. The future of sponsored conversations, whether on blogs, Twitter or other websites, may depend on the FTC's ability to establish consistent instructions that promote transparent truth in advertising.

References

Affiliate disclosure requirements and examples. (n.d.). *Bluehost.com*. Retrieved from http://www.bluehost.com/cgi/info/ftc.html

Agresta, S. (2009). *Exploring the FTC guidelines for social media*. Retrieved from www.scribd.com/doc/39244027/SelasTurkiye-Exploring-the-FTC-Guidelines-for-Social-Media-by-Porter-Novelli

American Marketing Association. (2012). Dictionary. Retrieved from http://www.marketingpower.com/_layouts/Dictionary.aspx?dLetter=W

Begley, A., Lanpher, L., & Heavner, C. (2011). *FTC continues to flex its enforcement muscle with regard to social media promotional activity*. Retrieved from http://www.tmtlawwatch.com/2011/04/articles/ftc-continues-to-flex-its-enforcement-muscle-with-regard-to-social-media-promotional-activity/

Bell, J. (2012). *The updated Ogilvy social media management code* [Web log post]. Retrieved from https://social.ogilvy.com/the-updated-ogilvy-social-media-engagement-code/

Bureau of Consumer Protection. (2010). *FTC's revised endorsement guides: What people are asking*. Retrieved from http://business.ftc.gov/documents/bus71-ftcs-revised-endorsement-guideswhat-people-are-asking

Carlson, N. (2011). The real history of Twitter. *Business Insider*. Retrieved from www.businessinsider.com/how-twitter-was-founded-2011-4

Cherenson, M. (2009, March 2). *PRSA submits comments to FTC on use of endorsements and testimonials*. Retrieved from http://media.prsa.org/article_display.cfm?article_id=1238

Clark, D. (2010). *In the matter of Reverb Communications, Inc.* Retrieved from http://www.ftc.gov/os/caselist/0923199/100826reverbcmpt.pdf

Clark, D. (2011). *In the matter of Legacy Learning Systems, Inc.* Retrieved from http://www.ftc.gov/os/caselist/1023055/110610legacylearningcmpt.pdf

Daitch, C. (2010). Why it's time to rethink viral marketing. *AdAge Digital*. Retrieved from http://adage.com/article/digitalnext/time-rethink-viral-marketing/147753/

Edelman Trust Barometer. (2012). Retrieved from http://trust.edelman.com/trust-download/executive-summary/

Federal Trade Commission. (2008a). *Protecting consumers in the next tech-ade: A report by the staff of the Federal Trade Commission.* Retrieved from http://www.ftc.gov/bcp/workshops/techade/reports.html

Federal Trade Commission. (2008b). *Guides concerning the use of endorsements and testimonials in advertising (16 C.F.R. Part 255).* Retrieved from www.ftc.gov/os/2008/11/P034520endorsementguides.pdf

Federal Trade Commission. (2009). *Guides concerning the use of endorsements and testimonials in advertising (16 C.F.R. Part 255).* Retrieved from http://www.ftc.gov/os/2009/10/091005endorsementguidesfnnotice.pdf

Federal Trade Commission. (2011). *Firm to pay FTC $250,000 to settle charges that it used misleading online "consumer" and "independent" reviews.* Retrieved from http://www.ftc.gov/opa/2011/03/legacy.shtm

Hawkins, S. (2011). *Are you disclosing? What you need to know about FTC rules and social media.* Retrieved from http://www.socialmediaexaminer.com/are-you-disclosing-what-you-need-to-know-about-ftc-rules-and-social-media/

Hespos, T. (2006). *Paying for blog juice could be illegal.* Retrieved from http://www.imediaconnection.com/content/12967.asp

Hobson, N. (2006). *The great PR cock-up.* Retrieved from http://www.nevillehobson.com/2006/12/28/the-great-pr-cock-up/

Indvik, L. (2010). *No fines levied in FTC's first blogger-advertiser investigation.* Retrieved from http://mashable.com/2010/04/30/ann-taylor-ftc-investigation/

Lasica, J. (2005). *The cost of ethics: Influence peddling in the blogosphere.* Retrieved from http://www.ojr.org/ojr/stories/050217lasica/

MacMillan, D. (2009). Blogola: The FTC takes on paid posts. *BusinessWeek.* Retrieved from http://www.businessweek.com/technology/content/may2009/tc20090518_532031.htm

McCarthy, C. (2009). Yes, new FTC guidelines extend to Facebook fan pages. *CNET.* Retrieved from news.cnet.com/8301-13577_3-10368064-36.html

McCarthy, C. (2010). Twitter cuts the cord on third-partyad networks. *CNET.* Retrieved from news.cnet.com/8301-13577_3-20005754-36.html

Naidu, P. (2012) Why Twitter is enforcing stricter guidelines for third-party developers. *Business2Community.* Retrieved from http://www.business2community.com/twitter/why-twitter-is-enforcing-stricter-guidelines-for-third-party-developers-0207808

Nielsen Wire. (2009). *Global advertising: Consumers trust real friends and virtual strangers the most.* Retrieved from http://blog.nielsen.com/nielsenwire/consumer/global-advertising-consumers-trust-real-friends-and-virtual-strangers-the-most/

Payne, K. (2010, April 20). *Measuring word of mouth.* [Web log post]. Retrieved from http://kdpaine.blogs.com/kdpaines_pr_m/2010/04/measuring-word-of-mouth-.html

Prochnow, J. (2011). *Endorsements, testimonials and the FTC.* Retrieved from http://www.bevnet.com/magazine/issue/2011/endorsements-testimonials-and-the-ftc-2

Ramirez, J. (2009). *Trusted mom or sellout?* Retrieved from http://www.newsweek. com/id/206786/output/print

Reverb Communications, Inc. (n.d.). Retrieved from http://www.reverbinc.com /ourclients/

Smillie, D. (2010). *Buzz patrol.* Retrieved from http://www.forbes.com/sites /bizblog/2010/02/23/buzz-patrol/

Smith, A., & Brenner, J. (2012). *Twitter use 2012.* Retrieved from http://pewinternet. org/Reports/2012/Twitter-Use-2012/Findings.aspx

Solis, B. (2009). *This is not a sponsored post: Paid conversations, credibility & the FTC.* Retrieved from http://www.techcrunch.com/2009/05/24/this-is-not-a-sponsored-post-paid-conversations-credibility-the-ftc/

Twitter. (2009, May 20). *Does Twitter hate advertising?* [Web log post]. Retrieved from http://blog.twitter.com/2009/05/does-twitter-hate-advertising.html?m=1

Twitter. (2010, May 24). *The Twitter platform* [Web log post]. Retrieved from http://blog.twitter.com/2010/05/twitter-platform.html

Twitter. (2012a). *About Twitter.* Retrieved from https://twitter.com/about

Twitter. (2012b). *Twitter for business.* Retrieved from https://business.twitter.com /en/basics/what-is-twitter/

Van Grove, J. (2010). Twitter to eliminate third-party ads in user timelines. *Mashable.* Retrieved from http://mashable.com/2010/05/24/twitter-third-party-ad-networks/

Vilaga, J. (2009). *FTC responds to blogger fears: "That $11,000 fine is not true."* Retrieved from http://www.fastcompany.com/1394286/ftc-responds-blogger-fears-11000-fine-not-true

Word of Mouth Marketing Association. (n.d.). *Social media disclosure: The WOMMA guide to disclosure in social media marketing.* Retrieved from http://womma.org /ethics/sm-disclosure-guide/

Yao, D. (2009). *FTC plans to monitor blogs for claims, payments.* Retrieved from usatoday30.usatoday.com/tech/news/2009-06-22-bloggers-free_N.htm

12

Legal Issues in Social Media

Genelle I. Belmas

If Internet time is like dog years (Kaplan, 1999), many social media applications have already lost the blush of youth and are well on their way into middle age. Sadly, the law rarely keeps pace with either technological or social developments. It is only in the last few years that legislatures and courts have begun to address the legal issues faced by companies and users of social media. With the numbers of social media users continuing to climb, and more and more companies taking advantage of these inexpensive and effective methods of contacting many current and potential customers, it is likely that the law will continue to struggle to keep up with new and emerging social media applications. Moreover, federal agencies have started to take notice of social media and of the potential impact of these applications on user privacy. Facebook in particular has been the target of several investigations by the Federal Trade Commission (FTC) in response to changes in its privacy policies over the past few years.

Advertisers and public relations professionals need to be aware of the legal pitfalls that could await them as they venture into the world of social media. How, for example, should a public relations firm deal with a nasty anonymous poster on its online message board? Can an employer order an employee to provide access to his/her social media? What liability could an advertiser incur if someone posts a libelous statement or a copyright infringement on its Facebook page? What about the use of social media information in making hiring – or firing – decisions?

It is probably no surprise that most traditional media law applies to the online environment. Sometimes the applications of current law to social media are very similar to applications to traditional media outlets, like newspapers and broadcast stations. Sometimes, however, they are very different. This chapter is aimed at addressing two fundamental and related questions: How has traditional media law adapted to address the unique characteristics of social media and its users? And, more importantly, what legal issues should strategic communicators watch for as they expand their offerings in social media? Court cases, statutes and administrative guidelines will be used to illustrate these potential dangers.

Libel

Some of the earliest law (1990s) that arose in response to the online environment dealt with online libel. Libel, the written form of defamation, is false material that tends to harm a person's reputation (Belmas & Overbeck, 2011). While the law of defamation itself remains basically the same when applied to an online publication as to a traditional publication (the plaintiff still has the burden of proof and must prove such elements as defamation, identification, publication, damages and fault), determining what organization, if any, has liability for allegedly defamatory material has proved to be more challenging. To what extent does an Internet service provider (ISP) or a social media platform have liability for third-party libels posted, anonymously or not, on its sites? As advertisers and public relations practitioners create new Facebook pages or YouTube channels for their goods and services, to what extent are they responsible for potentially libelous comments posted by visitors? The answer relies on whether the communicator acts as a publisher or distributor of those comments.

The law started out promisingly for websites in *Cubby, Inc. v. CompuServe, Inc.* (1991), in which CompuServe was found to be a distributor of defamatory content, not a publisher. The plaintiff had published defamatory information in the form of a database called Rumorville on CompuServe's Journalism Forum. CompuServe argued that it should be considered a distributor, not a publisher, for purposes of liability, and the federal district court agreed: "CompuServe has no more editorial control over [Rumorville] than does a public library, book store, or newsstand..." (*Cubby*, 1991, p. 140).

However, in 1995, a New York court came to a different conclusion about an ISP's responsibility for online postings. In an unpublished (non-precedential) case, *Stratton Oakmont, Inc. v. Prodigy Services* (1995), the court found that Prodigy was responsible for an anonymous posting that was defamatory about brokerage firm Stratton Oakmont. The *Stratton Oakmont* case caused an uproar. Many contemporary legal commentators (Hermann, 1996; Luftman, 1997) said that the court had caused serious damage to the growth of the then-nascent Internet community by making ISPs responsible for all postings on their sites, and they called for reform. Congress responded by passing the Communications Decency Act (CDA), part of the omnibus Telecommunications Act of 1996. Section 230 of the CDA, entitled Protection for Private Blocking and Screening of Offensive Material, states: "No provider or user of an interactive computer service shall be treated as the publisher or speaker of any information provided by another information content provider" (47 U.S.C. §230(c)(1)). The law is also broadly enough written to apply not only to ISPs but also to website owners and operators as well as social media.

The ISP protections in section 230 have been the subject of dozens of cases – and most of the time, the law is interpreted to provide virtually complete elimination of liability for ISPs in defamation cases, as long as the publisher does not exercise too much control over the third-party content. Section 230 protections have also been extended to social media in at least one case. In *Gaston v. Facebook, Inc.* (2012), the plaintiff sued Facebook for allowing a former colleague to post allegedly libelous comments about him. In denying the claim, the court provided a broad definition of the sites to which section 230 would apply:

> The CDA defines "interactive computer service" as "any information service, system, or access software provider that provides or enables computer access by multiple users to a computer server, including specifically a service or system that provides access to the Internet and such systems operated or services offered by libraries or educational institutions." 47 USC § 230(f)(2). Google, Facebook and Lexis Nexis clearly fall within that definition. (*Gaston*, 2012, p. 17)

However, the protections are not absolute, particularly when a court believes that actual editorial control has taken place. Facebook lost section 230 protection in a case in which plaintiffs alleged that Facebook used their actions on the site (such as liking a company) to create sponsored stories – advertisements that featured their names and pictures without their consent (*Fraley v. Facebook, Inc.*, 2011). In denying section 230 immunity, the court said that the act of creating the sponsored stories was beyond "a publisher's traditional editorial functions, such as deciding whether to publish, withdraw, postpone or alter content" (*Fraley*, 2011, p. 802).

The cases to date suggest that advertising and public relations companies operating Facebook or other sites in which comments are enabled should use a light hand in moderating comments on those sites, lest they forfeit the protections offered by section 230. It seems to be generally acceptable for these sites to moderate comments for allegedly defamatory, obscene, or other objectionable material, as most terms of service say that they will do. However if, for example, a company chooses to actively encourage negative comments about competitors or remove postings critical of it or its products or services, that company runs the risk of moving from being a mere distributor of content to being a publisher and sacrificing section 230 protection.

Thus, if someone posts negative comments on Facebook or YouTube that are not solicited or encouraged, there may be very little advertisers can do to fight those comments other than to provide content on that site or on their own websites that combats the harmful information. Should a company wish to unmask an anonymous poster for purposes of suing that person for libel, there are legal tests that courts have developed to address that issue.

However, anonymous online postings on websites are not the only forum for alleged defamation to take place. Even the 140-character limit on Twitter can be used to libel someone. The earliest recorded case is *Horizon Group Mgmt., LLC v. Bonnen* (2010). Amanda Bonnen found herself sued by her apartment management after she invited a friend to her apartment by tweeting, "You should just come anyway. Who said sleeping in a moldy apartment was bad for you? Horizon realty thinks it's okay" (*Horizon*, 2010, p. 2). Horizon sued her for $50,000, but a judge dismissed the case as too vague to be actionable as libel. But, perhaps the most high profile and colorful Twitter libel defendant is singer Courtney Love. Love's now infamous profanity-laced tweets, both threatening and defaming, about fashion designer Dawn Simorangkir, the Boudoir Queen, were sent after Simorangkir sent Love a bill for some clothing. Love tweeted, "oi vey dont f*** with my wradrobe or you willend up in a circle of corched eaeth hunted til your dead" (typos in original, profanity edited) (Lidsky & Friedel, 2011, p. 239). Love agreed in 2011 to pay Simorangkir $430,000 to settle the case, but that was not the end of Love's Twitter woes. A case is pending against Love by her former attorney, Rhonda Holmes, after Love tweeted: "i was f***ing devastated when Rhonda J Holmes Esq of San Diego was bought off," after the singer had fired and then tried to rehire her (Kahn, 2011, para. 9).

Twitter libel law suits continue to make news, even for those less famous than Courtney Love, even though none have gone to a full trial, to date. For example, a $1 million libel suit was dismissed by the plaintiff, an Oregon doctor, without comment in 2011. The defendant had blogged and tweeted about the doctor's disciplinary record, and the *Oregonian* reported that there would be no court costs or attorney's fees assessed but that the posts and tweets would remain online (Ho, 2011). While there may be challenges in determining who is at risk for suit in these cases, advertisers are entitled to the protections of section 230 for eliminating their liability for potentially libelous content.

Privacy

Perhaps the hottest legal topic in social media law, privacy has topped the list of issues of concern to the public. Hardly a week goes by without a news story about how this or that social media broke faith with its users and used their personal information in a way not permitted or intended by those users. Not only are adults concerned about their own personal information being distributed or used without their consent, they are worried about their children's information. Given how much data is gathered from social media sites, it should come as no surprise that both consumers and government agencies are watching these sites closely. Historically, traditional media outlets have been concerned about violating four privacy torts set out in a 1960 law review article (Prosser, 1960). Those torts are: publication of private facts, intrusion upon seclusion, false light, and misappropriation (Belmas & Overbeck, 2011). However, today's concerns are primarily about data privacy; concerns about how personal data, gathered online, is used and sometimes abused. Just one example: in 2011, Facebook settled charges with the Federal Trade Commission that it had made user information public that it had promised to keep private. Jon Leibowitz chairman of the FTC said in a press release:

> Facebook is obligated to keep the promises about privacy that it makes to its hundreds of millions of users. Facebook's innovation does not have to come at the expense of consumer privacy. The FTC action will ensure it will not. (Federal Trade Commission, 2011a, para. 3)

Facebook was charged with eight violations, including deceptive privacy settings, changes in privacy policies without sufficient notice, and sharing information with advertisers when it had said it would not do so. In the settlement, Facebook agreed, among other things, to 20 years of privacy audits.

The Children's Online Privacy Protection Act (COPPA) of 1998 was enacted to protect children's personal information from exploitation. To comply with COPPA, websites must obtain parental consent before gathering information from children under the age of 13, provide clear and comprehensive privacy policies on the site, provide parents with both access and the ability to delete their children's information, and protect that information's security from hackers (Federal Trade Commission, 2008). In 2012, the FTC called for updates to COPPA policies to address both new online developments in security and parental consent as well as developments in social media in which children can participate. For example, in a move that has implications for social media such as Facebook and YouTube, the FTC recommended that the COPPA rules be amended so that these and other sites that have both child and adult users can screen users so that COPPA regulations are enforced only on those users under the age of 13 (Children's Online Privacy Protection Rule, 2012). These rules were approved at the end of 2012 and will go into effect in 2013.

Other social media are not immune from FTC actions. In 2011 Twitter settled with the agency regarding allegations that it had lied to its users about their privacy settings and put user privacy at risk from hackers with lax email and account security procedures. Twitter agreed to implement a comprehensive security system with regular agency audits, according to an FTC press release (Federal Trade Commission, 2011b). In 2012 Google announced a new integrated, streamlined privacy policy to great fanfare; and dismay from some privacy advocates, including the Electronic Privacy Information Center (EPIC), who alleged that the new policy violated an earlier consent agreement between Google and the FTC. EPIC filed suit to stop Google from implementing the new policies. However, a judge refused to get involved, saying that the matter was not one for judicial review, and in fact the FTC was the one to consider whether one of its settlements was being obeyed or not (*Electronic Privacy Information Center v. Federal Trade Commission*, 2012). EPIC appealed, and courts have yet to rule on the appeal.

In March 2012 the FTC released its latest privacy report. Entitled, *Protecting Consumer Privacy in an Era of Rapid Change*, the report calls on online companies to revise and update their privacy policies (Federal Trade Commission, 2012). Companies, the agency says, should engage in what it calls "privacy by design" (Federal Trade Commission, 2012, p. vii), a consideration of consumer privacy issues from the earliest stages of product or service development through every phase of advancement. Privacy policies should be both simplified and transparent so consumers know what is being gathered and how the information is being used. Moreover, the FTC endorsed the development of, so-called, do not track mechanisms for consumers. Of particular concern to the FTC is the rapid development of facial recognition software. Because many social media, from Facebook to Yelp! to LinkedIn, encourage users to post pictures of themselves, the FTC issued this warning:

> The ability of facial recognition technology to identify consumers based solely on a photograph, create linkages between the offline and online world, and compile highly detailed dossiers of information, makes it especially important for companies using this technology to implement privacy by design concepts and robust choice and transparency policies. (Federal Trade Commission, 2012, p. 46)

It is obvious that as digital technology advances, social media will have the ability to gather more and varied types of data from their users.

However, courts have not assumed that privacy automatically extends to online communications in social media. In the 2009 case of *Moreno v. Hanford Sentinel*, a California court said that a public MySpace journal was just that, public. Cynthia Moreno wrote an entry on her MySpace journal entitled *Ode to Coalinga*, her hometown, that was disparaging of the town. She later took the entry down, but not before the principal of her high school submitted it to the local newspaper. The court denied her privacy claims, saying, "Cynthia's affirmative act made her article available to any person with a computer and thus opened it to the public eye. Under these circumstances, no reasonable person would have had an expectation of privacy regarding the published material" (*Moreno*, 2009, p. 1130). As discussed later in this chapter in the *Pietrylo* case, when affirmative steps are taken to make a group private, the outcome is different; courts are more likely to extend privacy rights when the users have made it clear they desire them.

Anonymity

"On the Internet, nobody knows you're a dog" (Steiner, 1993, p. 61). The caption to the now-famous *New Yorker* cartoon makes it plain: it is very easy to be anonymous online. Just make up a new name, use it to create a new email address on any of the dozens of free email services out there, and voilà, a new identity. Perfect for protecting one's *real* email address from spam, and ideal for engaging in mean-spirited, maybe false, maybe libelous, commentary on a news story, company website, or blog. But what if one of these comments crosses the line into libel or another tort, such as publication of private facts? Under what circumstances can an anonymous speaker retain that anonymity against attempts to reveal his/her identity?

Section 230, discussed above, usually immunizes ISPs from liability for third-party libels. However, an ISP may be subpoenaed to turn over identifying information for anonymous posters on their sites so that those posters may be sued by their victims. There have been many cases in the past decade that have dealt with ISP responses to subpoenas for identifying information, but a general test seems to be developing that has been adopted by a number of courts when asked to evaluate whether an ISP must reveal the identity of an anonymous speaker. This test essentially mandates that there be a good chance that the libel suit will succeed in court before the alleged libeler can be identified.

This test has been applied in at least one case involving social media, *Sinclair v. TubeSockTedD* (2009). In this case, Lawrence Sinclair, who had posted a video on YouTube that alleged he had done drugs and had sex with, then candidate, Barack Obama, sued several anonymous commenters on his video for libel. One of the defendants, TubeSockTedD, fought the subpoena for his identity, and won. The court, in ruling for TubeSockTedD, said that Sinclair simply had not pled a sufficient libel case to compel the release of the identity: "Where the viability of a plaintiff's case is so seriously deficient, there is simply no basis to overcome the considerable First Amendment interest in anonymous speech on the Internet" (*Sinclair*, 2009, p. 134).

Copyright

Under current copyright law, creators of copyrighted works may exploit their creations in any way they wish and may, or may not, license others to do so in whatever way they wish. If someone uses copyrighted work without the creator's permission or license, that person may be infringing the creator's copyright. However, under certain circumstances and subject to a legal test, copyrighted work may be used without infringing any of the owner's rights. For example, quoting part of a copyrighted article as part of a research paper is a fair use of that copyrighted work and not an infringement.

Since 1998, online copyright law has been governed by the Digital Millennium Copyright Act (DMCA). This law contains five parts, but most relevant for social media is Title II, Online Copyright Infringement Liability Limitation Act (17 U.S.C. §§ 512). This title provides protections similar to those provided for ISPs by section 230: if websites act in accordance with the rules of Title II, they cannot be sued for contributory copyright infringement if users post copyrighted materials on their sites. Like section 230, the DMCA provides protection for websites if they are merely acting as conduits for information. The law does not expect or mandate that a site monitor all postings for potential infringement. If a user posts infringing material on a website, the copyright owner provides notice to the website of the claimed infringement, and the website responds by removing or blocking access to the material, liability for the website itself is limited. This rule is sometimes referred to as the notice and takedown rule. The video poster may then counter-claim and ask for the video to be put back up. One other important element of the DMCA is the requirement that a copyright holder engage in a good-faith consideration of whether an alleged infringement is really a fair use, and therefore not illegal.

An excellent case study for how the DMCA works is video-sharing site YouTube. YouTube, owned by Google, is obviously very concerned about DMCA compliance. The site maintains a page entitled Copyright Infringement Notifications Basics (YouTube, n.d.) that provides information and a way to notify YouTube of alleged infringement and request a takedown. The site also has an automated Content Verification Program for use by companies who want to issue multiple takedown requests.

While many of the video takedowns are legitimate infringements, copyright holders have been caught requesting takedowns of videos without a consideration of whether those videos might actually be fair uses of the copyrighted material. Stephanie Lenz posted a 30-second clip of her young son dancing to Prince's song *Let's Go Crazy*. Prince, through his distributor, Universal Music, issued a DMCA takedown notice for the video, and YouTube took it down. Lenz counterclaimed, and the video was put back up. Then Lenz brought suit, alleging that her use of *Let's Go Crazy* was a fair use and that Universal had engaged in bad faith in ordering takedowns of all videos that used any Prince material without any consideration of whether, as in her case, the use was a fair use. A federal court found in her favor in *Lenz v. Universal Music Corp.* (2008).

In a case to watch (as well as a startling development in DMCA interpretation), the Second Circuit Court of Appeals in 2012 *reversed* the holding of a district court extending DMCA protection to YouTube (*Viacom Int'l, Inc. v. YouTube*, 2012). The appeals court said, in effect, that YouTube may well have been aware of infringing content posted on its site, which would reduce or eliminate any protection the DMCA offers. The court remanded the case to the lower court, asking for more information from the parties on whether YouTube actually did know about infringing material, and willfully turned a blind eye to that infringement. If it is determined by the lower court that YouTube did know about infringement and did nothing about it, some of the DMCA protections might not apply, leaving YouTube liable for contributory copyright infringement damages. The district court will reconsider the case in light of the holding by the Second Circuit.

Moreover, there have been allegations that YouTube has taken down videos in response to requests that were not based on concerns about copyright violations. In 2011, a promotional video created by alleged pirate site Megaupload and posted on YouTube was removed at the request of Universal Music Corp. Court filings suggested that the request had not been made for copyright violations but because of a private arrangement that Universal had with YouTube (Sisario, 2011). Megaupload accused Universal of abusing the notice and takedown provisions of the DMCA for its own benefit, because Universal did not like the content of the video (Sisario, 2011).

Special arrangements and potential for abuse aside, the DMCA governs any website that permits user-generated content, not only written content but images and videos. If they are followed the notice and takedown provisions protect a website from being sued for contributory infringement.

Advertising

Online advertising is big business. According to a 2012 report by the Interactive Advertising Bureau (IAB), the first quarter of 2012 set a new online advertising revenue record of $8.4 billion (Interactive Advertising Bureau, 2012). Most traditional advertising rules apply to the online advertising environment, including FTC rules against unfair or deceptive advertising. However, online advertising raises some other issues when it comes to social media and interactive consumers, including the gathering of data for behavioral advertising and endorsements.

Behavioral advertising is defined by the FTC as "the tracking of consumers' online activities in order to deliver tailored advertising" (Federal Trade Commission, 2009a, p. 2). While most of this tracking takes place using cookies, or small bits of data stored on surfers' computers and accessed by websites to serve up advertisements based on surfing habits, new technologies are tapping the connections created by social media. Called social retargeting, these technologies track the social contacts of a surfer to deliver ads to demographically similar friends (Regalado, 2012). For example, a woman visits an online sport shoe store and looks at several different styles of running shoes. A social retargeting company uses that information plus information from that user's Facebook profile and finds that 10 of her friends are of similar age and list running or jogging as interests. The retargeter can now aim advertising for such shoes at those 10 friends of the original surfer. While there are not yet FTC guidelines or policies on this technology, it clearly implicates a number of privacy concerns. There have been numerous calls for do not track policies or laws that would provide consumers with the opportunity to opt out of online tracking; in fact, the FTC's 2012 privacy report endorsed such a policy (Federal Trade Commission, 2012, p. 4).

In 2009, the FTC published updated guidelines on endorsements. This was not their first guidance on the ways in which advertisers must exercise online transparency; advertising companies have gotten guidance from the FTC in the form of a report called *Dot Com Disclosures* since 2000 (Federal Trade Commission, 2000), and the first guidelines on endorsements appeared in 1980. These guidelines were drafted to address potential deception and fraud in online advertising. The FTC has recently looked to revisit the Dot Com Disclosures document in light of new technologies. However, the endorsement guidelines outline the disclosures bloggers must make when endorsing products (Federal Trade Commission, 2009b).

The FTC will evaluate whether a positive message about a product or service is an endorsement and is subject to these rules. For example, the agency will look at any agreements in place and what the terms are; whether there is any compensation by the advertiser or its agent for the endorsement; and whether free products or services were provided. If the FTC determines that the message is an endorsement, then the endorser must disclose the elements of the relationship with the company. While the guidelines apply to all advertisers, the blogging community complained so loudly that the FTC issued a separate fact sheet to address their concerns (Federal Trade Commission, 2010). The FTC explained that the endorsement rules had not been revisited since 1980 and were in need of an update, and that the agency was not going to target or monitor bloggers. In 2011, the FTC fined Legacy Learning Systems Inc. $250,000 under the endorsement rules for advertising through online affiliates posing as customers or independent reviewers, and rewarding them with commissions for referrals without disclosing those relationships (*In the Matter of Legacy Learning Systems, Inc.*, 2011).

The potential for revenue draws advertising agencies and companies to the wealth of data available from their users' visits to their websites and social media, but the bottom line is that online advertising is an area being closely monitored not only by the industry but also by government agencies and privacy rights groups.

Hiring and Firing

While employment concerns involving social media are not unique to advertising and public relations firms, several recent legal developments merit a brief mention here. Can employers demand the passwords to their employees' social media? As of 2012 not in Maryland, the first state to pass such a law, or Illinois. The Maryland law forbids both the request of passwords from employees or job applicants and the refusal to hire a potential employee because of a refusal to turn over passwords (Md. Labor and Employment Code Ann. § 3–712, 2012). Illinois passed a similar law, an amendment to the Illinois Right to Privacy in the Workplace Act, effective on January 1, 2013 (Ill. Public Act 097–0875, 2012).

There has been at least one case that deals with the demand of an employer for the password to a private, social network employee gripe site. In *Pietrylo v. Hillstone Restaurant Group* (2009), several employees brought suit after another employee turned over the password to a private MySpace group that the employees used to complain about their jobs and managers, which resulted in those employees being fired. The court found that the employer violated the Stored Communications Act by intentionally accessing the private space without permission.

What about employer use of social media to screen potential employees? There are data brokers who are willing to sell information gleaned from social media to employers looking to screen (or screen out) potential employees. In 2012, the FTC settled with one of these brokers, Spokeo, for $800,000, alleging that it had violated the Fair Credit Reporting Act by not sufficiently monitoring the use of that data for violations of the act or warning that it should not be used inappropriately (*U.S. v. Spokeo, Inc.*, 2012). The decision raised the eyebrows of some commentators, who suggested that the Fair Credit Reporting Act should be revisited in light of new types of information available online (Ramasastry, 2012).

Most recently, a court said that liking something or someone on Facebook was *not* a speech act entitled to First Amendment protection, and therefore that firing employees based on this act was not unlawful retaliation (*Bland v. Roberts*, 2012). Six employees of the Hampton, Va., sheriff's department were fired for supporting the sheriff's opponent in a 2009 election by clicking the like button on the opponent's Facebook page. The judge dismissed the retaliation claims of the employees, saying, "It is the Court's conclusion that merely 'liking' a Facebook page is insufficient speech to merit constitutional protection. In cases where courts have found that constitutional speech protections extended to Facebook posts, actual statements existed within the record" (*Bland*, 2012, pp. 8–9). The case has been appealed to the Fourth Circuit Court of Appeals.

Discussion

The topics in this chapter demonstrate how the law is struggling to keep up with developments in both social media and technology and is not quite there yet. As more individuals share information with each other on social media, courts and legislatures will continue to be faced with cries about the loss of consumer privacy, laments about decreasing civility in public discourse, and concerns about speaking anonymously. Yet, the financial stakes are too high for advertisers and public relations firms not to use social media to connect with their current and potential customers.

While much of the media law that applies to traditional outlets is similar in its application to social media, there are some distinct differences. These laws were passed before the advent of social media, but courts have been relatively generous in expanding their scope to cover these sites. Section 230 protections have been interpreted robustly for all types of service providers as well as social media. The tests governing whether or not to unmask an anonymous commenter for purposes of libel or other suits are well established and protective of sites that function primarily as distributors of information. The burden is on the plaintiff in a libel case, for example, to establish that there are sufficient grounds for a successful suit before a court will force a company to reveal the identity of an anonymous poster. The DMCA contains protections for YouTube and other social media that host content against copyright infringement – subject to its requirements for notice and takedown and other requirements.

Much of the law and policy in this chapter did not arise from the actions of advertising or public relations firms, nor did it necessarily involve social media. However, because of the willingness of the courts to extend the protection of laws like Section 230 of the CDA and the DMCA to social media, as well as to sites that accept user-generated content, it is important to understand them. Moreover, it remains to be seen how the Federal Trade Commission will update laws such as COPPA, and it would be wise to watch for FTC updates on how the agency will interpret the mandates of COPPA for social media. The FTC will continue to be an active advocate for consumer rights and will issue additional guidelines for appropriate social media use; and penalties for its misuse. The FTC has made no secret of its concerns about consumer privacy in its 2012 privacy report, which is important reading for any company engaged in gathering information from consumers.

Current laws raise almost as many questions as they answer. For example, how will the FTC deal with social retargeting? How about facial recognition? Are we likely to see additional states follow the leads of Maryland and Illinois in social network password protection? Is it possible that the DMCA will be amended to deal with alleged misuse by private arrangement? What about a do not track online law? While there are no ready answers, it is clear that social media have changed the face of media law and continue to do so. It remains to be seen what those changes might be, and whether they will be a boon or a bane for strategic communication.

References

Belmas, G., & Overbeck, W. (2011). *Major principles of media law*. Boston, MA: Cengage.

Bland v. Roberts, 33 I.E.R. Cas. (BNA) 1435 (E.D. Va. 2012).

Children's Online Privacy Protection Act of 1998, 15 U.S.C. §§ 6501–6508 (2012).

Children's Online Privacy Protection Rule, 77 Fed. Reg. 46643 (2012).

Communications Decency Act of 1996, 47 U.S.C. § 230 (2012).

Cubby, Inc. v. CompuServe, Inc., 776 F. Supp. 135 (S.D.N.Y. 1991).

Digital Millennium Copyright Act of 1998, 17 U.S.C. §§ 512 (2012).

Electronic Privacy Information Center v. Federal Trade Commission, 2012 U.S. Dist. LEXIS 23126 (D.D.C. 2012).

Federal Trade Commission. (2000). *Dot Com Disclosures*. Retrieved from http://www.ftc.gov/os/2000/05/0005dotcomstaffreport.pdf

Federal Trade Commission. (2008, October 7). *Frequently asked questions about the Children's Online Privacy Protection rule*. Retrieved from http://www.ftc.gov/privacy/coppafaqs.shtm

Federal Trade Commission. (2009a). *Self-regulatory principles for online behavioral advertising*. Retrieved from http://www.ftc.gov/os/2009/02/P085400behavadreport.pdf

Federal Trade Commission. (2009b). *Guides concerning the use of endorsements and testimonials in advertising*. Retrieved from http://ftc.gov/os/2009/10/091005revisedendorsementguides.pdf

Federal Trade Commission. (2010). The FTC's revised endorsement guides: What people are asking. Retrieved from http://business.ftc.gov/documents/bus71-ftcs-revised-endorsement-guideswhat-people-are-asking

Federal Trade Commission. (2011a, November 29). *Facebook settles FTC charges that it deceived consumers by failing to keep privacy promises.* Retrieved from http://www.ftc.gov/opa/2011/11/privacysettlement.shtm

Federal Trade Commission. (2011b, March 11). *FTC accepts final settlement with Twitter for failure to safeguard personal information.* Retrieved from http://www.ftc.gov/opa/2011/03/twitter.shtm

Federal Trade Commission. (2012). *Protecting consumer privacy in an era of rapid change.* Retrieved from http://ftc.gov/os/2012/03/120326privacyreport.pdf

Fraley v. Facebook, Inc., 830 F. Supp. 2d 785 (N.D. Cal. 2011).

Gaston v. Facebook, Inc., 2012 U.S. Dist. LEXIS 23895 (D. Ore. 2012).

Hermann, R. P. (1996). Who is liable for on-line libel? *St. Thomas Law Review, 8,* 423–447.

Ho, S. (2011, October. 12). Million-dollar Twitter libel suit dismissed. *The Oregonian.* Retrieved from http://www.oregonlive.com/tigard/index.ssf/2011/10/million-dollar_twitter_libel_s.html

Horizon Group Mgmt., LLC v. Bonnen, Cook County No. 2009 L 8675 (Ill. Cir. Ct. 2010).

Ill. Public Act 097–0875, 2012.

In the Matter of Legacy Learning Systems, Inc., File No. 1023055 (2011).

Interactive Advertising Bureau. (2012). *Internet advertising revenues set first quarter record at $8.4 billion.* Retrieved from http://www.iab.net/about_the_iab/recent_press_releases/press_release_archive/press_release/pr-061112

Kahn, R. (2011, May 27). Lawyers claim Courtney Love defamed them. *Courthouse News.* Retrieved from http://www.courthousenews.com/2011/05/27/36895.htm

Kaplan, C. (1999, November 5). In Internet time, a year is much too long, judge finds. CyberLaw Journal, *New York Times.* Retrieved from http://partners.nytimes.com/library/tech/99/11/cyber/cyberlaw/05law.html

Lenz v. Universal Music Corp., 572 F. Supp. 2d 1150 (N.D. Cal. 2008).

Lidsky, L. B., & Friedel, D. C. (2011). Legal pitfalls of social media usage. In H. S. Noor Al-Deen & J. A. Hendricks (Eds.), *Social media: Usage and impact* (pp. 237–254). Lanham, MD: Lexington Books.

Luftman, D. B. (1997). Defamation liability for on-line services: The sky is not falling. *George Washington Law Review, 65,* 1071–1099.

Moreno v. Hanford Sentinel, 172 Cal. App. 4th 1125 (Cal. App. 5th Dist. 2009).

Md. Labor and Employment Code Ann. §§ 3–712 (2012).

Pietrylo v. Hillstone Restaurant Group, 29 I.E.R. Cas. 1438 (D.N.J. 2009).

Prosser, W. L. (1960). Privacy. *California Law Review, 48*(3), 383–423.

Ramasastry, A. (2012, July 17). Cyber-screening, social media, and fair credit reporting: Why we need to move beyond the FTC's recent Spokeo enforcement action. *Verdict.* Retrieved from http://verdict.justia.com/2012/07/17/cyber-screening-social-media-and-fair-credit-reporting

Regalado, A. (2012). Online ads that know who you know. *Technology Review.* Retrieved from http://www.technologyreview.com/news/428048/online-ads-that-know-who-you-know/

Sinclair v. TubeSockTedD, 596 F. Supp. 2d 128 (D.D.C. 2009).

Sisario, B. (2011, December 16). A YouTube takedown raises questions over media influence. Media decoder, *New York Times.* Retrieved from http://mediadecoder.blogs.nytimes.com/2011/12/16/a-youtube-takedown-raises-questions-over-media-influence/

Steiner, P. (1993). On the Internet, nobody knows you're a dog (cartoon). *The New Yorker, 69*(20), 61.

Stratton Oakmont, Inc. v. Prodigy Services, Inc., 23 Media L. Rep. 1794 (N.Y. Sup. Ct. May 26, 1995).

U.S. v. Spokeo, Inc., No. CV-12–05001 (2012).

Viacom Int'l, Inc. v. YouTube, 676 F.3d 19 (2nd Cir. 2012).

YouTube. (n.d.). Copyright Infringement Notification Basics. Retrieved from http://www.youtube.com/yt/copyright/copyright-complaint.html

Index